THRESHOLD
EDITIONS

# AMATEUR HOUR

## KAMALA HARRIS IN THE WHITE HOUSE

# CHARLIE SPIERING

THRESHOLD
EDITIONS

NEW YORK    LONDON    TORONTO    SYDNEY    NEW DELHI

THRESHOLD
EDITIONS
Threshold Editions

An Imprint of Simon & Schuster, Inc.

1230 Avenue of the Americas

New York, NY 10020

First Threshold Editions hardcover edition January 2024

THRESHOLD EDITIONS and colophon are trademarks of Simon & Schuster, Inc.

Simon & Schuster: Celebrating 100 Years of Publishing in 2024

For information about special discounts for bulk purchases, please contact Simon & Schuster Special Sales at 1-866-506-1949 or business@simonandschuster.com.

The Simon & Schuster Speakers Bureau can bring authors to your live event. For more information or to book an event, contact the Simon & Schuster Speakers Bureau at 1-866-248-3049 or visit our website at www.simonspeakers.com.

*Interior design by Erika R. Genova*

Manufactured in the United States of America

1   3   5   7   9   10   8   6   4   2

Library of Congress Control Number: 2023948833

ISBN 978-1-6680-4607-4
ISBN 978-1-6680-4609-8 (ebook)

*To my wife, Becca*

# CONTENTS

# AMATEUR HOUR

# INTRODUCTION

## THE PLACE: WASHINGTON, DC

## THE TIME: THE NEAR FUTURE—NEARER THAN YOU THINK

Chief of Staff Jeff Zients, Counselor Steve Ricchetti, senior advisor Mike Donilon, and senior advisor Anita Dunn gather in the White House to discuss their options with First Lady Jill Biden. Age and infirmity have finally caught up with her husband, despite every effort by family and staff to prop up the aging president. They can no longer hide the truth. President Joe Biden's time in office is over.

As they wait for everyone to assemble, they start revisiting how they arrived at this moment. Why did they push for him to run for reelection? Did they really think he could make it another four years? The signs of decline were already there. Staffers found him vacant and listless while attempting to brief him ahead of public events. They created note cards. "YOU take YOUR seat," "YOU give brief comments," "YOU depart," the instructions read. The teleprompter speeches grew shorter and simpler, and interactions with the public and even supporters were dialed back. Long stretches of rest were carved out of his schedule and the press was shut out to limit moments of embarrassment.

There was only so much they could do. The frequent coughing could no longer be stifled with a few cough drops. The stiffness grew more apparent as he walked to and from the podium. He lashed out angrily when questioned by the press and appeared lost and confused while aides directed him. The world was watching as the leader of the free world was repeatedly stumbling, falling on the stairs while boarding Air Force One, tipping over on his bicycle, and tripping and falling onstage.

Why did his trusted circle believe he could do it again? Because they wanted to. He was, after all, the only one who defeated former president Donald Trump. They thought—hoped—he could pull it off once more. Biden was passionate about driving Trump and his entire political movement into the dustbin of history. Defeat Trump, defend democracy, and restore the soul of the nation. That was all part of why they pushed the president to keep going. But deep down they knew the real reason he had to run again. Vice President Kamala Harris was not up to the job.

They should have known, they realized, that this was coming. In modern history, many vice presidents have stepped in and taken power suddenly in cases of ill health or national tragedy (or near misses). William McKinley's assassination elevated Teddy Roosevelt. Woodrow Wilson had a stroke. Dwight Eisenhower had a heart attack. Vice President Lyndon B. Johnson was sworn in as president just hours after President John F. Kennedy was murdered. Vice President Gerald Ford took office after President Richard Nixon resigned in disgrace. Ronald Reagan came within an inch of losing his life in 1981. Not since President Franklin Delano Roosevelt died at the age of sixty-three had a president died in office after struggling with health problems, requiring, in FDR's case, Vice President Harry S. Truman to replace him. Truman was ready and experienced. He served as a senator from Missouri for ten years before he was selected as the vice president, heir apparent to the aging Roosevelt as Democrats felt confident running him for a historic fourth term.

Vice President Kamala Harris's many struggles and mistakes during her first years in office were top of mind: the thin-skinned outrage, perceived grievances around every corner, the staff bullying and endless turnover, the mockery, the refusal to be a team player. A brain stroke away from the presidency, Harris appeared artificial onstage, never willing to engage or risk her brand, and constantly playing defense. Her speeches lacked conviction and spiraled into word salads. Tough questions were answered with laughter and dismissal. Harris barely suppressed her impatience and disdain for the president despite reading platitudes from the teleprompter. After less than four years in the Senate, she was not a dealmaker, a consensus builder, or even a conduit to activists. Her presidential campaign—where she launched a bitter but ineffective attack on Biden during one of the debates—was a notorious flop. Instead of playing dutiful backup to the president, Harris was trying to write her own political narrative according to her rules. She was in no position to take over for Biden and lead the Democratic Party into the future. But there was no way the Biden team could replace her on the ticket in 2024—that would be admitting a huge mistake.

It's a mistake that cannot be fixed. As Harris prepares to take the oath of office, Biden's aides realize that their power to manipulate their future is gone. They will be forced out of the White House and President Kamala Harris will take control.

———

Who knows if this scene will play out exactly as described. President Biden may win reelection and serve out a second term with no hiccups, retiring with grace at the age of eighty-six. He may run for reelection and lose. But whatever happens to Biden, Kamala Harris isn't leaving. And that should alarm us.

This book tells the story of the real Kamala Harris—the hilarious, incompetent, trailblazing radical who is now our vice president. It will examine in detail her disastrous and comical first years as vice president. It will investigate how and why staff fled her office and why Democrats lost faith in her leadership without publicly admitting it.

It will explore what Harris believes and chronicle her willingness to say anything to prove herself to the hard left by approving and adopting some of their most radical ideas. The book will chronicle her impatient journey into national politics and her disastrous presidential campaign. It will look at why Joe Biden selected her as his running mate in 2020, including how her allies worked behind the scenes to disparage other candidates until Harris looked like the best choice by comparison.

It will look back at how Harris began as a prosecutor and moved into local San Francisco politics and high society after dating California State Assembly Speaker Willie Brown. It will reveal how she positioned herself carefully as a politician in California, threading her social connections, her personal biography, and law enforcement record to rise quickly in state politics until she became a United States senator and ultimately vice president of the United States.

# CHAPTER ONE

# THAT GIRL WAS ME

*My mother used to—she would give us a hard time sometimes, and she would say to us, "I don't know what's wrong with you young people. You think you just fell out of a coconut tree?"*

—KAMALA HARRIS, MAY 10, 2023

Kamala Iyer Harris was born October 20, 1964. Two weeks later her parents filed an affidavit to change her middle name from Iyer to Devi, the name of a powerful Hindu goddess.[1] Harris's identity was already shifting to better position herself for success. It's unclear why her parents changed her name, but Harris's mother had a deep appreciation for Hindu goddesses. The name Kamala (pronounced Comma-la) also means "lotus flower" in Sanskrit. "I learned at that, you know, this flower sits on top of the water. But its roots are grounded in the mud," Harris explained later in life.[2] Kamala is also another name for the Hindu goddess Lakshmi, the goddess of wealth, fortune, power, beauty, fertility, and prosperity. Her parents were already expecting big things from their daughter.

One of Harris's favorite quotes that she shares in interviews is from her mother. "My mother used to say, you don't let people tell them who you are. You tell them who you are," Harris repeats. The way Harris likes to tell it, she was conceived in the civil rights movement and born into the fight for justice. From her earliest days as a politician, Harris introduces herself to audiences telling the story of her parents as young, idealistic students at the University of California, Berkeley. "They fell in love in that most American way, while marching together for justice during the Civil Rights movement in the 1960s," she wrote in her 2019 memoir, *The Truths We Hold*. It was a common refrain from her political stump speech. But Donald Harris and Shyamala Gopalan were more cerebral intellectuals than active community organizers.

Politicians frequently try to write their own stories and shape their early narratives as they reveal their preferred versions of themselves to the public. For decades, Harris has repeated that she grew up in the civil rights movement "marching and shouting for justice" and shares a version of a story recalling that as a child, she fell out of a stroller while her parents were marching at a civil rights protest with her. The adults kept marching on until they realized she was missing. When they returned, little Kamala was mad. "My mother tells the story about how I'm fussing," Harris says, "and she's like, 'Baby, what do you want? What do you need?' And I just looked at her and I said, 'Fweedom.'"[3]

Harris claims her mother told her that story, a version she shared with *Elle* magazine in April 2021. It's a cute vignette, but it has sparked some healthy skepticism about its origin. The similarities of her stroller story and a story about a child told by civil rights legend Dr. Martin Luther King Jr. prompted some accusations of plagiarism. "Read this too-perfect Kamala Harris story. Then click on this 1965 Alex Haley interview with MLK and search for the word 'fee-dom,'" Free Press editor Bari Weiss wrote on Twitter. The 1965 King interview was featured in *Playboy* magazine.

"I never will forget a moment in Birmingham when a white policeman accosted a little Negro girl, seven or eight years old, who was walking in a demonstration with her mother," King recalled.[4] "'What do you want?' the policeman asked her gruffly, and the little girl looked him straight in the eye and answered, 'Fee-dom.' She couldn't even pronounce it, but she knew. It was beautiful!"

Harris was born in the Civil Rights era, but not into struggle. She spent her early years raised by academics and neighbors who enjoyed the liberal haven of Berkeley. Her parents, Donald J. Harris, a young intellectual from Jamacia, and Shyamala Gopalan, an aspiring student from India, were ideologically radical leftists and part of the radical Afro American Association study group at Berkeley. A former member of the study group later told the Associated Press they admired communist dictators such as China's Mao Zedong and Cuba's Fidel Castro.[5] The association also gave intellectual backing to radical black nationalism and the rise of the Black Power movement, the creation of the Kwanzaa holiday, and the creation of the Black Panther Party. In a 1983 book by black studies professor Cedric Robinson, *Black Marxism: The Making of the Black Radical Tradition*, he listed and thanked Harris's mother as among his close friends. (Despite Harris's narrative that her parents "met at a protest," her father revealed to the *New York Times* that they actually met at college after Donald Harris delivered a speech on race in America at UC Berkeley.) Their ideas were radical, but their immigration and academic status prevented them from acting too practically on their ideas. "We were certainly very much aware of, and scrupulously careful about following, the rules and regulations governing our role as foreign students," Donald Harris wrote later in life.[6]

Donald Harris demonstrated a great appreciation for Marxist economic theory—even as a well-paid college professor. Born in Jamaica, he went to college at the University College of the West Indies and the University of London before he ended up in Berkeley, where he earned his PhD in economics. After teaching as a college professor in Illinois and Wisconsin, Harris taught at Stanford University, where he was granted tenure. The *Stanford Daily* described Donald Harris as a "Marxist scholar" in a 1976 article, noting he was a "charismatic" and even a "pied piper," leading students astray from neoclassical ideas.[7] His book *Capital Accumulation and Income Distribution* is a dense treatise of Marxist ideas and critiques of capitalism.

Donald Harris also appreciated radicals. He was a strong admirer of Malcolm X, despite widespread apprehension in American society about

7

the black nationalist. In the Jamaican newspaper the *Sunday Gleaner*, Harris wrote favorably about Malcolm X, noting that he converted to the Nation of Islam in prison. Harris wrote that the Nation of Islam "lumps together all white as 'blue eyed devils' and rejects the whole system of white institutions from the Christian Church to the white-owned business firm." Harris was sympathetic, praising the controversial figure for bringing "dignity and race pride" to the civil rights movement and the "rejects of American society." His black nationalist movement, Harris wrote, was "much maligned and misunderstood." Harris also boasted that he knew the man personally. "I had the privilege of knowing him personally and observing him in different situations," he wrote, noting that his "eloquence was electrifying." Malcolm was "as calm, cool, and incisive as a college professor" and had a "keen sense of humor."

But Donald Harris was not just a fan of radical relics. In an op-ed for the *Stanford Daily* in February 2008, Harris wrote favorably about then candidate for president Barack Obama's health care plan, praising him for his "well documented and highly regarded record of leadership" in his political career. "This record bodes well for his ability to do an outstanding job as president and to secure passage of path-breaking healthcare legislation," he concluded.[8] Despite demonstrating a keen interest in current policy and politics, however, Donald Harris never wrote about his daughter's political career.

When Kamala was only five, Donald Harris and Shyamala Gopalan Harris separated. They divorced when she was seven. Shyamala got full custody of the children. Kamala Harris has shared only scant details and few fond memories of her father. Donald Harris seemed to acknowledge that his intellectual productivity flourished after the divorce but was saddened by the impact it had on his children. "Finally, if there is any virtue in the writing of this book, it springs from the sacrifices knowingly or unknowingly made by my two daughters, Kamala and Maya. In return, it is dedicated to them," he wrote in his book.[9] Despite his radical political leanings, Donald Harris did not have a foundational impact on his daughter's intellectual development, due to the limited time he spent with his children. If Kamala Harris was closer with her father, she would have likely absorbed more radical ideals that she would have internalized and clung to later in life. But her distance from her professorial father also robbed her of a chance to develop a strong intellectual foundation as a child.

Harris was mostly raised by her Indian mother after the divorce but she was not always around. "I assume the divorce was very hard. I'm sure Kamala suffered. We did not have an orderly television family life. I was always working," Shyamala Gopalan Harris later explained.[10] After receiving her PhD, she was a breast cancer researcher at UC Berkeley, raising her children in Oakland. The way her daughters explain it, Shyamala was a no-nonsense, hardworking single mother who raised her children with high expectations. "I was raised that you do, you don't talk about yourself. You just do. You don't talk about it after you've done it. You just do the next thing," Harris would later recall.[11] The Harris sisters also revealed how their mother hated the word *exotic* to describe their heritage, viewing the term as racist. She also scorned the gender disparity in the workplace. Harris later shared a story of how her mother came home one day "raging mad" after she watched a man walk around the lab with a woman's uncovered breast on a tray. "She said, 'Do you think that they would have walked around with a man's—you know what,'" Harris recalled in a 2020 interview with former first lady Hillary Clinton, bursting into laughter. "'Without at least giving it the dignity of putting something over it or doing . . .' Right?"[12] It was a rather strange way to remember one's mother.

Gopalan also raised her girls with a strong connection to their Indian heritage, taking them to visit her childhood home and her grandparents. "Kamala comes from a long line of kick-ass women,"[13] Shyamala told the *Los Angeles Times* in 2004, noting that the Hindu culture of goddesses was strong in their household. "A culture that worships goddesses produces strong women." Gopalan described Harris as a "frequent visitor" to the elaborate Shiva Vishnu temple in Livermore, California, to an Indian media outlet in 2004. "She performs all rituals and says all prayers at the temple. My family always wanted the children to learn the traditions, irrespective of their place of birth," she explained.[14] Gopalan Harris had the spare time and money to routinely travel back to India with her daughters to visit family, "pretty much every other year," Harris recalled later in life. Harris is steeped in the Hindu tradition. In her early political career, she would refer to her Indian heritage from time to time, citing Hindu goddesses as an influence. Harris spoke about the Hindu goddess Parvati/Kali from during the Indus Entrepreneurs' first-ever Women's Forum in April 2004. Harris recalled growing up and hearing stories about Parvati, the benevolent goddess wife of the god Shiva. When Parvati was angry, she manifested the Mother Goddess in the form of the terrifying Kali. Kali is depicted as a dark-skinned, four-armed goddess wearing the skulls of her enemies and depicted holding a severed head and a sword. Harris said the story of Kali, which had been told to her many times as a child, inspired her to become a prosecutor. "Parvati and Kali can coexist in one woman," she said, using the myth to define herself as both a beautiful but deadly political figure.[15] As her national political career blossomed, however, Harris largely abandoned her Indian heritage in favor of her identity as a black woman in America.

As her birth mother was not black, Harris frequently refers to her "second mother" on the campaign trail. Growing up with a single mother who worked long hours in a lab, young Harris was frequently cared for by their neighbor Regina Shelton. "She was our community matriarch," Harris recalls, noting that Shelton took care of children in the community, offering "advice, support, a home-cooked meal, and sometimes even just a hug."[16] Shelton's background offered Harris a cultural connection to the black South, something she lacked from her black father, who was born and raised in Jamaica. In political speeches, Harris recalls how as a little girl, the Sheltons took her to the 23rd Avenue Church of God, where she sang in the choir, despite being raised by her mother in the Hindu temple. When traveling in the South and speaking to black audiences, Harris recalls her experience at the black church in San Francisco. "I sang in the choir about how faith combined with determination will always see us through difficult times," Harris recalled in a 2017 speech in Atlanta.[17] It was unclear when was the last time or if ever Harris had stepped into a choir robe.

With her father mostly absent, Harris was raised by a group of determined women even as other male figures in their lives faded to the sidelines. At the age of seventeen, Kamala's sister, Maya, gave birth to her daughter Meena. As the father was similarly not around, another girl entered the matriarchy of the Harris household. "A feminist household is all I've ever known," Meena later recalled about the Harris household. "Even the idea of men in power wasn't something I really learnt about until I got out into the world of work. Our little family unit was just women, fierce women: my grandmother, my mum, my aunt and me."[18]

Throughout her career, Harris has rarely spoken about formative male figures in her life. There is no record of Donald Harris appearing publicly to celebrate any of Kamala's political victories, even as she frequently singled out her mother for inspiring her achievements. "My father is a good guy," she told *SF Weekly* in 2003, "but we are not close."[19] Harris's niece, Meena, described the situation during an interview with the *New Yorker*: "He was not around after the divorce." Kamala Harris agreed. "I'm happy to talk about my father," she said, glumly. "But, ya know . . ." The *New Yorker* noted that Harris "raised her eyebrows, and said nothing."[20]

As Kamala's political career blossomed in California, Donald Harris appeared saddened that his daughters did not publicly share his deep love and appreciation of grassroots Jamaican culture, even though he tried to impart his heritage upon his daughters. "It is for them to say truthfully now, not me, what if anything of value they carried from that early experience into adulthood," he said in an essay published on Jamaica Global detailing Harris's Jamaican heritage from his perspective. Donald Harris recalled fondly a visit he made with his daughters to Jamaica in 1970 as he tried to share his love of his native country to them. But in the essay, Donald appeared bitter after the loss of the custody battle for his daughters, accusing the California justice system of being racist.[21] He wrote:

> This early phase of interaction with my children came to an abrupt halt in 1972 when, after a hard-fought custody battle in the family court of Oakland, California, the context of the relationship was placed within arbitrary limits imposed by a court-ordered divorce settlement based on the false assumption by the State of California that fathers cannot handle parenting (especially in the case of this father, "a neegroe from da eyelans" was the Yankee stereotype,

who might just end up eating his children for breakfast!). Nevertheless, I persisted, never giving up on my love for my children or reneging on my responsibilities as their father.

In his article, he posted a rare photo of him and an adult Kamala Harris together in a restaurant with his granddaughter Meena Harris. Donald was in the photograph, but not part of the bigger picture of his daughter's political career.

Imagine the horror Donald Harris felt when his daughter finally spoke about her Jamaican heritage as part of a joke to prove she was a not only a user but supporter of legalized marijuana.

"Half my family's from Jamaica—are you kidding me?" She laughed during an interview on *The Breakfast Club* radio show when asked during her presidential campaign if she smoked marijuana or supported making it legal. Her father was furious. "My dear departed grandmothers (whose extraordinary legacy I described in a recent essay on this website), as well as my deceased parents, must be turning in their grave right now to see their family's name, reputation and proud Jamaican identity being connected, in any way, jokingly or not with the fraudulent stereotype of a pot-smoking joy seeker and in the pursuit of identity politics," he wrote.[22] "Speaking for myself and my immediate Jamaican family, we wish to categorically dissociate ourselves from this travesty."

Her father's unvarnished opinion was deleted online soon after it was published, suggesting he was rebuked for revealing his true feelings. Kamala Harris remained mostly silent about her father's outrage, only saying that he was entitled to his opinion on the matter, when she was asked about it by the *New Yorker*. Harris never apologized. Months later, she discussed her appreciation for popular Jamaican singer Bob Marley, known for his enjoyment of giant blunts, in a *Washington Post* article about her Jamaican heritage. Recalling a concert she attended with her father when she was thirteen, Harris wrote in a statement, "We sat up top in the back of the theater and, as I watched the performance, I was in complete awe. To this day, I know the lyrics to nearly every Bob Marley song."[23] It was clear that when speaking about Jamaican heritage, Harris could not help but emphasize the stereotypes of weed and Bob Marley.

After experiencing her childhood in the safe confines of Berkeley, Harris left with her family for Montreal, Canada, after Shyamala got a job teaching at McGill University's medical department and researching cancer at Jewish General Hospital. In Montreal, Harris briefly attended a Fine Arts Core Elementary School in eighth grade before she was sent to a French school, Notre-Dame-des-Neiges, and ended up at Westmount High School, where she graduated. Harris spent her formative years not in the colorful culture of San Francisco but uprooted from the United States and living in an elite Canadian bubble in Montreal. The family lived in "a spacious Victorian home in an affluent neighborhood," bordering one of Montreal's wealthiest districts, the New York Times reported.[24] It was a complex upbringing as she traveled from liberal enclave to liberal enclave—hardly relatable to most Americans.

Harris's next step was to choose a college. She was drawn to Howard University for practical reasons, revealing that she admired a woman who showed her the advantages of attending a historically black university. "My aunt would talk about it because she went there, and so I always romanticized what Howard is and was," Harris said, referring to Christine Simmons, a family friend she called "Aunt Chris." When she was young, Harris participated in Alpha Kappa Alpha sorority events with her mentor, realizing the opportunity for valuable connections that would lead to a career path. Later in life, Harris told the Washington Post she chose Howard because she had attended "majority-white" schools her entire life and wanted to experience a life where everyone was black.[25] Speaking to journalist Jonathan Capehart in 2019, Harris spoke fondly about her memories of she and other students congregating in "The Yard," a safe space to be with her friends and grow into an adult. "We would all promenade and you know people would display their feathers and peacock," she recalled fondly, adding, "You would see that the football star was also on the debate team, you would see that the homecoming queen was also an extraordinary science student, you would see that there are no limitations and there are no choices in terms of false choices that one need make. And so you shouldn't be limited in your view and perspective of who is who and what is what."[26] Harris fulfilled her dreams of joining the

AKA sorority and worked her way into a network that would reward her professionally. As a candidate for political office, Harris used her experience at Howard to dismiss questions about her racial identity. "I reference often my days at Howard to help people understand they should not make assumptions about who black people are," she said in an interview.[27]

Harris was described by college friends as politically aware but not a passionate activist. She interned for then California senator Alan Cranston. She took interest in student government, running and winning for freshman class representative of the Liberal Arts Student Council. She even protested apartheid in South Africa with some of her friends in between the busy social life of a sorority girl in college. Harris graduated from Howard with a degree in political science and economics before returning to California to attend law school at the University of California Hastings College of the Law. She became the president of the National Black Law Students Association (NBLSA) in the college during her second year. She later reflected on a successful jobs fair under her leadership with law firms and black law students and advocating for more black students to attend the school. Harris's resume was that of a personal achiever, not an activist trying to change the world.

After graduating from law school, Harris hit her first major roadblock of her career when she failed the California bar exam. "I was a hard worker. A perfectionist. Someone who didn't take things for granted. But there I was, letter in hand, realizing that in studying for the bar, I had put forward the most half-assed performance of my life," she wrote in her memoir. Despite failing her bar exam, Harris still had a clerking position in the Alameda County District Attorney's Office. Failing up, it turned out, was possible. After more study, Harris retook the bar exam and passed the second time. Her career path was safe despite a setback. It was a practical choice as well. Serving competently as a public prosecutor was understood to be a path to career advancement. Succeed as a prosecutor and you may meet important people in the legal community. If you meet the right people, the job could even open doors to a political future.

# CHAPTER TWO

# THE REAL SLICK WILLIE

*Willie Brown is not going to be around. He's gone—hello people, move on.*

—KAMALA HARRIS, SEPTEMBER 24, 2003

Behind the success of every rising young politician is a political mentor—some experienced, well-connected person to give them advice, make introductions, open doors, and get them started in politics. For Kamala Harris, that mentor was Willie Brown. But Brown was no ordinary politician and was certainly no ordinary mentor.

Born in Mineola, Texas, into a segregated society, Willie Brown at the age of seventeen moved to California, where he attended San Francisco State University and Hastings College of the Law (now UC Law San Francisco) and avoided getting drafted to fight in the war in Vietnam. After law school he started his own firm, proudly representing prostitutes, pimps, and people on the wrong side of the law. "I believed that whether you are a criminal or not a criminal, you are entitled to the same rules and regulations," he said. Recalling the beginning of his legal career in a 2020 podcast interview, Brown said he was successful getting cases dismissed on the basis of selective prosecution, which led to a "magic set of circumstances."[1]

Brown's commitment to his clients, combined with his ability to get cases dismissed on technicalities, turned him into a local celebrity equal to that of the fictional lawyer Saul Goodman in the television series *Breaking Bad* and *Better Call Saul.* "The word spread throughout the hooker community, there's a guy down there on Sutter Street who has come up with something that keeps us out of jail, gets our cases dismissed," Brown recalled. Practicing law led to civil rights activism, and Brown was ultimately encouraged to run for political office. "I made cash money every day representing whores. I became the whores' lawyer . . . until I got elected," he later said in an interview with the *Los Angeles Times.*[2]

The "whores' lawyer" rose to become one of the most powerful politicians in the United States. First elected to the California State Assembly in 1964, Brown served as Speaker from 1980 to 1995, the longest reign of power in the state's history. He was unstoppable. "No politician dominated California politics longer or more completely than Willie Brown. No politician in California was more flamboyant or controversial or relished wielding power with more joy and zeal. None commanded more fear and hatred in his opponents," wrote James Richardson, a longtime reporter for the *Sacramento Bee,* in his biography of Brown.[3] The powerful figure nicknamed himself the "Ayatollah of the Assembly" and enjoyed lavish parties, fast cars, expensive suits, and attention from women while building a formidable political machine in San Francisco. To succeed in California politics, you needed permission and assistance from Brown. He walked comfortably amid accusations of cronyism and political favoritism but to him it was part of the way politics and the world worked. He was repeatedly investigated by the FBI when he was in power, as the aura of corruption accusations never left his side, but never arrested or convicted. His smooth persona dazzled San Francisco and made him untouchable. "Now I've met the real Slick Willie," former president Bill Clinton quipped, referring to one of his own political nicknames, after meeting Brown in California in 1992.[4] Brown was so successful and entrenched as a politician, it took a ballot proposition imposing term limits on members of the California Assembly and Senate to pry him out of office. In response, he ran for mayor of San Francisco, during which he started his relationship with Harris.

Harris started dating him at the age of twenty-nine in 1994, a transitional time for Brown, age sixty, who wanted to continue enjoying his life of power and prestige. Brown said he met the young and ambitious Almeda County prosecutor at a wedding. Their relationship was chronicled by the legendary *San Francisco Chronicle* columnist Herb Caen, who enjoyed frequent lunches with Brown as a source. Caen described Harris as "the Speaker's new steady" in his column even though Brown was still officially married to his estranged wife, Blanche. Brown had met Blanche at San Francisco State and they married in September 1957. They had three children, but Brown threw himself into his political career and preferred the busy lifestyle that followed. While Blanche was left home to raise the children, Brown was routinely spotted in public with young, attractive women on his arm and going into hotel rooms. Blanche and Willie Brown finally separated in 1980. It was clear he would not change, but they never divorced.

From the beginning, Harris represented something more to Brown's persona than just his latest fling. Caen wrote that at one swanky event actor Clint Eastwood "spilled champagne on the Speaker's new steady, Kamala Harris, an Alameda Co. deputy D.A. who is something new in Willie's love life. She's a woman, not a girl. And she's black. . . ." On Willie Brown's arm, Harris moved easily into the exclusive group of San Francisco socialites. Wherever Brown went, Harris was right beside him, soaking up the larger-than-life experience in California politics. She attended lavish parties, dinners, fundraisers, and events featuring the wealthy and powerful San Francisco elites. They approved of the relationship, as Caen wrote that Kamala Harris was "exactly the steadying influence he needs." Brown's campaign manager Jack Davis told the *San Francisco Chronicle* that Brown's "long-term relationship with a woman he cares about is an asset to the campaign."[5] It was an opportunistic relationship for both of them.

Brown relished the opportunity to boost the careers of women in his orbit, revealing in his autobiography his advice to young women seeking to advance. The best way to succeed in politics, he wrote, was to "cross over into the white community." He detailed the process:

I suggest black women lay the groundwork by looking to become active on the boards of social, cultural, and charitable institutions like symphonies, museums, and hospitals. It's the way to get respect from a world that otherwise is content to eschew or label you. You have to demand the opportunities to enter these worlds.[6]

Brown also wrote that he "worked hard not only to give women opportunities, but also to provide women with opportunities to grow with each other, learn from each other, and be empowered." Brown held annual "Women's Summits" in the city to bring women in the state together to socialize and network, celebrating his impact on the careers of political figures and businesswomen. "I was, of course, thrilled each year to be the only man among five thousand women," he added slyly.

Brown and Harris only dated for about a year, but he made a foundational impact on her political and financial future. In his last year as California Speaker of the Assembly, Brown appointed his new girlfriend to two positions in state government that all told paid her more than $400,000 over five years. "She took a six-month leave of absence from her Alameda County job to join the Unemployment Insurance Appeals Board. Brown then appointed her to the California Medical Assistance Commission, where she served until 1998, attending two meetings a month for a $99,000 annual salary," SF Weekly reported.[7] (A $99,000 salary in 1994 in 2023 dollars would be about $200,000.) As if that were not enough, Brown also gave Harris the keys to a BMW. As Brown's girlfriend, Harris was featured in all the gossip and high-society columns as Brown worked the city for his campaign for mayor. "She was the girlfriend, and so she met, you know, everybody who's anybody, as a result of being his girl," Brown's political consultant Jack Davis later told Politico.[8]

It was a mutually beneficial relationship. Harris was described as a youthful intelligent socialite, eager to tie herself to Brown, who still appeared to have a political future. Brown won his campaign for mayor, extending his political legacy even further. As he celebrated at his campaign victory party, Harris was right beside him, giving him a kiss and placing a blue hat emblazoned with gold letters that read "Da Mayor" on his head as he spoke to supporters.[9] Caen wrote that Harris was the "first-lady-in-waiting" and added, "keep an eye on these two."[10] But Brown's wife knew her estranged husband, as the mayor recounted in his autobiography. When asked by a friend about rumors that Brown would marry Harris, he recalled that Blanche replied, "Listen, she may have him at the moment but come inauguration day and he's up there on the platform being sworn in, I'll be the bitch holding the Bible."[11] It was true.

Brown broke news of the relationship ending the day after Christmas that year. "It's all over," Caen wrote, quoting Brown. "With those words, mayor-elect Brown let word get around over the weekend that his long affair with Kamala Harris, an Alameda County asst. district attorney, has ended." Caen lamented the end of the relationship, noting that friends viewed Harris as "attractive, intelligent and charming" and found her "the perfect antidote to whatever playboy tendencies still reside in the mayor-elect's jaunty persona." "The consensus: 'Kamala and Willie just looked right together,'" he concluded.[12] As she predicted, Blanche appeared at the inaugural ceremony in January and held the Bible while Brown took his oath of office. Kamala Harris was nowhere to be seen.

The romantic relationship was over, but Brown was never far away with a helping hand in her political career. Harris followed Brown's advice about showing up and demanding a seat at the table. She joined the boards of the San Francisco Bar Association, the San Francisco Museum of Modern Art, and Partners Ending Domestic Abuse and cochaired the Lawyers' Committee for Civil Rights.[13] She was still invited to the parties and fundraisers and moved comfortably in the world that Brown had introduced her to. Harris loathes the idea that she relied on Brown to launch her political career and does not mention him once in her 2019 political memoir.

# CAREER RISE

In February 1998, Harris was hired by District Attorney Terence Hallinan to work at the San Francisco District Attorney's Office career criminal division. Even though her relationship with Brown was over, few could forget the woman who handed Brown his "Da Mayor" cap at his campaign victory party. It raised questions from reporters, but Hallinan insisted that Brown did not have a role in her hiring.[14] Hallinan was the true image of a progressive prosecutor, one that would be celebrated by today's leftist activists. He chose not to prosecute nonviolent crimes like drug offenses in favor of mentoring and treatment programs. He favored decriminalizing prostitution and promoted legalization of medical marijuana. He tried to keep criminals out of prison. His approach to lenient crime prosecution triggered a nasty relationship with law enforcement groups in the city, but residents generally liked his progressive demeanor.

In 1999, Brown backed Hallinan for reelection and contributed five hundred dollars to his campaign, even though the local newspapers raised questions about his low conviction rate for violent crimes. Brown stuck by his man. "In terms of raw numbers, I'd have to assume that Terence Hallinan's office is as good as any in the state because we are obviously putting away a lot of bad guys and keeping them off the streets and making it unpalatable to come to San Francisco to commit crimes," Brown said.[15] It was hardly a ringing endorsement, especially as residents witnessed evidence to the contrary. Hallinan won reelection, but only by a thin margin.

In the meantime, Harris was struggling to climb the ladder within the district attorney's office. In her memoir, Harris laments the "toxic environment" in Hallinan's office and expresses shock and dismay that one day fourteen lawyers were fired at once. (She failed to mention that Hallinan fired them to shuffle up the status quo and make room for more minority lawyers like herself.)[16]

"It was devastating. People cried and yelled, and soon their fear turned to paranoia. Lawyers were afraid of one another—afraid of backstabbing by colleagues trying to protect their own jobs. Some people started skipping out on the goodbye parties of their fired compatriots, worried that their attendance would mark them as targets for firing, too," Harris wrote.

But what Harris did not reveal was her own contribution to the tumultuous office environment. Harris moved quickly within the district attorney's office after she was recruited by another one of her mentors, Richard Iglehart. When Iglehart left the office for a position as a judge, attorney Darrell Salomon took his place, even though Harris was angling for the job.[17] In response, Harris tried to rally attorneys in the office to overthrow Salomon, but her attempt at a coup failed.[18] Harris quit the district attorney's office in August 2000 complaining about "dysfunctional" leadership at the top. Instead, she took a job with the city attorney's office and began plotting her revenge.

Brown and Hallinan had been cautious allies, but Brown turned on the district attorney in October 2000 as more media outlets were reporting on the rise of illegal drugs and prostitution plaguing the city. Through a spokesman, Brown pointedly raised concerns of "either the perception or the reality that San Francisco won't prosecute those lawbreakers" on Hallinan's watch. He later rebuked Hallinan publicly, noting that "my support for him has absolutely nothing to do with the failure we as a city are experiencing with excessive prostitution or drug dealing, period." Brown was clearly trying to shuffle the blame on Hallinan but was it also a coincidence that Brown started pestering him publicly after Harris resigned?

Brown grew even more aggressive as San Francisco struggled with basic law-and-order problems. As the homelessness situation got worse and crime rose in the city, Brown continued flogging his chosen scapegoat. He did not hold back. "That son of a bitch should have been recalled by the very people who are currently outraged. I'm more disgusted than you'll ever believe," Brown said in a 2003 interview with the San Francisco Neighborhood Newspaper Association, blaming Hallinan for failing to prosecute people for urinating, defecating, and drinking on city streets.[19] It was quite a sudden turnaround—even for Brown.

Brown was not the only one upset by Hallinan's performance. The district attorney's relationship with the police department grew more toxic after "Fajitagate," a case that Hallinan pursued to embarrass the police leadership. Three San Francisco police officers got into trouble after drinking at a bar and spotting two men on the street with a bag of fajitas. After the officers demanded the food, the two men refused and the incident turned into a drunken brawl. No one was arrested, but when Hallinan learned that one of the officers was the son of the assistant police chief, he smelled a cover-up. It looked fishy, but Hallinan did not have enough evidence to bring them down. He brought charges against the police chief of obstruction of justice but that was ultimately dropped. The three officers were also acquitted of assault charges. It was a sign that Hallinan was thin-skinned, out of control, picking a losing battle with the police force regarding a fight over a bag of Mexican food. Things were not going smoothly in Brown's town.

Harris's seemingly audacious decision to challenge her boss for district attorney was not a risky proposition, but opportunistic. Hallinan had already embarrassed the office, lost the support of the mayor, and built a toxic relationship with the police, all while San Francisco residents watched problems like drugs, prostitution, and homelessness increase in the streets. It would not be long before he was replaced. Few were surprised when Harris announced the decision to run for district attorney of San Francisco. Harris's decision to run against her old boss stemmed from the long conflict she had within the office after she was looked over for a promotion. But Hallinan was not ready to leave. If he ran for a third term, it would be largely to defend his ideas, defy his critics, and beat Brown's abrupt betrayal. A more conservative prosecutor, Bill Fazio, also announced a campaign for district attorney. He'd lost to Hallinan twice before, but believed the public now viewed Hallinan as a disaster and that it was finally his turn.

Harris saw an opening, even in a three-way contest, and began connecting with police, the elite, and residents who were dissatisfied with the public perception of the office and the growing crime problems in the city. She arrived on the political scene and demanded a seat at the table. Brown was quietly behind her with the full support of his political machine. Even though he was term limited from running for a third term as mayor, Brown would never sit out a race that had not only Harris on the ballot, but his chosen successor for mayor, Gavin Newsom. Besides, who knew what Hallinan would do to Brown if the vengeful progressive won a third term? Harris kicked off her campaign arguing she was a competent progressive, pointing at Hallinan's low conviction rates and bitter relationship with the city police. She weaponized the city's dissatisfaction with Hallinan's lenient progressive approach to crime by proposing something different. Instead of being "soft on crime" or "tough on crime," Harris promised to be "smart on crime." Harris specifically criticized Hallinan's failure to prosecute the arrests of 2,300 protesters who rioted and destroyed city property during a protest against the Iraq War. "It is not progressive to be soft on crime," she said to voters on the campaign trail.

Harris ran to the right of Hallinan, just far enough to appear moderate compared with her old boss's failures. While Hallinan was more of an ideologue, Harris was a political opportunist and ready to fight. Part of being "smart on crime" was to attack Hallinan's lenient prosecution record. Harris played on the fears and anxieties of the city population's growing frustration with crime in San Francisco and fought dirty. Today's criminal justice reformers in the Democratic Party would ostracize a candidate voicing similar attacks on crime. Watch out, went the message: Terence Hallinan is allowing the rise of Mexican gang members and drug dealers. Hallinan is allowing criminals to beat up and kill women. Hallinan is failing children who are getting shot.

The campaign materials and staged political events made Harris look like a tough, dedicated, *Law & Order*–style crime fighter. One of Harris's political flyers featured a tattooed and shirtless man (who looked Hispanic) holding a gun and flashing a gang symbol. The message attacked Hallinan for a 30 percent rise in murders. "Who hears the cry for help?" the flyer asked. Kamala Harris was the proposed solution. Another flyer featured a chalk outline of a murdered corpse, calling Hallinan an "outline for disaster." "Which District Attorney has ranked last in convictions every year for the last eight years?" the flyer asked.[20]

During the campaign, Harris highlighted a mother whose twenty-eight-year-old daughter was killed in front of her children, allegedly by an estranged boyfriend. The woman had earlier filed two police reports about her boyfriend's behavior, but no action was taken. "Terence Hallinan is lying to us about his domestic violence record, and women are dying because of it," Harris said at a press conference on the steps of the Hall of Justice. The mother of the murder victim agreed. "If the district attorney's office had done its job, my daughter might still be alive," she said.[21] Harris also attacked Hallinan for failing to protect children. After a fifteen-year-old boy was shot and killed on a bus, she again appeared on the courthouse steps. "The district attorney should be one of the loudest voices of outrage that we have 24 cases this year alone involving people being killed who are under 25," she said, complaining of Hallinan's lackluster record of precutting gun crimes.[22] Compared to Hallinan, Harris was looking like San Francisco's "Dirty" Harry Callahan.

It was a three-way race, and Harris and her team knew that if they made it to the runoff in November she would have a good chance of winning in a one-on-one race against Hallinan. San Francisco elites who were tired of Hallinan's antics grew enamored with Harris and donated generously to her campaign. By doing so, they were supporting an opportunity to put a black woman in the position and make history. The time was up for the tired old white man currently in the position. Behind the scenes, Harris's political mentor was also betting on Harris despite her attempt to distance her connections to her former boyfriend. Brown personally donated five hundred dollars to Harris's campaign and a political consultant raising money on her behalf used a pitch letter signed by the former mayor to raise more money. The results were dynamite. By the time the campaign drew to a close, Harris raised over twice as much money as Hallinan, who protested that she had broken a voluntary spending cap on fundraising that she had pledged to honor. Harris had signed the form saying she would not spend anything more than $211,000. She exceeded the spending limit by more than $89,000. In response, Harris said she misunderstood the pledge and paid $34,000 in fines as the money kept rolling in.[23] The success of Harris's fundraising operation prompted Hallinan's suspicion. "If Willie Brown is raising hundreds of thousands of dollars for her—and has really created her that means she's indebted to him," he warned in a news article.[24] It was Hallinan versus the Brown machine.

Harris was making headway in the race, but she was furious when her opponents used her romantic relationship with Brown to suggest she was corrupt. The idea that Harris owed Brown made her angry, as she worked mightily to prove she was more than just Brown's ex-girlfriend who might return favors to the mayor and his allies. Harris had a different narrative of her first political campaign, one in which she was the hero. In Harris's version she tells the story of how she launched her campaign for district attorney out of the back of her car, using an ironing board as a stand-up desk as she pounded the pavement handing out flyers, speaking with voters, and asking them for support. "I knew I'd have to work hard to introduce myself and what I stood for to a whole lot of people who had no idea who I was," she wrote in her memoir, noting her main challenge was to explain who she was to voters in the city and boost her profile. But San Francisco journalists remembered Harris and her connections with Willie Brown and her opponents did too. Harris was faced with a problem. If she went to the press to boost her name ID, she would have to answer questions about Brown. If she shut out the press, she would only be known as the woman who dated Brown.

It was time to break free. Journalist Peter Byrne of *SF Weekly* had been contacting Harris for weeks to write a profile on her campaign, but she ignored him. When it was clear she was still lagging in the polls, she gave him a call. Together they spent about a week on the campaign trail as Harris pointedly voiced her frustrations with Brown. Bryne did not hold back, writing that Brown was "Harris' spurned ex-lover" even though he was still quietly working the levers of power for her campaign. Harris hated it. "The charge that she is Brown's puppet—that she's guilty by association with a mayor who has not been found guilty of anything—infuriates Harris," Byrne wrote, writing about her fight to "just get out from this damn Willie Brown thing."[25] Harris appeared resigned to the fact that she had to talk about Brown, but still she was not happy about it. "The mere mention of their former liaison makes her shoulders tense, her hands clench, and her eyes narrow," Byrne wrote, noting that she described her former boyfriend as an "albatross hanging around my neck." She asked voters to forget her past romance with Brown and step into the role of aliens visiting San Francisco from outer space. "Would it make sense if you are a Martian coming to Earth that the litmus test for public office is where a candidate is in their relationship to Willie Brown?" Harris asked in the article. "Willie Brown is not going to be around. He's gone—hello people, move on. If there is corruption, it will be prosecuted. It's a no-brainer, but let's please move on." She also argued that she would not criticize Brown because she believed it would appear inauthentic. "I refuse," she said vehemently, "to design my campaign around criticizing Willie Brown for the sake of appearing to be independent when I have no doubt that I am independent of him—and that he would probably right now express some fright about the fact that he cannot control me."

Yet Harris grabbed a shovel and started shoveling dirt on his political grave in an effort to prove her independence from Brown. "His career is over; I will be alive and kicking for the next 40 years. I do not owe him a thing," she insisted. But Harris had earned a big paycheck thanks to Brown and was still traveling the city in a stylish BMW—which she clarified for the article was not the 1994 model that Brown gave her when they were dating, but a 1997 that she traded it in for.

The women in the Harris family were also fiercely defensive of Harris's one-year relationship with a powerful man who was twice her age. "This hype around Willie Brown is such a distraction and so opportunistic, sexist, and ridiculous," her sister, Maya Harris, said. "When a woman dates an accomplished man, why are people so willing to assume it's only because of him that the woman is successful?" Maya's argument paled in front of the facts. Brown was the most powerful politician in California politics when he met Harris, who was then a prosecutor from Almeda County.

Harris's mother was also dismissive of the impact of the relationship, proudly noting that her daughter was brought up with the right manners and could thrive in high society. "Why shouldn't she have gone out with Willie Brown?" her mother asked. "He was a player. And what could Willie Brown expect from her in the future? He has not much life left."

Brown did have a lot of life left and he was still helping Harris and shifting a lot of political capital her way. He also may have encouraged Harris to do the interview with Byrne. "I later heard from her campaign manager that somebody had told her that [I was] a fair reporter. I suspect Willie Brown told her that—I wrote a lot about Willie Brown, and I was always fair," Byrne recalled later in life. The print cover version of the 5,600-word story was on every corner of San Francisco and proved to be a boost for Harris's campaign. Harris advisors later told Byrne that she would not have won if not for his journalistic epic and Harris agreed. Byrne recalled that while visiting Harris's campaign office on election night, she screamed with delight and gave him a hug.[26]

It was not the only assistance Harris got from the local press. The *San Francisco Chronicle* endorsed Harris in the early primary with a strong rebuke against Hallinan. "The district attorney's office can no longer afford to be a circus sideshow," the October editorial read. "Kamala Harris, a 38-year-old veteran prosecutor, offers the best hope of repairing the damage inflicted on that critical city office during the past eight years of Hallinan's reign."[27] Despite the launch of what looked like a long-shot campaign, Harris had successfully leveraged the city of San Francisco into the runoff election in a three-candidate race. She later beat Hallinan by ten points. Freed from the shadows, Brown appeared publicly at Harris's victory party and spoke to the press. "It is obviously a gender victory. It is obviously an ethnic victory. But it was her competence that defeated Terence Hallinan," he said.[28] Brown was too humble. Harris's election was proof that his political machine was still very powerful, powerful enough to get an unexperienced, unknown political figure elected as the next district attorney of San Francisco.

Brown has only teased details of his romance with Harris over the years. "It was a real love affair," he said in an interview with KCBS Radio in February 2019. "I loved me and she loved me."

He recalled that Harris was a wonderful companion who helped him focus on running his campaign and he enjoyed spending time with her but he could never get over her age. "She was much too young," he said. "Even I had a problem with age in that world." Brown also hinted in the interview that they had a contentious history. "I hope she becomes the president," he said, adding with a chuckle, "And I will move to another country."

Brown also wrote a column in January 2019 about his relationship with Harris more than twenty years prior, as the questions from the media piled up after she announced her run for president. "Yes, I may have influenced her career by appointing her to two state commissions when I was Assembly speaker," he wrote, recalling that he also helped her in her first race for district attorney. "I have also helped the careers of House Speaker Nancy Pelosi, Gov. Gavin Newsom, Sen. Dianne Feinstein and a host of other politicians," he wrote defensively. (To our best knowledge, Brown did not have romantic relationships with these political protégés.) Brown indicated Harris seemingly threatened him after she won her race for district attorney. "Harris is the only one who, after I helped her, sent word that I would be indicted if I 'so much as jaywalked' while she was D.A.," he wrote. "That's politics for ya."[29]

# CHAPTER THREE

# KAMALA THE COP

*We recognized . . . as a prosecutor in law enforcement I have a huge stick.*

—KAMALA HARRIS, JANUARY 14, 2010

Kamala Harris made history as the first black district attorney elected in San Francisco. The inaugural ceremony showcased her multicultural background. Harris took her oath of office on a bound copy of the Bill of Rights instead of the Bible, held proudly by her mother. The Black National Anthem was performed at the ceremony as well as the traditional National Anthem. A Hindu priest, Pandit Nageshwara Subramaniam Shastri, performed an ashirvadam ritual blessing and a Christian minister also offered a prayer. A traditional Asian dragon dance was performed by the Kie Lun Martial Arts group.[1] Harris delivered her inaugural speech with her canned campaign slogan.

"Let's put an end, right here, to the question of whether we are tough on crime or soft on crime. Let us be smart on crime," she said.

As district attorney, Harris's vow to be "smart on crime" appeared more like "smart on politics," as she carefully threaded her narrative to appear competent but progressive. It had mixed results. Often vowing personal and hands-on attention to important issues, Harris typically allowed issues to fade out when public attention waned. Rather than tackle monumental change, she appeared better at proposing and promoting new ideas rather than achieving results. When things went wrong in her office she feigned ignorance, blaming her staff for not keeping her informed. She became an expert at pandering to activists but also finding new ways to burnish her role as a tough law enforcement figure in California as she prepared to further her political career.

Despite running a campaign to the right of Hallinan, Harris began as a progressive. After just four months on the job, Harris took one of the toughest public stands of her career with a decision that damaged her relationship with law enforcement officers for years afterward. On the evening of April 10, 2004, two police officers approached two men acting suspiciously. One of them, a gang member, turned around and shot twenty-nine-year-old undercover police officer Isaac Espinoza with fourteen rounds from an AK-47. Police officers were heartbroken as they watched Espinoza's wife and three-year-old daughter at the funeral, and demanded the death penalty for his killer. But Harris had vowed to oppose the death penalty during her campaign and planned to stick with her position. She tried to win over the law enforcement community and the Espinoza family by issuing a statement.

"Today I want to be very clear: in the city and county of San Francisco, anyone who murders a police officer engaged in his or her duties will be met with the most severe consequences," Harris said.[2] The most severe consequence, however, was ruled out. Harris was not going to change her mind on the death penalty, not even after a police officer was shot in the streets. The police union was furious as officers would turn their backs to Harris when she appeared in public. Espinoza's mother was devastated. "She made the decision after just three days. My son wasn't even in the ground yet," said Carol Espinoza said afterward.[3]

Former mayor of San Francisco and now senator Dianne Feinstein felt differently. She appeared at Espinoza's funeral at St. Mary's Cathedral and berated Harris's decision while she sat in the audience. "This is not only the definition of tragedy, it's the special circumstance called for by the death penalty law," Feinstein said as the police officers gave her a standing ovation. After the service, Feinstein dug the knife in deeper, telling reporters she would have never endorsed Harris if she had known she would be so rigid on opposing the death penalty.[4] Harris felt betrayed, but her commitment to opposing the death penalty was firm.

Harris the progressive also turned a blind eye to violent protesters. For the first anniversary of the war in Iraq, Harris was faced with the problem of antiwar protesters who were arrested for violent disruptive behavior. San Francisco police arrested 124 of them for breaking the law, including some that had assaulted police officers. Whereas Hallinan, a year earlier, famously dragged his feet and ultimately dismissed the charges against violent protesters, Harris vowed to personally review each case. It did not matter. Days later, Harris dropped the charges, asserting that the burden of proof could not be met in any of the cases, despite detailed evidence captured on video.[5]

After campaigning on competence and commitment, Harris looked even more "smart on crime" as she began manipulating the numbers on conviction. If the district attorney prosecutes fewer cases and brings them to trial, the conviction rate goes up. The conviction rate also goes up when the prosecutor offers plea deals instead of taking it to court. Although she vowed to personally engage the backlog of murder cases, she gradually dismissed them at an astonishing rate. Harris began offering generous plea bargain deals to defendants, even those arrested for murder. Of the backlog of 73 homicide cases on Hallinan's watch, Harris cut a deal for 32 of them and only convicted 15 of the defendants for murder.[6] As a result, Harris boasted higher conviction rates even though she was bringing fewer cases to trial. Harris was also offering plea deals to gun offenders. During her first three years as district attorney, San Francisco's conviction rate jumped from 52 to 67 percent, which looked good on paper but baffled police officers.[7] Police officers making the arrests and filing casework found their efforts abandoned by a prosecutor who appeared less committed to justice than she was to her political future. It worked. By 2005, Oprah Winfrey featured "superstar prosecutor Kamala Harris" on her morning show, boasting of her "90 percent conviction rate" and praising her as California's "first African American female district attorney."[8] (Harris boasted about her "90 percent conviction rate" but it was only her record in homicide cases, not all criminal cases.)

Harris was quietly in the middle on most issues important to San Francisco residents. In 2004, she refused to prosecute a series of high-publicized police arrests for prostitution at a local strip club but went on the record in 2008 to oppose Proposition K, a ballot measure put to voters that would decriminalize prostitution in the city of San Francisco.[9] "I think it's completely ridiculous, just in case there's any ambiguity about my position," Harris said about the proposition. "It would put a welcome mat out for pimps and prostitutes to come on into San Francisco."[10]

Harris also publicly promoted an advertising campaign for San Francisco's sanctuary city status in 2008, reminding illegal immigrants they would not be treated as criminals for their immigration status, but she used the law to deport violent criminals. Harris defended a ballot proposition to legalize medical marijuana but defended federal raids on some of the "out of control" distributers in the city. Her cautious strategy worked. In 2007, Harris ran for reelection without a challenger—the first time that had happened in San Francisco since 1991—after collecting more than $500,000 in donations and lining up her endorsements. It was the kind of victory that encouraged her to dream about higher office.

As Harris began eying statewide office, she shifted to a new proposal that would frighten San Francisco families. The project began in 2006 when she announced she would start prosecuting parents of truant children, threatening them with a $2,500 fine and up to a year in jail. "It's a crime when a child goes uneducated—it's a crime," Harris said as she announced the program.[11] Fighting truancy was an easy target although the issue had not become a crisis.[12] It was a breathtaking use of power. Harris calculated that California voters statewide would approve of her idea of making sure more children went to school, and the campaign to terrify parents and truant schoolchildren began.

Harris later admitted in a 2010 speech that her proposal was "a little controversial in San Francisco," and that "my staff was going bananas," but she defended her willingness to get tougher on children and parents. She expanded her program after winning reelection, arguing that she had the political capital to do so. "I said, 'Look I'm done, this is a serious issue. I've got a little political capital and I'm going to spend some of it.'"[13] In other words: Watch out, kids. Kamala the Cop is going to throw your parents in jail.

Harris made a public show of using her authority to strike fear into the hearts of public-school-attending families. "We recognized that in that initiative as a prosecutor in law enforcement I have a huge stick," Harris explained during her speech, pointing out her stationery had the image of a badge, which she sent out to parents. Harris also laughed as she recalled a friend telling her a story about his wife using the letter to threaten her children. "'Kamala,'" her friend said. "'My wife got the letter, she freaked out, she brought all the kids in the living room, held up the letter, and said if you don't go to school, Kamala's going to put me and you in jail.'" Harris also explained why she wanted her toughest-looking homicide and gang prosecutors from her office to sit with school administrators and parents while they discussed truancy: "They went over there and I said, 'When you go over there, you look really mean,' and so they did and invariably the parents would say, 'Well who is the mean-looking dude?' And the principal would say, 'Well that's someone that mean DA Kamala Harris sent over because she says she's going to start prosecuting you if we can't figure this out.'"

Harris proudly celebrated her program as a smashing success, as she continued threatening children and families. "To date, I have prosecuted 20 parents of young children for truancy. The penalty for truancy charged as a misdemeanor is a fine of up to $2,500 or up to a year of jail," she boasted in a 2009 op-ed in a San Francisco paper.[14] Her enthusiasm on the issue was calculated as a way to show her commitment to California's children, but her callousness would later hurt her political brand.

A year after Harris was reelected as district attorney of San Francisco, she began to think about her run for attorney general of California. The political winds were in her favor. Harris was present in Grant Park in Chicago on election night to celebrate President Barack Obama's election victory over Senator John McCain and felt anything was possible. Harris was one of the few California elected officials who endorsed Obama instead of Hillary Clinton from the beginning, helping him campaign in Iowa when the idea of the nation's first black president seemed like a long shot. Despite her loyalty, Harris chose not to seek out a position in Washington, DC, as she felt ready to tackle statewide office. On November 12, 2008, just a week after Obama's election, she announced her decision to run for attorney general of California. With Obama's victory inspiring a new generation of political figures, Harris had her head in the clouds. "I am very proud to know that I provide a role model for those who identify with me for reasons of culture or ethnicity or gender," she said in an interview after announcing her campaign, adding that "the idea of being able to be inspirational to other people is something I think we all desire."[15]

While Harris was dreaming of statewide office, other problems were slipping past the district attorney's office, creating scandal. During her second term, Harris's prosecution of drug crimes took a major hit. Crime lab worker Deborah Madden had been convicted and jailed for domestic violence and also had problems showing up to work. Prosecutors knew her work was unreliable and flagged their office. On top of it all, Madden was allegedly skimming cocaine from the lab for personal use. But none of the information was revealed by the Harris's office until the police finally publicly admitted problems with the lab in 2010. Superior Court judge Anne-Christine Massullo was furious and blamed Harris for failing to report it. Thousands of cases would be affected due to Harris's negligence. "The District Attorney's failure appears to have been in part the result of lack of processes and procedures necessary to ensure that exculpatory information is timely provided to defendants which is solely the responsibility of the District Attorney's office," the judge wrote in her ruling, condemning "significant errors and misjudgments" by Harris and her office.

Senior officials within the district attorney's office knew of the problem and emailed Harris's top assistant about it, but Harris claimed ignorance, insisting she was not told about the problem by either her staff or police. Harris tried to downplay the seriousness of the scandal, initially saying it would only affect "dozens" of cases, but she soon realized the problem was much worse. As questions mounted, more and more cases were affected by the new information about the crime lab, affecting hundreds of cases which were being revisited one by one. In response, Harris suddenly dismissed about one thousand drug-related cases, including many in which convictions had been obtained and sentences were being served.

The city's head public defender, Jeff Adachi, a former tutor and friend of Harris, grew increasingly frustrated with her failure to turn over important information related to cases. Harris refused to turn over names of police officers with arrest records or a history of misconduct to public defenders. Harris, Adachi complained, was "unethical" for hiding the information and "putting the privacy interests of police officers who have misconduct records and who have been convicted of crimes above the rights of citizens to a fair and honest trial."[16]

In 2009, Harris was also exposed for critical mistakes in her signature "Back on Track" program, which placed first-time felony offenders in job-training programs instead of sentencing them to prison time." Alexander Izaguirre, an illegal immigrant in San Francisco, reportedly snatched twenty-nine-year-old Amanda Kiefer's purse as the driver of his vehicle ran her down and fractured her skull. Izaguirre was an illegal immigrant who pleaded guilty to selling cocaine four months earlier, earning him a spot in Harris's Back on Track program.[17] The incident flagged a critical issue with Harris's program as prosecutors were sending illegal immigrants to a job-training program for jobs they were not legally allowed to have instead of deporting them. Harris feigned ignorance about the issue but admitted it was a "huge kind of pimple on the face of this program" and promised to fix it.[18]

Harris was struggling to keep up with her existing job even as she was planning the next step of her political career. But her record was far from convincing as conviction rates were down in the district attorney's office, despite her best efforts to manipulate the numbers. Harris had run on competency, but her conviction rates were approaching Hallinan territory, even as she was offering more plea deals. *SF Weekly* savaged Harris as she was running for attorney general on her record of conviction rates. "Harris has won only 55 percent of murder trials since the beginning of 2009, and . . . in the first quarter of 2010 her office's conviction rate for *all* felony trials was only 53 percent. By contrast, the most recent statewide average for prosecutors was 83 percent," wrote reporter Peter Jamison for a cover story featuring Harris on the front page with the headline "Lack of Conviction."[19]

Despite her difficulties, Harris was making powerful connections at the top of the social ladder. An example of her social status was revealed by comedian Dave Chappelle in his comedy special *Sticks and Stones*, when he recalled how he once invited comedian and actor Chris Tucker to the Punch Line, a comedy club where he was performing. When Tucker asked if he could bring some friends, Chappelle agrees. Tucker arrived with Gavin Newsom, then the mayor of San Francisco, and Kamala Harris, the district attorney of San Francisco. Former vice president Al Gore was there as well as Google executives and NAACP president Ben Jealous. Chappelle recounted striking up a conversation with Harris, who flexed her political connections by telling him that "her friend" Barack Obama was running for president and even called Obama on her cell phone so that Chappelle could speak to him personally. (Obama did not answer the call from Harris's phone, but Chappelle left a voice message.) That's the kind of life a California politician lives. The biggest stars party with the biggest business executives, local politicians, and activists—and every year, the president of the United States cycles through for a series of fundraisers. Harris's connections to Obama continued to serve her well, as she met up with him any time he was in town. She also earned an invitation to a White House state dinner for the Indian prime minister in November 2009. Quite a pull for a local district attorney.

As her campaign for attorney general launched, Harris's political messaging machine also mobilized, despite bad headlines about her record. Donors did not care about the details and neither did the national media. During her second term as district attorney in San Francisco, Harris spent time turning her "smart on crime" message into a book in 2009 and the media tour began. Harris was learning the art of failing up. As she made her way through the media circuit, Harris started dazzling the national media as she was already being described as the "female Obama."

"She's brilliant, she's smart, she doesn't look anything like anybody you ever see on *Law & Order*, yet she's tough, she's got a great future, they call her the female Obama," PBS broadcaster Gwen Ifill said during an appearance on *Late Night with David Letterman* in March 2009. That was echoed in an interview with Matt Lauer on NBC's *Today* show.

Like Obama, Harris has a mixed-race heritage, but they are starkly different political figures. Obama was a Harvard Law School graduate who went into the Illinois legislature before running for the United States Senate. Harris had only served as a mediocre San Francisco district attorney, but she was workshopping a brand that offered something new. In her interview with Lauer, Harris celebrated her reform efforts but also reminded the audience she was also a career prosecutor and prepared to deal with crime. "If someone commits a serious crime, lock 'em up," she said, referring to the worst kind of criminals, like rapists and murderers. But she also had a record to defend. When Lauer brought up the case of illegal immigrants getting placed in her Back on Track initiative, Harris got defensive, noting there would always be problems with new systems. She assured viewers that everything was fixed. "When we learned that that happened, we fixed it. There you go," she said breezily.

Harris had already announced her campaign for attorney general, but first she had to face an unexpected primary challenger. In California, every politician is likely to face a particular kind of opponent at some point in their career: a self-funded multimillionaire. Republicans had their wealthy primary candidates, eBay executive Meg Whitman and HP executive Carly Fiorina. Democrats would always have their Tom Steyer, willing to light a few million on fire to run for a Democrat primary and lose. Harris's multimillionaire primary challenger was former Facebook attorney Chris Kelly. Kelly saw what most Californians were witnessing in San Francisco. Harris was struggling amid reports of poor conviction rates, the crime lab scandal, and (again) rising crime in the city. He felt there was an opening and as a Facebook executive he certainly had the money. Kelly's team collected a highlight reel of Harris laughing off tough questions from reporters and published a video on YouTube titled "We're Not Laughing with You" to emphasize her callousness.

Kelly believed Harris was a tough target, but beatable. He sank millions of his personal fortune into his campaign, believing he could saturate the airwaves in California with attack ads to break down Harris's substantial polling lead. The narrator in one ad said:

A scandal in the crime lab could release thousands of criminals back onto the streets. A judge blasted Harris for hiding the problems in her office. She has the lowest trial conviction rate of big-city DAs. Harris loses almost half of her felony trials—giving criminals a 50-50 shot of going free. San Francisco has the highest homicide and robbery rates in the state. And Kamala Harris wants to be your next attorney general?[20]

Kelly's message was strong enough to shake Harris's team out of a malaise and they ultimately responded with their own attack ads. Harris's team reminded Democrat voters she was endorsed by Dianne Feinstein, Nancy Pelosi, and every major newspaper in the state and was San Francisco's first African American district attorney. She insisted Kelly's claims were false, portraying him as a "rookie" who was "unexperienced" and not worthy of state office. The Harris team also ran campaign ads questioning Facebook's record on privacy while Kelly was working there, telling voters he would sell them out if given the chance. Kelly sank more than $12 million in his self-funded campaign against Harris in the primary, but he came up woefully short. Harris beat him by 18 points. Harris's victory over Kelly proved that competence did not matter to California votes as much as experience, familiarity, and endorsements from the entire California political machine. Harris retained her California support because she had not disappointed her donor base or her political base and remained on the right side of social issues important to Californians.

Harris's general election opponent, Republican Steve Cooley, was a much more formidable candidate, making this the toughest political race of her California career. While Harris was the career prosecutor from San Francisco with liberal sensibilities, Cooley had served three terms as district attorney for Los Angeles with a strong record as a prosecutor. Cooley ran as a Republican and was a competent law-and-order candidate who thought he had an easy fight against Harris. In the race against a fellow prosecutor, Harris worked hard to distance herself from her record as Cooley hammered her as a liberal idealogue because of her opposition to the death penalty, which, he reminded voters, was still the law of the land in California. In response, Harris proudly ran as a cop who was responsible for throwing people in jail. "I will not cede my law enforcement and crime fighting credentials to anyone," she said to local media in October 2010. "There are a whole lot of people spending a whole lot of time in state prison because of work I've personally done in the courtroom."[21] Those slogans played well early in her career but would prove problematic in her political future.

Cooley correctly identified Harris as a career politician who was using the attorney generalship as a stepping-stone to higher office. "She doesn't want to be attorney general," Cooley said at a speech at the Republican California Party convention, calling her a "radical." "She wants to be senator, governor, vice president. . . . But I would be very happy to stop her aspirations at an early point in her career. There's just too much at stake," Cooley concluded.[22] The attack might have been more effective in a state that was not California. Harris embraced the term *radical*. "I read that at the Republican convention he called me a radical, so I guess that is one difference between us," Harris said during a Google Talks event after Cooley's convention remarks. "And yeah, I am a radical. I do believe we have to get radical about what we are doing and take it seriously."[23]

Harris also had the support of elites from all over the country who wanted to meet the "female Obama" that everyone was talking about. Although she was running for state office in California, Harris took time off in the summer to cozy up to East Coast elites to broaden her fundraising base and political appeal. She earned the support of Jeff Zucker, then the CEO of NBCUniversal, who hosted a breakfast for her at the NBC office in August 2009 to boost her campaign. Zucker was all-in. "I believe Kamala is not just important for the city of San Francisco, the state of

California, but for the entire country," he said. Zucker admitted his endorsement was unusual, because he tried to stay out of politics, but did it anyway. Zucker recalled that he and his wife had met Harris four years earlier in San Francisco at a dinner, and that she "really knocked our socks off."[24] Harris also included a trip to Martha's Vineyard as part of her East Coast tour, sitting down for a *Vineyard Gazette* profile where she spoke about a kinship between California and Massachusetts. "They are both training grounds for Democratic Party leadership," she noted. Harris was already laying down groundwork for her national political future.

On the campaign trail in California, Harris criticized the current law enforcement system as in need of repair, campaigning as a reformer. She defended her opposition to the death penalty as personal, promising to defend and follow the law in state cases. She also promised to focus on white-collar crimes, like mortgage fraud, high-tech crimes, and even environmental crimes. Her campaign television ads featured a helicopter and a dramatic sound track as she walked confidently with law enforcement officers, hair blowing in the wind. "Our justice system needs drastic repair," Harris said in the ad, looking into the camera after footage featured police officers putting criminals into police cars.[25] Kamala the Cop was reporting for duty.

Harris also knew the importance of leaning left on social issues, despite swearing an oath to follow the law. But one law did not matter. Harris vocalized her opposition to Proposition 8, a law passed in California in 2008 banning same-sex marriage that was soon challenged in federal court. Knowing the law infuriated California liberals, Harris vowed she would not even defend the state law if she won the job as attorney general. It was a radical step to refuse to uphold the law, but it set a contrast with Cooley the lawman. Cooley said that if elected attorney general, he would defend Proposition 8 as the law of the land despite his personal views.

Cooley was a strong candidate who began the race leading the polls, so Harris and her team had no qualms about going on the offensive and lobbing attacks. Harris started attacking him as greedy and out of touch after he said he would take his district attorney pension on top of the attorney general salary, which was $150,000. She also started attacking

Cooley for accepting gifts of Lakers tickets, cigars, wine, and suits, which, while not illegal, were portrayed as unethical.[26] She also accused him of being indifferent to the environment, suggesting he was corrupt, ignoring environmental lawsuits in favor of land developers and oil companies. Cooley rested comfortably on accusations that Harris was soft on crime because she refused to seek the death penalty for a cop killer. The Republican State Leadership Committee ran a $1 million attack advertising campaign to help Cooley in late October, but the race was tightening.

Harris already had the support of President Obama, who endorsed Harris and rallied with her and other California Democrats on Cooley's home turf in Los Angeles at the University of Southern California campus in October 2010. During his rally speech, Obama called Harris out specifically as "a dear, dear friend of mine." He added, "So I want everybody to do right by her." Obama also attended a fundraiser for Harris in California on her behalf, charging $6,500 a person per ticket with a photo op.[27]

The race was close right down to the wire, and Harris nervously delivered an optimistic election night speech even as one newspaper had already declared the race for Cooley. Cooley gave a speech declaring victory even though there were more than 2.3 million ballots to be counted. For weeks the late ballots came trickling in and they finally helped push Harris over the edge. "On Election Night 2010, I lost the race for attorney general. Three weeks later, I won," Harris wrote in her book. After weeks of counting absentee and provisional ballots, Harris pulled ahead by a significant margin. Cooley called Harris to concede the race on November 25, right before Thanksgiving. He was bitter. "It is unfortunate that someone who is a nonpartisan, nonpolitician could not overcome the increasingly partisan tendencies of the state, even for an office that by its nature necessitates a nonpartisan approach," he said in his concession statement. In response, Harris thanked Cooley for participating in a "spirited campaign" and said she looked forward to working with him in the future. Harris barely scraped by a win, even though it was a big year for Democrats in the state of California. Senator Barbara Boxer beat her Republican rival Carly Fiorina by ten points, Gavin Newsom won his race for Lieutenant Governor by eleven points, and Jerry Brown beat Meg Whitman for California by thirteen points. Harris won her race by 0.8 percent.[28] She got the job as "top cop" in California, but her new position would present a challenge in the future of her career.

# CHAPTER FOUR

# TOP COP

*I now stand before you as the top cop of the biggest state in the country.*

—KAMALA HARRIS, JULY 27, 2016

As California attorney general, Harris was more cautious than ever about her political future even though she portrayed herself as a fierce champion for Golden State residents. Her near loss to Cooley served as a warning not to go too far left or else risk alienating moderate voters who would ultimately hold the future of her political career in their hands. But she also wanted to make a political impact on the top issue facing the country after the 2008 financial crisis. She was not alone. In 2011, Harris was one of many state attorneys general who had to weigh a decision that would have political ramifications across the country. There was a significant level of populist anger at the banks, particularly over their dubious foreclosure actions. State attorneys general had two choices: either pursue a legal settlement with the banks and get a lot of money for their state, or take the case to trial so angry voters could watch the fat cats be punished. President Obama and the Justice Department, anxiously approaching the president's reelection campaign, wanted a splashy deal done so they could run on a record of holding the big banks accountable. The Justice Department and state attorneys general began working up a multistate settlement with the nation's top five largest banks over their questionable servicing of home mortgages and foreclosure actions.

Harris had to weigh her position: She could either participate in the settlement and make headlines with billions of dollars for her state, or walk away and face a long exhausting legal battle by herself. In the beginning, Harris chose to walk away, but only after it was clear that her leading Democrat colleagues were planning something similar. Harris has since promoted the settlement as a huge moment of career political courage. But looking at the facts, it appears that Harris, as usual, carefully made her political calculations and was pressured by outside forces before acting. In early discussions, Harris made a point of appearing willing to stay away from the multistate settlement. But she was still in talks with the banks when New York State attorney general Eric Schneiderman made the first big splash by pulling out of the negotiations entirely. Schneiderman, not Harris, was described as the leader of the group of Democrat state attorneys general described as "renegade progressives" for using the settlement to score political points.[1]

Harris was more cautious and did not join Schneiderman by pulling out of the negotiations right away. On October 11, she went to Washington, DC, to meet again with the banks but was not satisfied with the response she was getting. Neither were activists in the state. Potential future political rivals like Lieutenant Governor Gavin Newsom joined activists in calling the deal a "deeply flawed settlement proposal,"[2] pressuring Harris to walk away from the negotiations. It was hardly a difficult choice, with Newsom exploiting a progressive populist political angle.

Harris returned to California and announced her decision to hold out for a better deal, spinning it as a moment of political courage when all forces were urging her to settle. Harris was hardly alone in her moment of "courage." Other state attorneys general were running a similar playbook: get tough on the banks and get a bigger settlement because it will enhance your political career. Massachusetts attorney general Martha Coakley was a holdout as well as Attorney General Catherine Cortez Masto of Nevada. President Joe Biden's son Beau, then the attorney general of Delaware, also joined the group of Democrats who wanted more from the banks. Harris loved Beau Biden, praising the vice president's son for siding with her, calling him "an incredible friend and colleague" and "a man of principle and courage." Aligning with the vice president's son, of course, certainly enhanced one's political career.

Harris also revealed a dramatic exchange she had over the phone with JPMorgan Chase CEO Jamie Dimon. "I took off my earrings (the Oakland in me) and picked up the receiver," Harris wrote in her book, casting herself as a changemaker who made "demands" during the call. Theatrics aside, the banks were ultimately willing to sweeten the pot, creating a deal attractive enough for both Schneiderman and Harris to fall into line. Of the so-called rebels, she was among the first to finally settle, not the last. With New York and California on board, it was easier for the banks to get Nevada, Massachusetts, and Delaware to join.

By February 9, 2012, the group of attorneys general announced an agreement to a settlement of $25 billion from the banks, and everyone involved had their moment to celebrate. "Under the terms of this settlement, America's biggest banks, banks that were rescued by taxpayer dollars, will be required to right these wrongs," Obama said proudly at the White House. Harris had secured $18 billion for the state of California, but she had not assuaged outraged activists. At the Democrat state convention in 2015, activists unfurled banners berating Harris. "$18 Billion Settlement Is Not Justice" and "Kamala Harris $ Sold Out Homeowners $ Protected Wall Street $," they read. During her convention speech, activists shouted, "Sold out! Sold out! Took money from Wall Street!"[3] The so-called tough, no-nonsense prosecutor had settled.

In some cases, Harris outright ignored highly questionable behavior by the banks. A leaked memo from her office published by the Intercept revealed that she inexplicably ignored a yearlong investigation of OneWest that uncovered illegal foreclosures of mortgages in the state. From 2009 to 2012, the bank acquired thousands of troubled loans in California and began foreclosing them. During the crisis, OneWest had foreclosed on

35,000 homes in the state and opened foreclosure proceedings on another 45,000. The memo cited "evidence suggestive of widespread misconduct." The CEO of OneWest at the time was Steven Mnuchin, who at the time was also a Harris campaign donor, and later the Secretary of Treasury for President Donald Trump. Leftist billionaire George Soros was also an investor.[4] Harris decided against prosecuting the case, prompting accusations from her political opponents that she was willing to look the other way on issues facing her friends and political donors. In May 2011, Harris announced the creation of a Mortgage Fraud Strike Force that would investigate and prosecute people trying to take advantage of the crisis. "Families are losing their homes, while those who perpetrated crimes and frauds against them walk free," Harris said as she announced the new force of twenty-five attorneys and investigators. But the task force had a slow start, only prosecuting three cases in ten years.[5] Not surprisingly, Soros and Mnuchin were not on the list.

In 2012, Harris wanted to use her record on "fighting" the banks as a springboard to national political stardom. Thanks to her loyalty to Obama, she earned a coveted speaking role at the 2012 Democratic National Convention. But instead of a self-promoting speech, Harris was asked to deliver a six-minute speech scripted by Team Obama to help savage his rival, Mitt Romney. Harris dutifully read the scripted speech but mistakenly referred to the former Republican governor of Massachusetts and future Utah senator as "Miss Romney" before correcting herself. Convention crowd conversations and noise continued on the floor as Harris spoke, as only a few people in the crowd clapped and cheered at her applause lines. It was hardly a repeat of Obama's 2004 Hope and Change speech that catapulted him to superstardom.

Hope and Change, however, was not Harris's brand at the moment. She was focused on a tougher law-and-order record that would look out of place in the modern Democratic Party. Teaming up with Democratic governor Jerry Brown, Harris fought the courts to keep inmates in California's overcrowded prisons. Brown certainly did not want to be responsible for any horrific crimes committed by released prisoners, and Harris, with her political future on the line, had the same goal. On May 23, 2011, the US Supreme Court ruled in *Brown v. Plata* that California's overcrowded prison system was unconstitutional, affirming a three-judge federal court ruling ordering the state to reduce the prison population to 110,000. The Supreme Court argued that California was breaking the Eighth Amendment's ban on cruel and unusual punishment. "A prison that deprives prisoners of basic sustenance, including adequate medical care, is incompatible with the concept of human dignity and has no place in civilized society," Justice Anthony Kennedy wrote in the majority opinion.

Governor Brown led the fight against the ruling and Harris, three months into the job, was the lawyer. They defied the Supreme Court ruling, fighting a three-person federal panel designed to force the release of prisoners early to reduce overcrowding. Despite many failures in court, they managed to stall enforcement of the order. The *Atlantic* reported in 2013 that Harris "has authorized or permitted the filing of a series of dubious motions and briefs on behalf of the state as it tries to weasel out of its constitutional requirements to the inmates."[6] The panel complained in a 2013 ruling that "defendants have repeatedly found new and unexpected ways to frustrate this Court's orders," and accused them of "protracting these legal proceedings to a time that could hardly have been imagined."[7] While the courts were trying to wrest the prison doors open, Harris was slamming them shut. In 2014, her lawyers fought against the new parole program by arguing in court that they could not release prisoners because the prisons "would lose an important labor pool" and "severely impact fire camp participation" for inmates to fight fires. When there was an uproar in the press, Harris feigned ignorance. "I will be very candid with you, because I saw that article this morning, and I was shocked," she responded to BuzzFeed News, insisting she was "very troubled by what I read." It was a familiar response for those following the career of Kamala Harris. Instead of taking responsibility, she always returned to the notion she had no idea what was going on in her own office. "The idea that we incarcerate people to have indentured servitude is one of the worst possible perceptions," said Harris. "I feel very strongly about that. It evokes images of chain gangs. I take it very seriously and I'm looking into exactly what needs to be done to correct it."[8] She needed to take it seriously. The state's first black attorney general was playing the role of a chain gang boss.

Despite her "top cop" branding, Harris also tried to appear as a lenient prosecutor in front of corporate and activist audiences, a merciful lawyer willing to give nonviolent criminals a chance. At the Ford Foundation in May 2014, she delivered a speech about criminal justice reform acknowledging the struggle with the court decision. "This as you can imagine presented a crisis in California and the way the discussion played out was, 'Oh bleep, what are we going to do?'" she said, bursting out laughing. "'We got all these bleep-bleeps that we gotta . . . what are we going to do?'"[9] Harris promoted her Back on Track initiative as the solution, even though she was actively fighting against releasing criminals from California's prisons. Harris also tried to earn laughs from older generations in the room by ridiculing young people. "Remember, age is more than just a chronological fact. What else do we know about this population eighteen to twenty-four? They are stupid," she said with a laugh. "That is why we put them in dormitories and they have a resident assistant! They make really bad decisions!" Harris did not appear to be set on winning the hearts and minds of the youth.

In the summer of 2014, as Harris was running for reelection as attorney general, she was presented with a different career path. President Barack Obama's US attorney general, Eric Holder, phoned her and asked if she was interested in his job. Holder had suffered a host of political scandals, including his stonewalling of congressional Republicans on their investigation of the Department of Justice's gun-running Operation Fast and Furious—in which federal agents let more than 2,000 guns get sold illegally, some of which were later used in crimes. For that, Holder was officially held in contempt of Congress. (The Justice Department announced they would not prosecute him despite the contempt of Congress vote.) Holder emerged as an embattled partisan who survived the controversy, but needed to leave before Obama's reelection campaign. Harris appreciated the offer but decided against the idea. The move would be a career dead end, and she had bigger plans. Why join Obama when you can *be* the next Obama?

That same summer, social media and public protests fueled a new movement challenging the system of law enforcement. In July 2014, forty-three-year-old Eric Garner died after a New York City police officer used a chokehold on him, sparking a series of angry protests. In August 2014, eighteen-year-old Michael Brown was shot to death by police in Ferguson, Missouri, sparking days of rioting in the community. In response to the public outcry, leftist activists formed the Black Lives Matter movement, mobilizing against police officers and law enforcement. Leftist donors joined the fight, fueling a full-scale rejection of modern policing in the Democratic Party.

One might expect that Kamala Harris, as a black attorney general of a Democrat-controlled state, would take the lead in the Black Lives Matter movement, but she did not use her position to make any important reforms. Earlier in her career, Harris was on the record explaining why she believed it was a "myth" that there was a conflict between police and black people, calling it a "false choice." "I think there is a myth among the entire population, that African Americans don't want law enforcement. We do," she said in a 2006 event with talk-show host Tavis Smiley. "We just don't want excessive force," she continued. In her book *Smart on Crime*, Harris wrote that more cops on the streets was a good thing. "[I]f we take a show of hands of those who would like to see more police officers on the street, mine would shoot up," she wrote.[10]

Harris, while running for reelection, did not initially engage with the Black Lives Matter movement or even meet with activists who challenged her. Activists began rallying against police shootings of young men in California, demanding further scrutiny after the deaths of Mario Romero, twenty-three; Ezell Ford, twenty-five; and Mario Woods, twenty-six. They demanded that Harris independently launch investigations into the incidents, but she did not act. Activists were further annoyed at Harris failing to use her position as attorney general to step up and investigate police shootings, choosing instead to let local prosecutors handle the cases. She also criticized AB-86, a bill proposed in the state of California in 2014 requiring the attorney general to appoint special prosecutors to examine deadly police shootings. "I don't think it would be good public policy to take the discretion from elected district attorneys," she told the *San Francisco Chronicle*, backing the existing system of justice that activists were raging against.[11] Instead Harris offered lip service to more moderate reforms, encouraging local governments to enact body camera policies, improve racial sensitivity programs, and recruit a more diverse police force.

Throughout her career, Harris spoke warmly to audiences of activists about how she chose to work as a prosecutor so she could be the government official opening the doors to activists demanding change. But as attorney general, Harris left the doors shut. "Her absence is noticeable," state senator Holly Mitchell of Los Angeles, a Democrat member of the black caucus, told the *Los Angeles Times*. "People are looking to her for guidance and direction." Democratic assemblyman Kevin McCarty of Sacramento, another member of the black caucus, also expressed his frustration. "The African American and civil rights community have been disappointed that [Harris] hasn't come out stronger on this."[12]

As attorney general, Harris also defended the concept of cash bail even as activists fought it as a discriminatory policy that disproportionately affected people of color. A true "progressive" prosecutor would have joined efforts to reduce cash bail, since the left views it as a discriminatory way to keep poor people of color in jail. A cautious moderate or a conservative would warn that eliminating cash bail would only allow more criminals on the streets. Harris was polishing her law enforcement credentials. "Neither the bail law nor the bail schedule discriminate on the basis of wealth, poverty, or economic status of any kind," she wrote, defending the practice.[13] Notably, Harris was also quiet on law enforcement issues that the police unions may have opposed, as she was preparing for the next step in her career. Harris's shift on law and order won her the respect of the police unions and organizations. When it came time for her reelection campaign, Harris was endorsed by the Peace Officers Research Association of California and the California Statewide Law Enforcement Association.[14]

Harris kept her promise not to defend Proposition 8 in court, delighting LGBTQ activists in the state. Although a US district court found Proposition 8 unconstitutional, there was a stay on the case by the Ninth Circuit Court of Appeals until the Supreme Court ruled on it. In June 2013, the Supreme Court dismissed the appeal from private groups attempting to defend Proposition 8, arguing they did not have standing to do so. Harris delivered a speech celebrating the news, calling for the Ninth Circuit to lift the stay. "As soon as they lift that stay, the wedding bells will ring," she said.[15] Despite the Ninth Circuit initially stating it would take twenty-five days to lift the stay, they moved quickly to lift it just two days later. Harris officiated the first same-sex wedding in California since 2008 that evening, marrying two of the plaintiffs in the case, Kris Perry and Sandy Stier. It was an easy political boost for a politician in California, further evidence she would soon run for higher office.

Harris's support for LGBTQ issues, however, only went so far as was politically popular. While she was a tireless advocate for same-sex marriage, supporting the right to transgender surgeries for prisoners was a bridge too far. In May 2015, Harris joined California prison leaders to file a request before the Ninth Circuit to block sex reassignment surgery for convicted murderer Michelle-Lael Norsworthy, a biological male formerly named Jeffrey who was transitioning into a female. "I know that I am a woman trapped in a man's body," Norsworthy said.[16] "I know that I need (the surgery). I can never achieve any kind of normalcy without it." Harris lost the case, as a federal judge in San Francisco ordered the California prison system to provide the surgery.[17]

As promised, Harris defended death penalty cases in court as attorney general despite her public disagreement with it. Harris announced in August 2014 she would appeal a federal judge's ruling declaring California's enforcement of the death penalty to be unconstitutional. "This flawed ruling requires appellate review," she said in a statement. It was a sharp turnaround for Harris, who ten years earlier refused to pursue the death penalty for a cop-killer in San Francisco.

In 2014, Harris ran for reelection but did not face any serious politi-

cal challengers. Obama was already appearing at star-studded fundraisers in California with Harris, significantly boosting her political career.
"She is brilliant and she is dedicated, and she is tough, and she is exactly
what you'd want in anybody who is administering the law, and making
sure that everybody is getting a fair shake," Obama said in April 2013 at
a fundraiser for Harris. "She also happens to be by far the best-looking
attorney general in the country," he added, prompting laughter in the
audience. "It's true! C'mon," Obama said defensively. Obama ultimately
had to apologize for his remark, which was interpreted as "sexist," but
one thing was clear: he was a big fan of Harris. (Obama's comment
and subsequent apology might have had the effect of propelling Harris to *Maxim* magazine's top Hot 100 women that year with a No. 54
slot, just above actresses Rachel McAdams, Cameron Diaz, and Emilia
Clarke.)[18]

Harris ran for reelection with no serious opponent. Her Republican
challenger was Ron Gold, a former deputy attorney general and private attorney with no political experience. Harris ignored Gold, refusing to even
debate him. Harris's political atrophy reappeared on occasion on the campaign trail. During an August 2014 meeting with the *Sacramento Bee*'s editorial board, Harris appeared unprepared to answer even basic questions.
When asked about internet gambling and legalizing marijuana, Harris
froze, then began circling her rhetoric and stalling without answering the
questions. "I am not prepared to form an opinion and express one right
now because we are studying it and with issues like that want to be very
well informed about exactly where it's going and the potential of where
our opinion would be," she said about online gambling. Journalists in the
room struggled to maintain their composure as Harris rambled on. When
asked whether she believed the death penalty was constitutional, Harris
replied, "I am not going to express an opinion as the attorney general on
the constitutionality of the death penalty."[19] The important issues brought
up by journalists in the room were all part of her job, but she did not want
to talk about them.

Meanwhile, Ron Gold got a lot of press by being a Republican candidate who supported the legalization of marijuana, while Harris did not.

She did not take the bait. "Your opponent, Ron Gold, has said that he is for the legislation of marijuana recreationally. Your thoughts on that?" a KCRA-TV reporter asked Harris at an event. "Uh, I . . . he is entitled to his opinion," Harris replied, laughing off the question and moving on.[20] By October 2014, Harris had more than $3.6 million in the bank and was running ads almost as a courtesy to her donors. "Kamala Harris. A Prosecutor with Convictions," the ad's narrator read, noting that as attorney general, Harris "cracked down on predators who victimized the vulnerable," and was again "endorsed by law enforcement." Despite targeting children and families for truancy, Harris featured schoolchildren in her political ads exchanging high fives with her as she celebrated her record. In November, Harris easily won reelection by 15 points.

After cruising through her reelection campaign, Harris shifted her principles again as she started eying the next step in her political career. Her first step was to shift her position on marijuana. Immediately after the election, Harris described legalization as "inevitable," despite refusing to take questions about the idea during her campaign. "It would be easier for me to say, 'Let's legalize it, let's move on,' and everybody would be happy. I believe that would be irresponsible of me as the top cop," Harris said in an interview with BuzzFeed.[21] But she signaled she was ready for a change. "I don't have any moral opposition to it or anything like that. Half my family's from Jamaica," Harris added with a laugh. The comment about her family went largely unnoticed until she repeated it later in her career.

Harris also started offering lip service to proposals from Black Lives Matter activists. On the issue of body cameras, Harris announced a pilot program in 2015 for California Department of Justice agents to wear the cameras. "I'm going to start in my own backyard," she said. But only twenty of Harris's state agents were involved in the program.[22] Harris actually opposed state legislation that would have required all officers to wear body cameras, much to the chagrin of activists. "I don't think we can have a one-size-fits-all approach to this," she said.[23] In 2016, she announced a website to collect data on law enforcement uses of force that led to serious injuries or death. "As a country, we must engage in an honest, transparent, and data-driven conversation about police use of force," she said.[24] Harris hardly acted on her own to make the reform happen. A new state law passed in 2015 that made the release of the data mandatory. She was, however, willing to take credit for the idea.

In her second term as attorney general, Harris began using her office to pick fights with her political enemies, even though they rarely earned significant results beyond a favorable headline. It was a useful way to show leftist activists she not only cared about their political issues but would fight for them in her political future. Chief among her enemies was the pro-life movement. Harris wielded her bully pulpit to champion California's Reproductive FACT Act, a bill requiring pro-life pregnancy centers to provide information on abortion services against their will. It was rare to have an attorney general so vocal on the issue, but Harris was determined to demonstrate her commitment to abortion activists. The contentious law was overturned by the US Supreme Court in 2017. "[T]he people lose when the government is the one deciding which ideas should prevail," Justice Clarence Thomas wrote in the court's majority opinion. Justice Anthony Kennedy agreed. "Governments must not be allowed to force persons to express a message contrary to their deepest convictions. Freedom of speech secures freedom of thought and belief. This law imperils those liberties," he wrote in his concurring opinion. Harris did not care. She had already proved herself to the pro-abortion lobby.

Harris also weaponized her office to investigate the Center for Medical Progress, after CMP activists David Daleiden and Sandra Merritt secretly filmed videos of Planned Parenthood officials discussing the cost and delivery of fetal tissue and body parts for medical research. Planned Parenthood had a major scandal on their hands after the videos were released, as Republicans and pro-life activists reacted in horror to what was revealed on the tapes and vowed investigations. It was one of the greatest scandals in Planned Parenthood's history. Harris predictably sided with Planned Parenthood after it begged her to prosecute the nonprofit. "We will carefully review the allegations raised in your letter to determine whether there were any violations of California law," Harris wrote in a letter to Planned Parenthood activists in July 2015. Harris was not finished.

In April 2016, she sent California state agents to raid the apartment of Daleiden and seize video files in his possession.

Harris also worked to enhance her record on tackling gun control. In early 2013, Democrats struggled to make political progress on their dream of banning and limiting guns in response to mass shootings that were taking place in schools, particularly after the massacre at Sandy Hook Elementary in Newtown, Connecticut. Some Democrats took political risks to address the aftermath. California senator Dianne Feinstein debuted a bill proposing a national ban of 157 different "assault weapons" and magazines holding more than ten rounds. Harris had a different, more practical idea. In January 2013, she unleashed a group of state special enforcement agents to enter the homes of Californians, using a state database of people convicted of a felony or violent misdemeanor, placed under a domestic violence or other restraining order, or suffered from serious mental illness. Since it was illegal for people on the list to have firearms in their homes, Harris's team entered and seized any guns in their possession and brought them in to the attorney general. The special enforcement group, named the Armed Prohibited Persons System, invited journalists to join them on the raids, ensuring press coverage. The operation allowed Harris to stand victoriously for photos with stacks of seized guns to prove she was making the state safer.[25] In January 2013, Harris even sent a letter to Vice President Joe Biden to describe the program, promoting it as a model for the rest of the country. One thing was clear: Harris was eager for more national approval.

# THE "ONE": DOUG EMHOFF

As she weighed her political future, Harris also weighed carefully the ramifications of being a single woman in politics. She spent most of her political career trying to avoid disclosing or making any boyfriends public, after the relationship with Willie Brown broke up in 1996. The rare exception was in 2001 when Harris appeared with TV talk show host Montel Williams. The couple went public as they attended a fundraiser together and were photographed on the red carpet. The relationship did not last long.

Harris believed having a public boyfriend as a single female politician was a disadvantage. "As a single, professional woman in my forties, and very much in the public eye, dating wasn't easy. I knew that if I brought a man with me to an event, people would immediately start to speculate about our relationship," she wrote in her memoir. It also had political ramifications. If she ran for governor of California, a single Harris would have to compete with her old friend Gavin Newsom, who was already comfortably in his second marriage with film director Jennifer Siebel after divorcing his first wife, Kimberly Guilfoyle. Harris expressed dismay in her book about how society treated single women in politics. "I also knew that single women in politics are viewed differently than single men. We don't get the same latitude when it comes to our social lives. I had no interest in inviting that kind of scrutiny unless I was close to sure I'd found 'the One.'"

"The One" ended up being Doug Emhoff and the romance blossomed swiftly (and conveniently) right before she ran for her next political office. At the age of forty-nine, Harris decided to go on a blind date with Emhoff, an entertainment lawyer and divorced father of two. Harris recalled that her friend set them up and urged her not to look him up on Google. (Harris did anyway.) Emhoff recalled texting her from a Los Angeles Lakers game and leaving a nervous voice mail introducing himself and asking her to go on a date. The romance was hardly a sweeping fairytale as the couple exchanged emails and texts. After their first date, Doug recalled, "the next morning, I pulled the move of emailing her with my availabilities for the next four months, including long weekends. And I said something like, 'I'm too old to hide the ball. You're great. I want to see if we can make this work. Here's when I'm available next.'" Harris said she was "terrified," but the couple moved their relationship forward quickly.[26]

In March 2014, Emhoff proposed to Harris at her apartment and five months later they were married. The ceremony was at a Santa Barbara courthouse, where they exchanged vows that they wrote themselves. The officiant was Harris's sister, Maya. Harris placed a flowered garland around Emhoff's neck, a nod to her Indian heritage. Emhoff also gave a nod to his own, Jewish heritage, breaking a glass at the end of the private ceremony. Harris later shared a blurry photo online of the two embracing in the courthouse, indicating the informal nature of the event.

Harris explained later that she uneasy with the term *stepmother* so she became "Momala" to Emhoff's two children, Cole and Ella, even though she never had children of her own. Harris also emphasized she remained friendly with Emhoff's ex-wife, Kerstin Emhoff. "We sometimes joke that our modern family is almost a little too functional," she said.[27] Doug and Kamala were now a political power couple ready for the next step of her political career.

Modern California is a state governed by one party, so Democratic leaders do their best to avoid any conflicts between their top talent. But Kamala Harris and Gavin Newsom were seen as barreling down a one-way street in opposite directions, each waiting for the other to blink. Both were Willie Brown protégés looking for the next step in their political careers. Newsom, then lieutenant governor and former mayor of San Francisco, was eager for another shot at the governor's mansion after he abandoned his 2008 primary campaign for governor. He settled for running as lieutenant instead, waiting in the wings as Governor Jerry Brown took the lead. By 2014, it was clear that both Harris and Newsom were eying a campaign for governor in 2018, both confident in their ability to beat the other. Harris refused to talk about it. "I am superstitious," she said to the *Los Angeles Times*. "I believe you must do what's in front of you, and do it well, and the next thing will come." The next thing did come. On January 8, 2015, Senator Barbara Boxer announced she would retire at the end of her fourth term, after more than two decades in office. The opportunity for a Senate seat in Washington, DC, was open. Newsom made it clear he had no interest in the job, citing his "unfinished work" in California. His announcement opened a lane for Harris, if she wanted it. She did.

Harris had just won reelection as attorney general, but she had her political future to think about. She could run for California governor, but the Senate could serve as a pathway to the presidency, as it had done for President Barack Obama. It would not be a difficult campaign, as the Republican Party in the state proved no longer able to field competitive candidates. By beating Steve Cooley, Harris had defeated the last relevant California Republican for a statewide race and so the only serious contest would be against a fellow Democrat. Without Newsom in the race, it promised to be an easy coast to victory. Just eight days after taking her oath of office for her second term as attorney general, Harris announced her campaign for Senate.

# CHAPTER FIVE

# SENATOR KAMALA HARRIS

*Excuse me. I'm asking the questions.*

—KAMALA HARRIS, JUNE 6, 2017

Kamala Harris did not need a serious campaign effort to beat any challengers for Senate. She had already lined up support from California's top donors in Hollywood, Silicon Valley, and from President Barack Obama himself. She was granted fawning interviews in the national media and maintained a noncontroversial political profile in California. The general complaint in the local press was that Harris was too cautious and unwilling to risk her political brand to excite activists. She did not care about complaints from the press.

Other prominent California Democrats quietly decided to stay out of the race, knowing that running against Harris was not an easy task. But Harris had no experience in Washington, DC, which prompted Representative Loretta Sanchez, a ten-term veteran Democratic congresswoman, to make her case. Sanchez felt it unfair that Harris was essentially getting coronated by the state elites. "This is too important a state, and too important a position for someone to get on-the-job training," Sanchez said. Harris relished a primary fight with Sanchez. "I always start my campaigns early, and I run hard," Harris told the *New York Times*. "Maybe it comes from the rough-and-tumble world of San Francisco politics, where it's not even a contact sport—it's a blood sport."[1]

Harris did not need to use her familiar playbook of brutal tactics to take down Sanchez. To the elites in the state, Sanchez was already embarrassing and weird. Just days after her campaign announcement, Sanchez deployed a Native American war whoop during a meeting with Indian Americans at the California Democratic convention in Anaheim. Sanchez was telling a group of Indian American Democrats of experiencing a moment of confusion between Native Americans and Indian Americans during a meeting with an Indian American. "I'm going to his office, thinkin' that I'm gonna go meet with woo-woo-woo-woo, right?" she said, clapping her hand to her mouth repeatedly to imitate a war whoop. "'Cause, he said, 'Indian American.'" A video of the moment blew up on social media as Native Americans condemned the negative stereotype and demanded an apology. Sanchez made the political gaffe even worse as she literally ran away from a reporter attempting to question her and slipped into a nearby building to avoid confrontation. Pressured by local media and critical Democrats, Sanchez finally apologized.[2]

Harris quickly lined up a flood of support in her favor. US senators Elizabeth Warren, Cory Booker, and Kirsten Gillibrand endorsed her in the first few weeks of her campaign, which only added to national attention on the race. Democratic donors responded too. Harris raised three times as much money as her opponent. With her coffers flush with campaign cash, Harris began living the life of luxury at her donors' expense. In October 2015, the alarm bells started going off about the campaign's spending. The money was not just going to expensive television ads, but also toward pampering Harris with the luxurious life of a celebrity.[3] A *National Journal* report in December revealed the Harris campaign was paying over a thousand dollars a pop for luxury hotel rooms, such as at the St. Regis in Washington, DC, and the Waldorf Astoria in Chicago. Other receipts showed expenses for high-priced air travel and luxury car services. Further reports revealed Harris had already burned through more than 40 percent of her $6 million that she raised for her campaign. She was also paying extraordinary consulting fees to SCN Strategies, a veteran firm in the state representing top California political Democrats.[4] Why was so much donor money getting wasted on an easy political race? As easy as the campaign for Senate appeared, Harris was also having problems with her staff. She was already on her third financial director by the end of the year. She ultimately parted with her campaign manager, Rory Steele, after stories about her expenses emerged and replaced him with her then senior advisor Juan Rodriguez.[5] The rocky stories about her lavish campaign spending and staff turnover, however, did not affect the love coming from the Democratic establishment.

As Harris's national profile rose, she grew annoyed as fellow politicians and media figures continued to mispronounce her first name. In May 2016, she and her team devoted some of her campaign funds to correct the world on the proper pronunciation of Kamala. "It's not Cam-el-Uh, it's not Kuh-MAHL-uh, it's not Karmel-Uh, it's Kamala," a group of children paid by the campaign explained to the audience in a YouTube ad. If Kamala Harris was going to be a star, the world had better pronounce her name right.

Harris easily won her Senate primary against Sanchez by 20 points in June 2016, but the race was not technically over. In 2010, voters in California had changed the state election law so the top two vote-getters could run again for the general election in November regardless of party. That left more time for Harris and Sanchez to campaign before the final vote and also participate in a debate in October 2016. Most California voters had made up their minds, but Sanchez fought through the debate and clashed with the moderator as Harris played it safe. But Sanchez had one more weapon to deploy before it was over. During her closing statement, she dropped a "dab," to wrap up her performance. The "dab" was a trendy pose at the time popularized by young athletes and celebrities. It was hardly a move for a ten-term congresswoman trying to get elected to the United States Senate. Harris raised her eyebrows and smirked as she turned and looked into both cameras as the crowd laughed.

"So there is a clear difference between the candidates of this race—" Harris said with a bemused look on her face as she began her closing statement.

"There definitely is," Sanchez interrupted.

"And I think voters will make that decision," Harris continued.

They did. Harris beat Sanchez again in November by 25 points.

Harris won her Senate race the same night as Hillary Clinton lost to Donald Trump in the presidential campaign. That shook up what Harris was expecting to be a big party night after celebrating her easy victory. "This is some sh-t," Harris said to her staff behind the scenes, as they started rewriting her victory speech.[6] As she ascended the stage to declare victory, Harris tried to seize the mantle of the next great leader of the Democratic Party. "Do not despair. Do not be overwhelmed," she said to her supporters. "Do not throw up our hands when it is time to roll up our sleeves and fight for who we are." Harris did her best to rally her party, but back at her home, she was less enthusiastic as she turned to her "go-to stress food," she later revealed—a family-size bag of Nacho Cheese Doritos: "I sat on our couch. I didn't share one chip with anyone. I was just like: 'This. Can't. Be. Happening.'"[7]

Trump's victory sparked a trope on social media from adults on the left, where they told stories of their children crying or "literally shaking" at the thought of Trump or something he planned to do. The stories frequently earn mockery from the right, as they appear insincere or made up. Harris shared a similar saccharine story about her nine-year-old godson, Alexander, that night: he was literally asking her about Trump with tears in his eyes and trembling. "Auntie Kamala, that man can't win. He's not going to win, is he?" Harris recalled the young boy telling her. In response, Harris played the superhero to bring hope to the frightened children.

"Alexander, you know how sometimes superheroes are facing a big challenge because a villain is coming for them? What do they do when that happens?" she recalled saying.

"They fight back," he whimpered.

"That's right," she replied. "And they fight back with emotion, because all the best superheroes have big emotions just like you. But they always fight back, right? So that's what we're going to do." It's another one of those personal family stories shared by Harris that are too good to check. Hollywood could not have scripted it any better.

In January, Harris arrived in Washington looking for a fight. She soon got her chance as leftist activists swarmed into Washington, DC, the day after Donald Trump's inauguration, for the first "Woman's March." "What a beautiful sight I see, what do my eyes behold," Harris said after taking the podium for her speech, celebrating the throngs of women wearing their signature pink "pussy hats" and shouting. "There is nothing more powerful than a group of determined sistas, marching alongside with their partners and determined sons and brothers and fathers, standing up for what we know is right," she said. It was a preview of the fight ahead.

Once in the Senate, Harris surprised her colleagues in how obviously she was pursuing a future run for president instead of doing the work in the Senate. Longtime staffers were familiar with the "showboat" senators who were using the position as a political springboard. But even senators like Elizabeth Warren, Hillary Clinton, and Barack Obama spent their first few years trying to demonstrate seriousness and substance for the job they had. Senate Democrat leadership assigned Harris to four committees—Homeland Security and Government Affairs, Environment and Public Works, Intelligence, and Budget. Harris arrived impatient, eager to make a political impact while Republicans took power.

Since the dawn of C-SPAN, which opened up committee hearings to the general public, politicians of both parties have tried to leverage their time to make an impact on the political scene, counting on a specific moment in a hearing to boost their political career. The advent of social media only increased attempts for theatrics, since now the goal of "going viral" online was a badge of honor. As a senator, Harris tried valiantly to generate the most noise and heat she could in committee hearings and she started by confronting Trump appointed cabinet officials seeking Senate confirmation.

Former general John Kelly, who served as the commander of the United States Southern Command, was chosen by the Trump administration to serve as the secretary of the Department of Homeland Security. Kelly, a native of Boston who retained his gruff accent, was a well-respected general who had lost his son, First Lieutenant Robert Kelly, in Afghanistan and was given a wide berth by Democratic senators, who praised him as a patriot and a valued public servant who would help the administration. Harris was not interested in Kelly's record and pressed him about what he would do about the removal of DACA, the Obama administration's Delayed Action for Childhood Arrivals program, which allowed children of illegal immigrants to remain in the United States. "I'll follow the law," Kelly replied, but admitted that illegal immigrants who had not broken the law would be less of a priority. Harris reminded Kelly that she was "a career prosecutor, formerly attorney general of California," and asked him how he would use his resources to work with illegal immigrants (instead of deporting them). Kelly repeated that he would be guided by the law. Harris had a different philosophy. "I would encourage that not only the law but how it would practically apply in the streets," Harris replied. Harris was unimpressed with Kelly, choosing to join ten other Senate Democrats who voted against his confirmation.

Harris continued clashing with the former general, tormenting him inside and outside political hearings. On January 27, 2017, President Trump signed an executive order suspending the admission of refugees to the United States and temporarily banning some travel from several Middle Eastern countries. The executive order created leftist fury and protesters gathered at airports to express their outrage at the Trump administration. Harris seized the moment by calling Kelly's personal phone to confront him directly. "I called him up at home 'cause I got the number," Harris later bragged at a political forum in California. "I was really unsatisfied with the conversation," she added.[8] In her book, Harris explained that she made the call because she "needed to find out what was going on." Kelly, she revealed, responded, "Why are you calling me at home with this?" and ended the call. It was hardly the drama that would launch a political career, but Harris kept trying.

Harris's opposition to Kelly appeared more personal in later hearings as she exhausted him with seemingly pointless interruptions. On June 6, 2017, during a hearing on the Homeland Security budget, Harris repeatedly interrupted Kelly as he tried to answer her questions about back-channel communications with local governments. Kelly grew frustrated. "Can I finish what I was saying?" he asked, when Harris interrupted. Harris ignored him, speaking over Kelly and asking a different question entirely.

"Had you not cut me off, I would have said the same thing you would have said. Probably not as eloquently but I would have said the same thing as you did," Kelly replied tersely, adding that he would likely have "below-the-radar" conversations to assist local governments.

"What do you mean by 'below-the-radar'?" Harris began.

"Probably on the phone," Kelly replied patiently.

Harris paused. "Excuse me, sir," she shot back, visibly annoyed that Kelly was making her look foolish, and repeated her question.

When the bewildered Kelly started to explain the process of having a phone call with local law enforcement, Harris interrupted again.

"Can you let me at least finish once before you interrupt me?" Kelly replied.

"Sir. With all due respect," Harris replied, raising her eyebrows pausing for emphasis.

"With all due respect, Senator," Kelly replied, leaning back in his chair with frustration.

Harris asked another question. As Kelly began replying, Harris interrupted again.

"Can you let me finish once, Senator?" he asked.

"Excuse me. I'm asking the questions," Harris replied.

"I'm trying to answer the questions," Kelly continued. Harris ignored Kelly and asked another question.

"Okay, before I start to answer, will you let me finish?" Kelly asked cautiously.

"If it's responsive to the question, of course," Harris replied, allowing him to finish before her time expired.[9] It was obvious that Harris delighted in tormenting Trump officials with interruptions even though she had no clear objective to her line of questioning.

Republican representative Mike Pompeo, Trump's appointee for director of the Central Intelligence Agency, appeared at his Senate confirmation hearing with the respect of many in Congress. A graduate of the US Military Academy at West Point, Pompeo served as a tank commander in the US Army before attending Harvard Law School and beginning his career in the House of Representatives after getting elected in Kansas in 2010. Harris was not interested in his military credentials, choosing instead to grill Pompeo about his views on global warming. She asked Pompeo about whether he was aware of former CIA director John Brennan's warnings about climate change and data from NASA that pointed to human activity as a cause of global warming. It was clear that Pompeo had little interest in directing the CIA to fight climate change. "As the director of CIA, I would prefer today to not get into the details of climate debate and science," Pompeo said. "My role is going to be so different and unique from that. It is going to be to work alongside warriors keeping Americans safe." Harris also confronted Pompeo for his views on same-sex marriage, trying to paint him as a bigot who would persecute LGBTQ employees in the CIA. "Can you commit to me that your personal views on this issue will remain your personal views and will not impact internal policies that you put into place at the CIA?" Harris asked. Pompeo replied he had a long history of treating all people and employees with dignity and respect and would do the same at the CIA.[10] In Harris's mind, climate change and discrimination seemed to be the foremost threats to the security of the United States.

Harris continued her grilling of Trump officials as if racists, sexists, bigots, and white supremacists were around every corner. In November 2018, Harris tried to compare the Immigration and Customs Enforcement agency to the Ku Klux Klan during the confirmation hearing for Trump's nominee to head the agency, Ronald Vitiello. Harris was never a fan of ICE, telling NBC reporter Kasie Hunt in June 2018 she believed it was time to reimagine the agency and "probably think about starting from scratch."[11] Harris was determined to smear Vitiello during the hearing, and brought up a joke he had made on social media about the Democratic Party being "neo-Klanist." Setting him up, Harris asked Vitello to explain why the KKK was bad. "Are you aware of the perception of many about how the power and the discretion at ICE is being used to enforce the laws and do you see any parallels?" she asked. Vitiello was shocked, denying there was any perception that ICE was in the same category of the KKK, which he described as domestic terrorists. "I do not see any parallels between sworn officers and agents," Vitiello began, before Harris interrupted him.

"I'm talking about perceptions," she said. Harris lamented there was a "perception" from immigrants that ICE is administrating its power "in a way that is causing fear and intimidation."

"I do not see a parallel between the power and authority that ICE has to do its job and agents and officers who do it professionally and excellently with lots of compassion—" Vitiello began before Harris interrupted with incredulity.

"Sir, how can you be the head of an agency and be unaware of how your agency is perceived in certain communities?"[12] Harris described illegal immigrants as "innocent people arriving at our border fleeing harm" and urged Vitiello to work to change the reputation of the agency. Vitiello was used to politicians using hearings on border security to grandstand for their open-borders agenda, but Harris's question was unprecedented. By speaking about ICE and the KKK in the same question, she was trying to turn false perceptions about overtaxed border security agents into a reality.

On the warpath, Harris was getting more attention from activists fighting to resist Trump. In May 2017, Harris appeared at a live podcast recording in San Francisco for *Pod Save America*, which is hosted by former staffers for President Barack Obama, to talk about her fight against Trump and the Republicans.

"They're engaged in all of this happy talk which is bull . . . not truth," she said, hesitating before bursting into laughter.

After the hosts encouraged her to swear, Harris went R-rated.

"What the fuck is that?" she said, laughing profusely, after quoting a Republican congressman on health care.

When asked to describe the first one hundred days of President Trump's administration, Harris replied, "I was told one should not say 'mothafucka' in these kinds of interviews." Harris burst into laughter again. "So I'm not going to say."

"Trump is president, you can say whatever you want!" one host responded.

The audience of young progressives cheered wildly. Clearly she was successful at channeling their rage.

# FAREWELL, FRANKEN: A #METOO STORY

Kamala Harris joined a group of Democrat senators who used the #MeToo movement to further their political careers. The #MeToo movement was a way for victims of sexual abuse, harassment, and rape to push back against powerful men in society who were accused of sexual misconduct. The movement began after mega–Hollywood producer Harvey Weinstein was finally exposed for his long history of predatory behavior with women, as prominent actresses began publicly revealing it. Now California politicians scrambled to distance themselves from Weinstein, whom they had been cozy with for years. Harris was not unscathed, as Weinstein donated $2,500 to Harris in 2014 when she was running for attorney general and another

$2,500 during her run for Senate in 2017. (A Harris spokesperson claimed she would donate the funds to charity.) Harris joined the movement that urged Americans to believe women's accusations of abuse instead of dismissing them as unfounded or demanding due process for men.

As perpetually outraged Democrats struggled through their first year of President Donald Trump dominating the headlines, the media punditocracy was already in search of their "Trump Slayer" who could revive the party and beat the president in 2020. One name included in the mix was Senator Al Franken of Minnesota. As Democrats struggled to rediscover their identity, Franken, long famous as a comedian before he entered politics, was singled out as a senator who had successfully buried Republicans in Minnesota with his unique brand of midwestern populist politics. In early 2017, Franken published a book, as most politicians eying the presidency do, with a media tour that boosted his national profile even as he insisted he had no intention of running for president. His political future was clearly on the rise.

That all changed on November 16, 2017. Los Angeles radio talk show host Leeann Tweeden released a shocking photo of the comedian appearing to grope her while she was sleeping, grinning widely at what he thought was a hilarious joke.[13] The incident took place during a 2006 USO tour and Tweeden finally went public with her accusations against Franken, including a claim that he forcibly kissed her and forced his tongue in her mouth during a rehearsal. Franken denied the accusations, but he was immediately criticized by his Democrat Senate colleagues. "Sexual harassment is inappropriate in every circumstance, in every way, whomever is involved," Harris told reporters after the scandal broke.[14] It looked like some Democrats viewed the awkward but affable Franken as a threat to their political career, particularly as a male candidate. In the weeks that followed, more women came forward to accuse Franken of unwanted touching and groping during appearances with the senator. Franken said he would submit to an investigation by the Senate Ethics Committee and abide by their ruling, but more allegations kept surfacing.

After three weeks of the controversy, a group of Democrat women senators rallied together to demand his resignation. Senators Kirsten Gillibrand, Kamala Harris, Claire McCaskill, Mazie Hirono, Patty Murray, Maggie Hassan, and Catherine Cortez Masto met with Minority Leader Chuck Schumer to demand Franken's resignation.[15] Harris was not the first, but she was not the last to turn on Franken. Gillibrand was first to break the dam, posting a lengthy statement on Facebook on the morning of December 6 at 11:26 a.m. urging Franken to step aside in the wake of the accusations. (Gillibrand's leading role in pressuring Franken to resign would later damage her relationship with Democrat donors.) Other Democrats followed, including Senator Kamala Harris, who weighed in just before noon. "Sexual harassment and misconduct should not be allowed by anyone and should not occur anywhere. I believe the best thing for Senator Franken to do is step down," she wrote on Twitter. Harris further reflected on her decision to call for Franken's resignation while speaking with reporters. "I respect Sen. Franken for the work that he has done as a senator on issues that are right now, issues that we are fighting . . . but frankly the numerosity of the complaints and allegations against him I found to have weight, bearing weight." When it was clear that none of his Senate colleagues, including Leader Chuck Schumer, felt it necessary to give him due process, Franken announced his resignation the following morning. After his speech, his Democratic colleagues tearfully bid him farewell, including some of the senators who called for his resignation. Franken never forgot how his colleagues turned on him. He reflected on Harris's role in his ouster in a 2020 interview with PBS anchor Judy Woodruff. "Of course, I took issue with that, my colleagues who said I shouldn't have due process. I think that was wrong, especially from people that were lawyers, etc.," Franken said.[16] In politics, the only rule of law is the politics of personal advantage.

Harris was hardly a #MeToo champion, as she had her own #MeToo moment in December 2018. The *Sacramento Bee* revealed that one of her top staffers, Larry Wallace from California, was responsible for a $400,000 harassment and retaliation settlement with his former female assistant at the California Department of Justice. The California Department of Justice denied the claims, but the lawsuit was settled in May 2017. Wallace was not just a random advisor. He was one of Harris's "closest professional confidants," according to the *Bee*, and was part of her inner circle.[17] The department was first notified about the complaint on October 3, 2016, three months before Harris left the attorney general's office. As a senator, Harris hired Wallace in March 2017, even after the harassment lawsuit had been filed in December 2016. After the *Bee* reported news of the settlement, Harris insisted she had no idea about the allegations until she was contacted about it by reporters. "I'm frustrated that I wasn't briefed," she said. "That's what makes me upset about this. There's no question I should have been informed about this. There's no question. And there were ample opportunities when I could have been informed." Harris moved swiftly, as her office announced by the end of the day that Wallace had resigned. There was no evidence that Harris had prior knowledge of the lawsuit, but either she may have looked away from an alleged case of harassment or she had failed to vet her Senate staff properly.[18] Once again, Harris's excuse was that she was completely oblivious about something that may have been happening in her own office. Congressional staffers knew it was not possible. How many times would this defense work?

With Franken gone, Democrats now faced an empty slot on the Senate Judiciary Committee. Harris was conveniently positioned for the job, but Cory Booker of New Jersey, who was first elected in 2013 was more senior. Congressional Black Caucus chair Representative Cedric Richmond of Louisiana sent a letter to Schumer encouraging him to appoint either Booker or Harris to the committee, saying it was "a pivotal moment in American history" in the Trump era that demanded more black representation on the committee. Schumer ultimately yielded to his demands. On January 9, he announced that both Harris and Booker would join the veteran Democrats on the Senate Judiciary Committee. Harris had not achieved much in the Senate, but Schumer appreciated her willingness to bring the heat into hearings with Trump officials that were getting a larger audience.

## THE CLOWN CAUCUS

Senators Booker and Harris both arrived at the Senate Judiciary Committee in 2018 eyeing a 2020 run for president. Both were sardonically branded as members of the "clown caucus" by staffers, as each senator tried to upstage the other to demonstrate their presidential chops on the national scene. Booker crafted the demeanor of an eager, principled civil rights defender, earning him the nickname "Spartacus" for his repeated dramatic speeches and willingness to break Senate precedence. Harris, however, adopted the theatrics of an erudite and determined prosecutor, questioning highly qualified judicial and administration nominees as if they were criminals.

Harris could not hide her distain for pro-life nominees to the courts. President Trump appointed Senator David Vitter's wife, Wendy Vitter, to be a judge on the US District Court for the Eastern District of Louisiana. Wendy Vitter worked as the general counsel of the Roman Catholic Archdiocese of New Orleans from 2012 to 2019 and was active in the pro-life movement. During her confirmation hearing, Harris looked with disgust at Vitter, noting that she had moderated a panel of women on a pro-life discussion forum in which one of the participants featured a brochure warning of the dangers of birth control. Referring to the pamphlet's contents, Harris asked, "Do you believe that birth control pills cause women to have extramarital affairs?" Vitter said she had no prior knowledge of the views of the women on the panel. Harris's eyes narrowed as she repeated the question. Vitter tried to distance herself from the pamphlet, but Harris interrupted her repeatedly, demanding that she answer whether she thought that women who were on birth control were more likely to have extramarital affairs. "No, I do not," Vitter finally replied. Harris was digging deep.

She then brought up a 2010 commencement speech Vitter delivered in which she used a common analogy about graduates learning to be "turtles" who had to "stick out your necks" to move forward in their careers.

"As a judge, are you suggesting you would stick out your neck and fight for pro-life cases?" Harris asked with a smirk. "What, what, what—how should we interpret your statement as it would be applied to your work as a judge?"

Vitter and judiciary staffers in the room could barely smother their amused reactions to Harris's line of questioning. Vitter explained that the turtle analogy was a common exhortation for graduates, citing sex therapist Dr. Ruth Westheimer as a possible source for the quote.

"Whoever said it," Harris said dismissively. "Would that apply to you if you were confirmed to your work?"[19] Vitter denied that it would.

It was not the only time that Harris would attack Catholic judicial nominees for their beliefs. In January 2019, Harris posed a series of written questions to Brian Buescher, a nominee for a judgeship for the US District Court for the District of Nebraska, challenging his membership in the Catholic fraternal charity group the Knights of Columbus. Harris referred to the Catholic institution as "an all-male society comprised primarily of Catholic men," pointing out that it was pro-life and opposed to same-sex marriage.[20] Buescher's response was straightforward, that he would remain impartial as a judge enforcing the law despite his personal faith and beliefs and membership in the Knights. Catholics were outraged and even journalists criticized her attacks on the group. "For those who know the Knights of Columbus, this is a bit like accusing your Aunt Harriet's knitting circle of being a Mexican drug cartel," *Washington Post* columnist Michael Gerson wrote, accusing Harris and her colleagues of "anti-Catholic bigotry."[21] Rabbi Mitchell Rocklin decried the "troubling precedent of intolerance" in Harris's line of questioning in a *Los Angeles Times* op-ed, calling it "unconscionable in principle and terrible in practice." "This practice has no place in America," he wrote, decrying Harris's attempt at posing a "religious test" for judicial nominees.[22]

As Harris continued interrupting government officials, many other senators grew tired of her antics. They already knew she was a showboat, but as the months went on, she was clearly resting her laurels on behavior they viewed as unprofessional, particularly as the audience for the hearings increased. In June 2017, Harris participated with the same demeanor in a hearing with Admiral Mike Rogers and Deputy US Attorney Rod Rosenstein on the issue of the ongoing investigation of the Trump administration and Russia. Harris first asked Rogers about conversations he had had with the president in New York City; was he willing to share details of the conversation? "If it's not classified," Rogers replied. "You can keep trying to trip me up. . . . Senator, if you could, could I get to respond. Please, ma'am?"

"No," Harris said, extending her finger in the air to shut Rogers down. "No. No," she repeated. Harris turned to Rosenstein, asking him if he was willing to sign a letter giving Special Counsel Robert Mueller the power to conduct his investigation completely independent from the Justice Department.

"Senator, I'm very sensitive about time and I'd like to have a very lengthy conversation and explain that all to you," Rosenstein began. "I tried to do that in a closed briefing—"

"Can you give me a 'yes' or 'no' answer please?" Harris interrupted.

"Well, it's not a short answer, Senator," Rosenstein replied. "The answer is—" Harris again cut him off.

"It is," she replied. "Either you are willing to do that or not as we have precedent in that regard."

Senator John McCain grew annoyed. "Mr. Chairman, they should be allowed to answer the question," he said disapprovingly, addressing Chairman Richard Burr. Rosenstein continued answering the question, before Harris interrupted again to get an answer of whether he would sign a letter. As Rosenstein again tried to explain, Harris interrupted again. "Yes or no, sir," she demanded. "Are you willing to do as has been done before—"

Burr intervened. "Will the senator suspend?" he interjected. "The chair is going to exercise its right to allow the witnesses to answer the question, and the committee is on notice to provide the witnesses the courtesy, which has not been extended all the way across, extend the courtesy for questions to get answered."

Harris was furious. "Mr. Chairman, respectfully, I'd like to point out that this witness has joked . . . as we all have, his ability to filibuster—"

"The senator will suspend," Burr shot back. "Mr. Rosenstein, would you like to thoroughly answer the question?" Rosenstein reassured Harris and the committee that Muller was safe and independent, but Harris was not satisfied. "So, is that a no?" she quipped as her time expired.[23]

As the interrupting Harris was interrupted herself by her male colleagues, furious Harris supporters depicted the veteran pair of senators as racist and sexist. Harris and her staff seized the moment to raise her political profile—and raise money. "The women of the United States Senate will not be silenced when seeking the truth," she wrote on social media, linking to a fundraising page. "Fight back."

In June 2017, Attorney General Jeff Sessions sat before the Senate Intelligence Committee to discuss conversations he may have had with President Donald Trump about Russia. Harris's rapid-fire prosecutorial style immediately clashed with Sessions's slow southern drawl as he tried to cautiously answer questions from the committee panel. Sessions served in the Senate for twenty years before he was appointed by Trump, so he was not about to be pushed around by the freshman senator from California. Harris tried anyway, and pressed Sessions about whether he had conversations with Russians during the Republican National Convention in 2016. "I don't believe I had any conversation with Russian businessmen or Russian nationals," Sessions began.

Harris interrupted, "Are you aware of any communications . . ."

"Although lot of people were at the convention," Sessions continued, frustrating Harris with his slow and careful rhetoric. "It's conceivable that somebody came up to me—"

"Sir, I just have a few minutes," Harris said impatiently.

"Will you let me qualify it?" Sessions replied. "If I don't qualify it, you'll accuse me of lying. So I need to be correct as best I can."

"I do want you to be honest," Harris replied.

"And I'm not able to be rushed this fast. It makes me nervous," Sessions replied.

Harris asked Sessions whether he had any knowledge of Trump campaign officials or associates with any Russian officials or nationals.

"I don't recall that," Sessions replied. "At this moment."

Sessions had spent the day dodging most of the Democrat questions about Russia and Trump by citing a long-standing Justice Department policy of executive privilege regarding his conversations with the president. In response, Harris demanded that Sessions provide evidence of a written policy that allowed him to do so. "Is that policy in writing somewhere?" she asked.

"I think so," Sessions replied.

"So did you not consult it before you came before this committee, knowing we would ask you questions about that?" she asked.

"Well, we talked about it," Sessions said. "The policy is based—"

Harris interrupted. "Did you ask that it would be shown to you?"

Sessions tried again. "The policy is based on the principle that the president—"

Harris interrupted again. "Sir, I'm not asking about the principle. I'm asking when you knew that you would be asked these questions . . ."

Sessions grew frustrated. "Well, I'm unable to answer the question."

Harris continued, ". . . and you rely on that policy, did you not ask your staff to show you the policy that would be the basis for refusing to answer the majority of the questions that have been asked of you?" McCain, clearly annoyed by Harris's repeated interruptions, again begged Chairman Burr to intervene.

"Mr. Chairman, the witness should be allowed to answer the question," McCain said. Burr hesitated, as he had already been singed by critics for stepping up a week earlier.

"Senators will allow the chair to control the hearing," Burr replied to McCain. "Senator Harris, let him answer."

Sessions explained that the Constitution provides the head of the executive branch the privilege of confidentiality of communications.

Harris was unimpressed as she interrupted again.

"Mr. Chairman, I have asked . . . Mr. Sessions for a yes or no. Did you ask your staff to see the policy?"

"Well, the answer is yes, I consulted," Sessions said.

"Did you ask your staff to see the policy?" Harris repeated, as the chairman informed her that her time expired. "Apparently not," she replied.

Harris was angry as she felt unfairly interrupted just as she was squeezing out the truth about whether Sessions had asked his staff to show him a written document. Her time had expired in the hearing, but her staff realized she had generated another viral moment. "It was a simple question," Harris wrote on Twitter. "Can Sessions point to the policy, in writing, that allows him to not answer a whole host of our questions today."

Hundreds of sympathetic headlines followed. The *New York Times* wrote about "The Universal Phenomenon of Men Interrupting Women."[24] Vox reported, "People keep interrupting Sen. Kamala Harris," and asked, "Now, why might that be?"[25] Harris posted video of her exchange with Session on her social media accounts. "I questioned Attorney General Jeff Sessions," she wrote. "The American people don't deserve evasion—we deserve the truth." It did not matter that Harris's question was mostly irrelevant. What mattered was that she had her viral moment. Her contentious moments in the Senate continued going viral online, dazzling the establishment media. "California's very junior senator has emerged as the latest iteration of a bipartisan archetype: the Great Freshman Hope, a telegenic object of daydreaming projection—justified or not—for a party adrift and removed from executive power," *New York Times* reporter Matt Flegenheimer wrote, adding that the "casting call came early" when she first won her Senate race in California.

## KAMALA REBOOT: JOYFUL WARRIOR

Although Harris delighted in picking fights with Trump officials, she soon realized she needed to move her political brand in a different direction if she was ever going to run for president. At the end of 2017, after workshopping her political identity, she tried to seize the mantle of a "joyful warrior." "At the end of the year, I thought back to 2017, and I was like, 'Bye, Felicia,'" she said, trying to implement a dismissive quote from the 1995 comedy film *Freaky Friday* to wave off her anger and rage in a *Vogue* magazine profile in March 2018. "This year, I'm just gonna be a joyful warrior."[26] In April 2018, Harris appeared on Ellen DeGeneres's show to showcase her new brand of politics. "We have to be joyful warriors, you know, I decided at the end of last year, there was so much that was creating anxiety and depression and anger. I was like, I'm done with that, I'm done with that, I don't like that feeling, I don't think any of us do. Let's just go into 2018 and be joyful warriors," she said. As the audience applauded, Harris turned to the cameras and smiled broadly. "We have to remember it's not about fighting against something, it's about fighting for something," she continued warmly, trying to inspire the audience with her deep thoughts. "And it is fighting for a spirit of love of country, and that is really important to remember. We love our country. And part of being a patriot, love of country is about fighting for the ideals of our country, fighting for the best of who we are. We are a great people; we are a great country." The new brand, however, was put to the test when DeGeneres posed a series of quick questions to the senator.

"If you had to be stuck in an elevator with either President Trump, [Vice President] Mike Pence, or Jeff Sessions, who would it be?" DeGeneres asked.

Harris glanced sideways before replying, "Does one of us have to come out alive?" She burst into laughter.[27] The joyful warrior was looking more like the Joker.

# CHAPTER SIX

# STOP KAVANAUGH

*You have been a true patriot in fighting for the best of who we are as a country.*

—KAMALA HARRIS TO CHRISTINE BLASEY FORD,

SEPTEMBER 27, 2018

Kamala Harris's attempt to seize the mantle of a joyful warrior did not last long. On June 27, 2018, Supreme Court justice Anthony Kennedy, eighty-one, announced his decision to retire. The announcement kicked into motion a ferocious battle for his successor that would shake up Washington, DC, and set the Supreme Court to be aligned to a more originalist interpretation of Constitution. In response, Harris and Senate Democrats launched the most outrageous personal smear of a Supreme Court nominee since the failed attempt to block Justice Clarence Thomas in 1991.

It did not matter who President Trump selected to replace Kennedy. The left was preparing an all-out war against the president's second nominee to the Supreme Court, the first being Neil Gorsuch in 2017. Trump ultimately selected Judge Brett Kavanaugh, a well-known figure in Washington, DC. After graduating from Yale Law School and clerking at the Supreme Court, he worked for independent counsel Ken Starr's investigation of President Bill Clinton and served on the legal team of Governor George W. Bush's recount battle in Florida for the 2000 presidential election. He ultimately joined the Bush administration as a legal counsel and a staff secretary. He was later nominated by Bush to the US Court of Appeals for the District of Columbia Circuit, firmly establishing his position in the DC legal community. "Throughout legal circles, he is considered a judge's judge, a true thought leader among his peers. He is a brilliant jurist with a clear and effective writing style, universally regarded as one of the finest and sharpest legal minds in our time," Trump said at the White House on July 9 after announcing Kavanaugh as his nominee.

The Kavanaugh hearings served as a proving ground, almost a primary race as Democratic presidential hopefuls tried to prove themselves as the left's most committed champions. Harris was determined to make an impact, as she was still largely unknown outside California. It was her chance to make a bigger name for herself. Harris took a lot of swings but ended up striking out.

Harris went public with her opposition to Trump's choice just a half an hour after it was announced. "Judge Brett Kavanaugh represents a direct and fundamental threat to that promise of equality and so I will oppose his nomination to the Supreme Court," she wrote in a statement, decrying him as a "conservative ideologue."[1] As part of the Supreme Court confirmation process, senators are expected to meet with a nominee to learn about them, question them, kicking off a rigorous examination of their credentials as a judge. It was a real struggle for Democrats to follow precedent, with the future of the Court in the balance. When the White House reached out to Harris's office on the phone to set up a meeting, someone in the office answered and reportedly replied, "We want nothing to do with you." They were speaking directly to White House Counsel Don McGahn.[2] Harris's office denied it, but the report demonstrated the tone she was setting ahead of the process. Harris ultimately met with Kavanaugh on August 21, but she had already made up her mind. "[N]othing in my meeting with Judge Kavanaugh changes my read of his record—he is well outside the mainstream and threatens hard won rights and protections for all Americans," she said in a statement.

The Senate confirmation hearings for Kavanaugh began on September 4 with Democrats making their best effort to upstage the hearing and derail the process. It did not take long. Just ten seconds after Senator Chuck Grassley began his opening remarks, Harris led the charge. "Mr. Chairman," Harris began. "Mr. Chairman. I'd like to be recognized for a question before we proceed." Harris continued speaking over Grassley, as senators grumbled in the background about regular order. Harris complained that the committee had received tens of thousands of documents the previous evening and that Senate Democrats had not had the chance to review them.

"You're out of order, I'll proceed," Grassley said, continuing his opening statement as Harris continued protesting the hearing. Harris's action kicked off over an hour of interruptions from Democrats on the committee, at which point a visibly annoyed Grassley stated that the hearing had been taken over by "mob rule."

"How long do you want to go on?" he asked his Democratic colleagues. "Can I proceed, members of the Democratic caucus?" Grassley asked, looking disapprovingly at his colleagues. Some of the veteran Democrats on the committee looked almost sheepish for the unprecedented level of political theater taking place but Harris was not deterred. "Mr. Chairman, if I may be recognized for one final point," she interrupted.

"After you are done, can I proceed to my opening statement?" Grassley asked. Harris continued speaking, complaining that Democrats had already raised concerns about the timing of the hearing and the documents made available at the last minute. Despite Grassley's plea, Harris objected to the hearing, repeating her motion to postpone it. When the hearing ultimately resumed, Harris devoted a portion of her introductory remarks to reflect on her memories as a little girl riding a bus to school. "As you know, as we all know, this is a week where most students in our country go back to school, and it occurs to me that many years ago right around this time I was starting kindergarten, and I was a bus—in a bus, a school bus, on my way to Thousand Oaks elementary school as part of the second class of students as busing desegregated Berkeley, California public schools." It was unclear what her experience as a child in kindergarten had to do with Kavanaugh's Supreme Court nomination, but she ultimately got to the point, noting that using busing to desegregate schools was a result of the 1954 Supreme Court case *Brown v. Board of Education*. If Chief Justice Earl Warren had not been on the court at the time, she explained, the decision could have affected her entire life and political career. "Had that decision not come down the way it did I may not have had the opportunities that allowed me to become a lawyer or a prosecutor. I likely would not have been elected district of San Francisco or attorney general of California, and I most certainly would not have been sitting here in the United States Senate," she added, noting that the seriousness of the hearings was "personal" to her life story. Harris was going for an emotional moment during the hearing but it was mostly ignored. It was not the last time, however, that she would use her bus story to score political points.

Harris wanted Americans to see Kavanaugh as corrupt and connected to Trump, even though the judge was a George W. Bush acolyte. But the perfect way to question his character was to connect him to an ongoing bogus narrative about Trump colluding with Russia to steal the 2016 election and the special counsel investigation by Robert Mueller. All she needed to do was connect the dots.

"Have you discussed the Mueller investigation with anyone at Kasowitz, Benson, and Torres, the law firm founded by Marc Kasowitz, President Trump's personal lawyer?" Harris asked Kavanaugh during the confirmation hearing. When a puzzled Kavanaugh looked back at her and hesitated, Harris continued. "Be sure about your answer, sir."

Kavanaugh was wary of falling into a trap, as Harris might have knowledge of such an event actually occurring. "I'm not remembering but if you have something, you want to . . ." Kavanaugh began, adding, "I'm not sure if I know everyone who works at that law firm . . . I'm not remembering."

Kamala the prosecutor was back.

"I'm asking a very direct question. Yes or no," she pressed.

When Kavanaugh asked to reveal details about her question she refused.

"I would like to know the person you're thinking of," he replied.

"I think you're thinking of someone and you just don't want to tell us," Harris shot back, eliciting chuckles in the room. "Who did you have a conversation with?"

It was an awkward moment as Kavanaugh struggled to move forward. Republican senator Mike Lee of Utah intervened, noting that Washington, DC, was full of lawyers who worked for many different firms. Harris was vexed. Raising her eyebrows at Lee, she demanded that her time be reserved. The proceedings were interrupted by a protester who was escorted out of the room. "They're like rabbits," Lee continued, sharing his thoughts about DC lawyers. "They spawn new firms. There's no possible way we can expect this witness to populate an entire firm."

When Harris recovered her time, she again directed her question to Kavanaugh. "Sir, please answer the question." Kavanaugh noted he had many relationships within the legal community, and likely spoke about the case with fellow judges. "I don't know everyone that works at that law firm, Senator," he replied. Harris repeated her question, but Kavanaugh refused to play along.

"You ask me that, I need to know who works there," Kavanaugh replied.

"I think you can answer the question without me giving you a list of all employees of that law firm," Harris replied.

"Well, actually I can't," Kavanaugh replied.

"Why not?" Harris said.

"Because I don't know who works there," he replied.

Harris reasserted her question, saying it was a "very direct" question that he should be able to answer.

"I'd be surprised but I don't know everyone who works at that law firm, so I just want to be careful because your question was and/or and I want to be very literal," he said.

Harris repeated her question again.

Kavanaugh said he was not "remembering" any conversation.

"So, you're not denying that you've spoke with anyone," Harris said, trying to lead her witness.

"Well, I said, I don't remember anything like that," Kavanaugh replied with a chuckle of disbelief.

"I'll move on," Harris replied sardonically. "Clearly you're not going to answer the question." The moment drew attention online, as Harris's fans again celebrated her "tough" questioning that confused Kavanaugh.

Behind the scenes, the White House war room team was puzzled. Who was Harris thinking about? After some research, they believed Harris was likely trying to get Kavanaugh to admit that he had spoken to Edward McNally, a partner in the firm who worked in the Bush White House when Kavanaugh did. As authors Mollie Hemingway and Carrie Severino reported in their book *Justice on Trial*, the war room team contacted McNally, who confirmed that he had not discussed the Russia investigation with Kavanaugh.[3]

The following day, Harris appeared eager to sink her claws into Kavanaugh and gloated about her viral moment in front of him during the hearing. "As I'm sure you've noticed, your lack of a clear answer to a question I asked you last night has generated lots of interest," she told Kavanaugh with a smirk. Harris continued speaking, springing the perjury trap, like a villain who had finally captured her prey, revealing she had received "reliable information" that Kavanaugh had spoken about the investigation with the firm and that he had still not answered her question. "I will ask you again. And for the last time. Yes or no. Have you ever been part of a conversation with lawyers at the firm of Kasowitz, Benson, Torres about special counsel Mueller and his investigation," she asked dramatically.

Kavanaugh was ready, but still curious about who she was asking about. "Are you referring to a specific person?" he asked.

Harris again refused to answer Kavanaugh's question.

"I'm referring to a specific subject and the specific person I'm referring to is you," she replied.

"Who was the conversation with?" Kavanaugh asked. "You said you had information . . ."

"That is not the subject of the question, sir. The subject of the question is you and whether you were part of a conversation regarding special counsel Mueller's investigation," she repeated.

"The answer is no," Kavanaugh replied confidently.

"Thank you," Harris replied, looking down at her papers, and smirked. "And it would have been great if you could have said that last night."

"In my . . ." Kavanaugh hesitated, clearly ready to defend his decision to be cautious but realized that Harris had finished pressing the topic. "Never mind," he added.

"Let's move on," Harris agreed.

Harris never revealed her source of her "reliable information," proving her attack to be a dud. She was either likely relying on a source that was not reliable or just making the whole thing up to confuse Kavanaugh. Reporters were also puzzled. "This moment, viral as it was, sit up in your chair as it was, the person who hasn't produced any documentation or evidence of it yet has been Senator Harris," CNN congressional correspondent Phil Mattingly explained on camera after the exchange. It was all a stunt.

Like many Democrats, Harris tried to prod Kavanaugh on his view of *Roe v. Wade*, but he repeatedly cited the precedent of not signaling how he would rule on a specific case. Harris instead tried to shake him with her unfounded opinion, that government regulations on abortion were unfair and sexist. "Can you think of any laws that give government the power to make decisions about the male body?" she asked.

"I'm happy to answer a more specific question," a baffled Kavanaugh replied.

"Male versus female," Harris added.

"Medical procedures?" asked Kavanaugh.

"That the government has the power to make a decision about a man's body?" Harris asked.

"I thought you were asking about medical procedures that are unique to men," said Kavanaugh.

"I'll repeat the question," said Harris with a smile, enjoying Kavanaugh's discomfort. "Can you think of any laws that give the government power to make decisions about the male body?"

"I'm not aware—I'm not—thinking of any right now, Senator," he replied.

Harris and Senate Democrats were struggling. Despite all their protests and Harris's perjury trap, which came up empty, the path to confirm Kavanaugh was being paved. The hearings were over, and the next step was a confirmation vote that they expected to lose. But Democrats had one more card to play.

"I believe her," Harris announced on *CBS This Morning* on September 18, less than two days after California professor Christine Blasey Ford had gone public to accuse Kavanaugh of sexual assaulting her when she was a teenager in high school.[4] The path for Ford to identify herself and go public with her accusation was arduous, but it was clear that Senate Democrats betrayed her wish to remain anonymous as reports of a letter she wrote to Senator Feinstein forced her out into the open.

Ford had first called Representative Anna Eshoo in early July to reveal her accusation against Kavanaugh, but said she wished to remain anonymous. Eshoo informed Feinstein about the accusation; Feinstein then instructed her to have Ford write her a letter. Feinstein included the information for Kavanaugh's background check, but the details of the letter were never made public. Feinstein also appeared not to have informed Harris of the letter.

After the initial Kavanaugh hearings were over, Eshoo spoke to Harris about the letter from Ford, expressing interest in the reason why it was never used. Ruth Marcus of the *Washington Post* reported in her book *Supreme Ambition* that Harris confronted Feinstein about the letter and demanded details. "There are going to be repercussions from this," Harris reportedly told her. "You've got to figure this out."[5] It was never publicly revealed who first leaked information about the letter to the press, but the details kept trickling out despite the woman's stated desire to remain anonymous. Someone believed this was the kill shot against Kavanaugh, despite the thin accusation. In response to some of the outrage from her colleagues, Feinstein briefed Democratic senators on the letter and more details were leaked to the press. The Intercept published a report by Ryan Grim on September 12 revealing that Feinstein was aware of a letter from a constituent describing "an incident involving Kavanaugh and a woman while they were in high school."[6] The letter was dated July 30, proving that Democrats had been holding the card for a while and deployed it after the hearings were concluded.

Subsequent reporting from BuzzFeed and the *New Yorker* teased out details of the allegations. On September 16, Ford had contacted the *Washington Post* through a tip line, but she refused to go on the record to discuss her allegation. When it was clear her identity had leaked after reporters started contacting her, she decided to go public with the *Post* with her allegations. Ford claimed that when she was in high school, she was at a party of teenagers at a house in Montgomery County, Maryland, where a visibly intoxicated Brett Kavanaugh pinned her to a bed and tried to remove her clothing while other boys in the room laughed. When she tried to scream, she claimed, Kavanaugh put his hand over her mouth. "I thought he might inadvertently kill me," said Ford to the *Post*. "He was trying to attack me and remove my clothing." Ford recalled that she ultimately fought free from the bumbling teenage boys and fled.

It was all Harris needed. She hailed Ford as a hero, praising her for the "courage" of coming forward and challenging a person of power. "She's doing it, I believe, because she knows that this is an important matter. It's a serious matter. And she has the courage to come forward. She has nothing to gain. What does she have to gain?" In the interview with CBS, Harris raised doubts about "who Brett Kavanaugh really is," suggesting that the entire committee had been led astray. "I want to know about this guy's background . . . we need to know are we about to put somebody on the United States Supreme Court who committed sexual assault," she demanded. Kavanaugh had already been through six different background checks before taking positions in legal and government circles, which came up empty. But for Harris, it was enough to condemn him. "I believe her," Harris repeated during her interview, but admitted she had not even spoken to Ford yet or met with her. Harris also downplayed the need for a burden of proof for Ford's claims, or due process for Kavanaugh: "I have had many cases where there was enough evidence to believe something happened but not necessarily prove it beyond a reasonable doubt in a courtroom, but it doesn't mean it didn't happen." Harris demanded a delay. "A vote on Kavanaugh's nomination must be delayed until there is a thorough investigation," she wrote in a statement.

Democrats successfully derailed Kavanaugh's confirmation vote, as Senator Chuck Grassley and Senate Republicans negotiated to put Ford on the stand and testify to her allegations. Harris had already made up her mind, appearing to channel John F. Kennedy's dramatic treatise on courage. "You have been a true patriot in fighting for the best of who we are as a country. I believe you are doing that because you love this country, and I believe history will show that you are a true profile in courage at this moment in time in the history of our country and I thank you," she told Ford during her opening remarks at the hearing.[7] It was the language typically reserved for war heroes.

When it came time to question Kavanaugh, Harris had no interest in his character witnesses, witness statements, or repeated denials of the sexual assault accusations. She wanted to paint the widely respected husband, father, and coach as a drunken and abusive frat boy.

"Do you agree that it is possible for men to both be friends with some women, and treat other women badly?" Harris asked, suggesting that he could have a dark, secret past of abusive behavior.

"Of course," Kavanaugh said, but stressed he had multiple character witnesses from women who defended him. Harris was not interested in his side of the story, instead painting him as hardened and unfeeling.

"Did you watch Dr. Ford's testimony?" she asked Kavanaugh.

"I did not," Kavanaugh replied. "I plan to."

As the testimony continued, Democrats paraded to the media, repeating that they believed Ford and that Kavanaugh was not fit for the Supreme Court. Senate Republicans, however, were on defense, and restrained themselves from challenging Ford's credibility.

President Trump had seen enough. At an October 2 rally in Southaven, Mississippi, he delighted his supporters by fighting back. "Guilty until proven innocent, that's very dangerous for our country," he said as the crowd roared their approval. Then Trump mocked Ford for remembering that she had one beer before the attack but did not know any other key details of it. Parroting her testimony, he said, "How did you get home? I don't remember. How'd you get there? I don't remember. Where is the place? I don't remember. How many years ago was it? I don't know."

The crowd cheered. "I don't know. I don't know," Trump continued, imitating Ford's voice. "What neighborhood was it in? I don't know. Where's the house? I don't know. Upstairs, downstairs—where was it? I don't know—but I had one beer. That's the only thing I remember."

Trump lamented the fact that Kavanaugh and his family were shattered by the accusations, shaming Harris and Senate Democrats for their vicious tactics. "They destroy people," Trump said. "They want to destroy people. These are really evil people."[8]

Harris seized on Trump's remarks and denounced them at the Atlantic Festival the following morning during an interview with *Atlantic* magazine funder Laurene Powell Jobs. "Stop being mean," Harris pleaded, as the audience applauded. Harris reminded the audience of Ford testifying that Kavanaugh's friends were laughing as he assaulted her and compared her story to the same laughter that Trump had elicited by mocking her testimony. "And so now we have, last night, the president of the United States urging a crowd to laugh at her!" Harris said sadly. "I can't think of anything more—inappropriate is not descriptive enough. It's mean. It's mean and it's completely without any level of empathy." Harris went even further, joining Democrat senators to attack Kavanaugh's credibility as a human being. She questioned whether Kavanaugh could even be "honest and truthful" on the Supreme Court and raised concerns about his "temperament" and whether he would be influenced by "emotion" rather than "facts" in important cases.[9] At this point in the fight, it was Harris and the Democrats who were running on emotional fumes, not facts.

Kavanaugh's nomination continued moving forward. With the Senate Judiciary Committee vote scheduled on September 28, the outrage demonstrated by protesters reached a new peak. Led by Senator Mazie Hirono, Harris joined a walkout from the committee room, joined by

Senators Richard Blumenthal and Sheldon Whitehouse. As reporters swarmed around the group of senators, Harris expressed her outrage. "This is a sham what's going on right now," she said, waving her finger in the air. "From top to bottom this has been about bullies. Listen to the people, all that we have asked for is an FBI investigation," she said. But when reporters asked if the Democrats would return to the final committee vote, they demurred. "Haven't decided yet," Hirono replied. Harris interrupted to change the subject and deliver another passionate speech. "This has been about raw power," Harris said, jabbing her finger, expressing her frustration with the nomination process. "It's been pushing and pushing and ramming this thing through, because they have the power as opposed to the integrity . . . this is a failure of this body." Behind the scenes Harris was even more upset, as it appeared that Democrats were losing their case. People in the room recalled Harris cursing and dropping f-bombs, ordering around Senate staffers who did not even work for her. "Anyone who's staff, get the fuck out of here!" Harris yelled at staffers in the Senate anteroom after a particularly emotional moment during the hearings.

On social media, Harris and her staff were also busy. "Moments ago, I walked out of the Senate Judiciary Committee hearing on Kavanaugh," Harris wrote on Twitter. "This hearing is a sham and Dr. Ford and the American people deserve better." She also used the moment to build up her email list and do some fundraising. "This is a disgrace," the Harris email read. "So, instead of sitting through this farce . . . I walked out." The email linked to an ActBlue digital fundraising page.[10] The walkout only increased the left's outrage. Protesters flooded into the Capitol Building as two women accosted Senator Jeff Flake in the Senate elevator, screaming and pleading that he act to halt the vote. The entire moment was captured on camera and Flake was rattled. Behind the scenes, the worried Flake made a deal with his Democratic colleagues to support advancing the nominee to the full Senate vote but only if they could wait for a week for the FBI to investigate the allegations before the final vote. With concern and agony displayed on his face, Flake announced that his decision to vote to advance Kavanaugh's nomination to the floor would be conditional on a limited FBI investigation. Harris and all the Democrats on the committee returned to the hearing to vote no.

Days later the limited FBI investigation was complete, with no concrete evidence that Kavanaugh was a rapist. In her Senate floor speech, Harris denounced the investigation as "incomplete and insufficient." Harris spoke about her career as a prosecutor, trying to elicit emotion as she evoked the sadness of prosecuting cases of sexual assault. "Dr. Ford's experience in this regard is not different from sexual assault victims and she should be believed," Harris said. "When it comes to Dr. Ford's allegations, we fell short. We fell short. We did not do her justice, we did not do the American people justice," she added. Despite their rage and emotion, Democrats ultimately ran out of gas. On October 6, the full Senate finally voted to approve Kavanaugh to the Supreme Court with a vote of 50–48.

Kavanaugh was ultimately confirmed but Harris was not finished with him. On September 15, 2019, nearly a year later, Harris publicly called for his impeachment after a new report surfaced in the *New York Times* featuring dubious new claims that Kavanaugh had exposed himself in front of a female student at a college party at Yale. (The *Times* later corrected the report to note one alleged victim declined to be interviewed for the story, and her friends told reporters she did not recall the incident.) Kavanaugh denied the allegation, but once again, it was enough for Harris. "Brett Kavanaugh lied to the U.S. Senate and most importantly to the American people. He was put on the Court through a sham process and his place on the Court is an insult to the pursuit of truth and justice," she wrote on Twitter. "He must be impeached." Harris's demands sparked a series of fellow Democrats to join her, including Representative Julian Castro, Senators Elizabeth Warren and Amy Klobuchar, and former Texas representative Beto O'Rourke.

Harris finished the fight but did not succeed in stopping Kavanaugh. She was directly responsible for turning up the heat on the confirmation process but proved woefully unprepared for any serious attempt at challenging his confirmation. Instead, she generated more attention for herself, crafting more viral moments to prove to leftist activists that she was their champion in the fight—and the champion they would want in the future. She abandoned any professionalism or courtesy for her Senate colleagues to boost her own brand as she pursued the idea of running for president. The emerging profile of Harris was a person who was vengeful, angry, and aggressive—just the type of person the angry left wanted to challenge Trump for president. But was the rest of the country ready?

# CHAPTER SEVEN

# RADICAL LEFTIST REBRAND

*As Robert Kennedy many years ago said, "Only those who dare to fail greatly can ever achieve greatly."*

—KAMALA HARRIS, JANUARY 27, 2019

When Harris was not focused on abusing her position in the Senate to go viral, she spent her time crafting a new brand to appeal to progressives in time for the 2020 election. The key to success, she believed, was to run to the left as far as she could. Like a new kid in high school, freshman Senator Harris was ready to cosponsor anything that would help bolster her progressive credentials—even if it was in direct opposition to her previous work as a California attorney general and district attorney. Everything was on the table for a reboot. Her "Smart on Crime" agenda had to go, replaced by a newfound horror of racism in the judicial system that she spent her entire career working in. In January 2017, Harris went from acknowledging the inevitable legalization of marijuana in California to crusading for decriminalizing and ultimately making marijuana legal nationwide. She was now the cool lawmaker, ready to legalize pot despite her record of throwing people in jail for smoking it. In May 2018, Harris announced her decision to cosponsor legislation with Senator Cory Booker to federally legalize marijuana. "Making marijuana legal at the federal level is the smart thing to do, it's the right thing to do," she said in a statement. "I know this as a former prosecutor and I know it as a senator." Smart on Crime had gone to pot.

Harris also cozied up to the Senate's most popular socialist, Senator Bernie Sanders, in April 2017 to introduce the College for All Act, a bill she cosponsored to drastically cut student debt interest rates and offer free college. In August 2017, Harris announced her decision at a town hall in Oakland that she would be the first Democrat senator to cosponsor Sanders's Medicare-for-all bill to give Americans single-payer health care. "This is about understanding, again, that health care should be a right, not a privilege," she said. "And it's also about being smart." Harris's colleagues were surprised to see her align herself with Sanders but viewed it as a prelude to running for president. She also drafted a plan of her own to offer free money to low-income Americans. Then, in October 2018, Harris proposed the LIFT (Livable Incomes for Families Today) the Middle Class Act, a bill that would dramatically change tax policy to give $250 a month or $3,000 a year to individuals without children making less than $50,000 a year, and $500 per month or $6,000 a year to married couples making less than $100,000 a year.

Harris also worked to soften her law-and-order image. After defending the use of cash bail as attorney general of California, Harris teamed up with Senator Rand Paul in July 2017 to push pretrial bail reform. "In our country, whether you stay in jail or not is wholly determined by whether you're wealthy or not—and that's wrong," she said in a statement. It was a sharp shift from her efforts as attorney general to keep inmates in California's overflowing prisons.

In December 2018, Harris even signaled her willingness to support the Green New Deal, one of the most dramatic spending and regulatory proposals championed by Representative Alexandria Ocasio-Cortez with the goal of ending use of fossil fuels in ten years. When contacted by reporters about supporting the massive spending agenda, estimated to cost $93 trillion, Harris's staff indicated that she was "broadly supportive" of the idea and would take a "close look" at legislation to address it.

Harris's attempt at a liberal rebrand worked. In 2019, GovTrack, a nonpartisan organization that tracks bills in Congress, ranked Harris as the "most liberal compared to all senators"—more liberal than even Bernie Sanders or Elizabeth Warren. The new Kamala Harris was a far cry from the competent moderate progressive image she spent years cultivating with San Francisco's elite.

## WEAPONIZING IDENTITY POLITICS

As a mixed-race Democrat, Harris leveraged her identity to boost her political profile as she prepared a run for president. She challenged Democratic Party leaders with the "uncomfortable truth" on their relationship with minorities during an August 2018 speech at Netroots Nation, a gathering of leftist grassroots bloggers and activists. Taking the stage, Harris challenged the party for resisting the pursuit of "identity politics."

"I have a problem, guys, with that phrase, 'identity politics,'" she said. "Because let's be clear, when people say that it's a pejorative. That phrase is used to divide, and it is used to distract. Its purpose is to minimize and marginalize issues that impact all of us. It is used to try and shut us up."

Referencing past Democrat political victories, Harris reminded Democrats that "black women have been putting in the work, going door to door, organizing even when the cameras were focused elsewhere." The party, she argued, was already in debt to women of color and it was time to pay up.

"The truth is, we shouldn't just be thanking women of color for electing progressive leaders. In 2018, we should be electing women of color as those leaders," she said as the audience applauded.[1] It was not a uniting speech, but the message was clear. Harris wanted a bigger seat at the table.

Why was Harris considering a run for president? She had only been in the Senate for two years and her political record was extremely thin. Her call to "speak truth" was hardly a product of lived experience but rather a crafted message trying to elicit feelings of the civil rights era. She had leveraged her Senate career into some viral video clips but had not earned much respect from her colleagues. She was not seen as a leftist champion, a bipartisan dealmaker, or a national healer. She had not even visited the White House as a senator. The only way to rise was to show up and demand a seat at the table, which was a strategy Harris was accustomed to.

As she eyed a run for president, Harris continued workshopping her softer side. In early January 2019, she also tried to bring back her "joyful warrior" brand she tried to sell in early 2018. It fit in well with her book tour for her memoir, *The Truths We Hold*. "I came up with that term because you know, I said, I'm tired of being mad all the time. And being kind of upset, and I said you know we gotta find time to sing and dance and laugh and have a little fun," she reminded journalist Jonathan Capehart at a book event interview.[2]

Harris also published a new children's book in January 2019, *Super-heroes Are Everywhere*. At a time when Marvel superhero movies were earning billions at the box office, Harris jumped on the trend to promote her own superhero franchise. Everyone was a superhero in Kamala's book. The normally hard-nosed senator prosecuting the case from the Senate hearings was now sitting barefoot on a couch using an earnest, friendly voice to attract children.[3] She pointed out that the last page of the book was a mirror, reminding them they were heroes too. "You're a hero by being the very best you. Now that's pretty super. You are a hero." If Harris looked in the mirror on the page, she would see herself as the hero in her own book. She later told Capehart: "I grew up reading comic books I love comic books. I'm a nerd. I pretend not to be," Harris said. "You don't have to look at a CGI screen to see a superhero."[4] It was plain to see that Harris was auditioning as the biggest superhero for the Democratic Party.

## CAMPAIGN LAUNCH

On January 21, 2019, Harris celebrated Martin Luther King Jr. Day by announcing a run for president before heading back to California for her campaign kickoff event, a rally in her hometown of Oakland. A grinning, laughing, waving Harris took the stage to Mary J. Blige's "Work That" as supporters in the crowd started shouting "Kam-a-la!" The location for her announcement demonstrated that Harris was trying to recapture a moment she experienced twelve years before when she was a young San Francisco district attorney, sitting front and center at a rally of thousands of supporters in the exact same place, chanting the name of Obama. Harris also tried to channel Obama's claim to destiny, as if she was the candidate defying the party establishment. "Of course, we know this is not going to be easy, guys. It's not going to be easy. We know what the doubters will say. It's the same thing they've always said. They'll say it's not your time. They'll say wait your turn. They'll say the odds are long," she said. "They'll say it can't be done. But—but America's story has always been written by people who can see what can be, unburdened by what has been." Harris also parroted Robert Kennedy to argue it was time for a new generation of bold leadership. "As Robert Kennedy many years ago said, 'Only those who dare to fail greatly can ever achieve greatly,'" Harris said proudly.

When Harris spoke about her record as a prosecutor and her attempts to reform a "deeply flawed" justice system, a person in the crowd began shouting, interrupting her speech. Harris began laughing as the crowd of supporters responded by chanting her name to drown out any opposition. Harris pivoted to a promise to "speak truth" about issues facing the country, repeating the phrase over a dozen times. "In this moment, we must all speak truth about what's happening. Seek truth, speak truth, and fight for the truth. So, let's speak some truth. Shall we?" she said, promising to speak the truth about drug addiction, climate change, racism, sexism, homophobia, transphobia, and antisemitism as well as problems with criminal justice in minority communities. Harris highlighted her career as a prosecutor as evidence she was only ever a tireless public servant. "In my whole life, I've only had one client: the people," she said, declaring her campaign slogan as "Kamala: For the People." Even San Francisco knew that was insincere. Harris's number one client was herself.

As she eyed her presidential campaign, Harris chose close advisors she felt she could trust. She selected the former head of her California Senate campaign, Juan Rodriguez, as her campaign manager. Rodriguez brought his business partners Averell "Ace" Smith, Sean Clegg, and Laphonza Butler to the table—all titans in California politics but without much experience running a national campaign. Harris brought her family to the campaign team as well, as she chose her closest advisor and sister, Maya Harris, to be the campaign chair. Maya Harris had served as a policy advisor for Hillary Clinton during her failed 2016 presidential campaign, helping Clinton try to navigate the pitfalls of the modern left. While Harris was the prosecutor and cop of the family, Maya was the professional activist, serving as the executive director of the Northern California American Civil Liberties Union and then as the vice president of the Democracy, Rights and Justice program at the Ford Foundation. She also served as a senior fellow at the leftist think tank Center for American Progress. She was even hired as an MSNBC analyst for a year before leaving the network to help lead her sister's presidential campaign.

Maya Harris is married to Tony West, who had a long career at the Justice Department in the Bill Clinton and Obama administrations. West leveraged his career at high levels of government to end up in the private sector. He worked at PepsiCo in 2014 as general counsel, corporate secretary, and executive vice president for public policy and government affairs and then shifting into the tech sector to work as the chief legal officer and corporate secretary at Uber in 2017. When first considering a campaign for president, West argued against Harris running, warning that her record as a prosecutor could hold her back, according to author Edward-Isaac Dovere. "Yeah," Harris replied. "I locked up some mothafuckas."[5] Harris was already famous in the Senate for her love of expletives and teased her "favorite curse word" in interviews across the country. The answer, although she never explicitly vocalized it, was "motherfuckah."

"It starts with an 'm' and ends with 'ah,'" Harris said in a July 2019 interview with NowThis News as she burst into laughter. "Not '-er.'"

Harris signaled early in the campaign that she was aware of her political liabilities, speaking about her record in law enforcement in a March 2019 interview with Star Jones at the Black Enterprise Women of Power Summit.

"But I think that part of what happens is, you know, there are those especially in this race especially as it is gearing up, people are going to say, 'Oh you know, Kamala is po-po,'" she said, bursting into laughter.[6] It was one more example that further provoked justice activists when it was clear Harris was not taking their concerns seriously and was even mocking them.

Harris repeatedly cited her ability to grill Trump officials on Capitol Hill as proof she was ready to be president, even though she failed to stop any of them from getting confirmed by the Senate.

"For me it's about being there and just trying to get to the truth, and you know, like that old movie about, you know, 'You can't hide from the truth!'" she said in an interview with podcaster Jemele Hill, misquoting the famous "You can't handle the truth" line from actor Jack Nicholson.

"*Few Good Men*," Hill replied, naming the movie.

"Right. *A Few Good Men*, you know?" Harris added. Harris clearly did not know.

Journalists grew more curious about Harris's identity as she kicked off her campaign, but she was sensitive about answering questions about her race. After an appearance at her alma mater, Howard University, one reporter questioned her about how she identified herself.

"You're African American, but you're also Indian American," a reporter said.

"Indeed," she replied.

"How do you describe yourself?" the reporter asked.

"Did you read my book? How do I describe myself? I describe myself as a proud American," she said sharply.[7]

But as Harris was reluctant to discuss her identity, prominent black figures began asking questions of their own. Despite her efforts to appeal to the black community, there were still some critics. In a February 2019 interview, CNN's Don Lemon challenged Harris's right to identify herself as an African American in an interview with veteran White House reporter April Ryan.

"To want that distinction, to say, 'Is she African-American or is she Black,' or whatever, there is nothing wrong with that! There's a difference between being African-American and being Black," he said.

Ryan replied that Harris was in fact a woman of color and a black woman.

"I agree with that . . . but is she African-American?" Lemon questioned. "There is a difference, and there's nothing wrong with that. No one's trying to take anything away from her. I think you're falling into the trap of that."

As Ryan pointed out that slaves from Africa were also taken to the Caribbean, as well as the United States, Lemon interrupted with a patronizing tone: "Jamaica's not America. Jamaica's not America. Jamaica did not come out of Jim Crow, I'm just saying."[8] One of the highest-profile black broadcasters was openly questioning Harris's identity, despite her long history of identifying as an African American.

Lemon's challenge represented how some in the black community viewed Harris. Dr. Charisse Burden-Stelly, then an assistant professor of Africana studies and political science at Carleton College, explained how Harris was perceived by some in the black community in an interview with podcaster Briahna Joy Gray in 2021. "Kamala is just a failed Condoleezza Rice. It's like 'You suck, you're a Condoleezza in Chucks,'" she said, pointing out that black people struggled to connect with her as "an authentic African American." Not only did she have a white husband, Burden-Stelly explained, but "she was primarily raised by her mother, and her mother was not black."[9]

Harris had little patience for the questions about her race. "For other people who can't figure out am I 'black enough,' I kinda feel like that's their problem, not mine. Maybe they need to go back to school to figure it out," she said in her interview with Hill. "And maybe they need to learn about the African diaspora and maybe they need to learn about a number of other things. But it is challenging and to be honest with you, it's also hurtful and it is real."

## MODERN-DAY LYNCHING

Harris vowed to "speak truth" during her presidential campaign, but that was immediately put to the test when one of her friends in Hollywood was embroiled in one of the most bizarre and embarrassing celebrity controversies ever. On January 29, actor Jussie Smollett approached Chicago police claiming he was the victim of a hate crime in the city at 2 a.m. as he walked to a Subway for a sandwich. Two masked assailants, he insisted, poured bleach on him, wrapped a noose around him, and shouted "This is MAGA country!" Sources connected to Smollett told TMZ that when he walked out of his house, someone yelled, "Aren't you that f***ot 'Empire' n*****?" and beat him badly and fractured his rib even as he fought back.[10] Despite her record as a prosecutor, Harris threw caution to the wind and was the first presidential candidate to voice her outrage at the alleged attack and offer support for Smollett. "Jussie Smollett is one of the kindest, most gentle human beings I know. I'm praying for his quick recovery," she wrote on social media. Harris went further, choosing not to use the word *alleged* when discussing the attack. "This was an attempted modern day lynching. No one should have to fear for their life because of their sexuality or color of their skin. We must confront this hate," she added. Harris was already close to the young ambitious gay actor. In January 2018, the two had protested together at a Kingdom Day Parade in Los Angeles, as Smollett was one of a group of celebrities with Harris wearing a pink "Time's Up" T-shirt to support women's rights.[11]

As police began investigating the details of Smollett's story, a growing number of reports indicated the incident was likely a staged hoax. Harris remained silent on the campaign trail. When questioned by WMUR's Adam Sexton if she was angry by the news, Harris feigned ignorance about the story. "I think the facts are still rolling themselves out, so I don't actually know what happened," Harris said. Despite her background as a prosecutor, Harris was treating the "facts" as inconvenient. Harris was confronted about her defense of Smollett on February 18 by a reporter in New Hampshire who asked her if she stood by her "modern day lynching" post on Twitter.

"Which tweet? What tweet?" Harris asked, looking around for her press secretary, Ian Sams, to intervene. Sams did not react, looking away as Harris was forced to stammer out a response. "Uh. Uh. OK, so, I will say this about that case. I think that the facts are still unfolding, and, um,

I'm very, um, concerned about obviously, the initial, um, allegation that he made about what might have happened," she said weakly.[12]

As more questions were raised, Harris stated she would not comment further until the investigation was complete because any allegation of a hate crime should be taken "seriously." On February 21, Harris had lunch with Al Sharpton, but fled from cameras afterward, ignoring all questions about Smollett. That evening, however, Harris finally conceded to address the developments of the case after Smollett was arrested by police. In a lengthy statement, Harris described it as a "tragedy." "Like most of you, I've seen the reports about Jussie Smollett, and I'm sad, frustrated, and disappointed. When anyone makes false claims to police, it not only diverts resources away from serious investigations, but it makes it more difficult for other victims of crime to come forward," she said in a statement. The episode demonstrated Harris's weakness as a candidate in the rush to be "first" and go viral instead of waiting for the facts.

Rather than owning up to her mistake, Harris pivoted to try to make her mistaken judgment about more than just one person's reputation. "Part of the tragedy of this situation is that it distracts from that truth and has been seized by some who would like to dismiss and downplay the very real problems that we must address," she said. "We should not allow that. I will always condemn racism and homophobia. We must always confront hate directly and we must always seek justice. That is what I will keep fighting for." The real tragedy was that Harris was fooled by an embarrassing hoax and was only offering excuses. It was one more sign she was not ready to run for president.

The establishment elite did not care. Straight out of the gate, Harris's big crowds in California, and her fundraising, caught their attention. "I think that you are going to be a formidable contender. I will just say honestly I think that there's a good chance that you are going to win the nomination," MSNBC's Rachel Maddow gushed after interviewing her on her show.[13] As a candidate, Harris quickly made the rounds among the top influencers in Democrat activist circles and got rave reviews. After lunching with Al Sharpton, the famed black activist compared her to Obama, noting they both ordered chicken and waffles when they met with him.

"Clearly, a lot of people that came [to see them lunch], the reaction shows that she has a lot of people like Barack Obama did," he said.

Harris appeared in person on February 11 on the popular New York City radio show *The Breakfast Club*, where co-host Charlamagne Tha God, asked her to respond to people who believed she opposed the legalization of marijuana. "That's not true. Look, I joke about it, I have joked about it. Half my family is from Jamaica, are you kidding me," she said, bursting into laughter. She was then asked if she had ever tried smoking weed. "I have. And I inhaled. I did inhale," she responded with a laugh. "It was a long time ago, but yes." "I just broke news!" She added with a laugh, appearing delighted with her response. "It was a joint," she volunteered. The former California attorney general who had a history of prosecuting marijuana smokers was now openly honest about her own personal drug use and remained supportive of legalizing the drug. "Listen, I think it gives a lot of people joy," she added. "And we need more joy."

But Harris's remarks did not bring joy to her Jamaican father, Donald Harris, who expressed his fury at his daughter for shaming her entire family, issuing a statement that was published on the Jamaica Global website:

> My dear departed grandmothers (whose extraordinary legacy I described in a recent essay on this website), as well as my deceased parents, must be turning in their grave right now to see their family's name, reputation and proud Jamaican identity being connected, in any way, jokingly or not with the fraudulent stereotype of a pot-smoking joy seeker and in the pursuit of identity politics. Speaking for myself and my immediate Jamaican family, we wish to categorically dissociate ourselves from this travesty.

The article was soon taken down from the website without an explanation, and Donald Harris shrank back out of the public conversation. Most of the media allowed the awkward moment to pass without much fanfare. When Harris was asked about her father's thoughts, she replied simply, "He's entitled to his opinion."[14]

As a US senator for California, Harris made a splash on the Hollywood funding circuit. She already had relationships with the top donors of the state, and they rewarded that relationship right out of the gate. Universal Pictures' Jeff Shell hosted one of Harris's first fundraisers in Los Angeles on January 30. Film producer J. J. Abrams and his wife, Katie McGrath, hosted a fundraiser for Harris in March, along with Endeavor superagent Ari Emanuel and ICM's Chris Silbermann. Famous actors and actresses lined up with checks supporting her in the first three months of her campaign. Ben Affleck gave $2,800; Elizabeth Banks donated $5,600; Eva Longoria Baston gave $5,400. Actors Jon Hamm, William Macy, and Pedro Pascal also donated. Other supporters included actresses Reese Witherspoon, Jessica Alba, and Mindy Kaling. By July, the *Hollywood Reporter* reported that Harris had raked in 48 percent of donations from presidential campaign donors on their top 100 list of Hollywood's most influential power players for $73,580.[15] The rich and powerful were already well-connected with Harris, enjoying a close relationship from her previous political career. She appeared ready to succeed on the presidential level, propped up by the same people who already supported her.

Harris felt like a celebrity herself as she pursued her historic campaign. On the stage at the Black Enterprise Women of Power Summit, Harris spoke about her experience on the campaign trail, including what it meant to experience "Black Girl Magic," a term used to describe that aura of top celebrities like Beyoncé. "I will say that the moment that I feel it, it's a reflective moment, meaning that when I see you I feel it, right? It's like a reflection of myself. When we see it in each other I think that's when we see it, right? 'Cause it really is not about one as an individual, it is about us as a collective," she said.

When it came to taking a position on her policies, however, the magic dimmed. Harris was the first to cosponsor Senator Bernie Sanders's bill to provide Medicare for All and even suggested that it was time to get rid of private insurance in a town hall meeting with CNN in January. "Let's eliminate that. Let's move on," she said, citing the frustrations of people working with the private health care industry. After she learned how unpopular voters found the idea of losing their private insurance, Harris tried to walk back the notion in a later interview with CNN. "I know it was interpreted that way. If you watch the tape, I think you'll see that there are obviously many interpretations of what I said," she said defensively.[16] She argued that theoretically there was always room for private insurance to exist alongside a government paid plan, which was not an honest assertion.

The confusion about where Harris stood on Medicare for All continued. In June, Harris raised her hand when the candidates were asked by debate moderators to signal whether they supported getting rid of private health insurance. The following day, Harris again worked to walk back her response. this time in an interview on MSNBC's *Morning Joe*, saying she had misunderstood the question.[17]

Harris was experienced enough on the single-payer health care issue to try to avoid the political pitfalls, but it was incomprehensible that she did not have command of the issue as she was the first to cosponsor the bill proposed by Sanders.

Harris continued trying to be all things to every radical leftist activist in the primary. Every talking point was on the table. "There's no question I'm in favor of banning fracking," she said during a CNN town hall on climate change in September. That year, climate change activists were wringing their hands at the amount of methane produced by cow farts and proposed dietary restrictions on beef as a solution. For a candidate trying to get traction in the farm state of Iowa, the concept was laughable, but not for Harris. When asked if she would support the federal government changing dietary guidelines to reduce the consumption of red meat, Harris replied, "The answer is yes." Another popular restriction favored by leftist climate activists was reducing the use of plastic straws. As Americans struggled to suck their drinks through insufficient paper tubes, Harris supported the idea of banning plastic straws. "I think we should, yes," she replied, adding, "We do need to ban the plastic."

In February 2019, Harris endorsed the idea of decriminalizing prostitution during an interview with the black news outlet the Root despite her history of advocacy against the same idea in San Francisco. She clarified that she did not support the "ecosystem" of the sex trade that followed decriminalization of prostitution, "But when you're talking about consenting adults? Yes, we should really consider that we can't criminalize consensual behavior as long as no one is being harmed." It was a far cry from her dismissal of the idea as "completely ridiculous" when she was in San Francisco just a few years earlier.

Harris had already shifted her position toward the legalization of marijuana but further dismissed concerns about its effect on the developing brains of children. Her argument was the only way to study marijuana was to legalize it. "If we don't study it though, and we don't legalize it, we can't study it," she told the Root. "And that's one of the reasons why I think you know what, there might be some harm but the benefit of legalizing it is worth the harm," she said.

Harris was already an abortion warrior, supporting the right to abortion until just before birth and the use of taxpayer funds to pay for them. As one of the few women running for president, Harris felt she could earn points for being the most aggressive abortion promoter in the race. At a Planned Parenthood presidential forum in Iowa, Harris applauded the idea voiced by an audience member of abortions being "free, on-demand, and accessible to all people at all times." She promised activists to "do the work on the defense and to fight, but also my intention is to work on the offense."[18] As part of her efforts to go on offense, Harris proposed a law that would require the Justice Department to approve state abortion laws, which would effectively cut down any abortion restrictions in the states.[19] The constitutionality of the idea was dubious, but that did not matter. It was an obvious play to one-up the other candidates on the issue.

Harris was also aggressive on the issue of guns, supporting a nationwide mandatory buyback program for some semiautomatic rifles. She also vowed to use executive action to restrict gun sales, directly challenging Biden's objections to the idea. When Biden tried to explain to her during a debate that effective restrictions on guns would require an act of Congress, not executive power, Harris appeared indignant. "Hey, Joe, instead of saying, 'No, we can't,' let's say, 'Yes, we can,'" she replied before laughing off his concerns about the Constitution.

Harris moved rapidly to smother her "po-po" persona by supporting an incredible swath of criminal justice reform. She voiced support for fundamentally "reimagining" policing and applauded a plan to cut police funding in Los Angeles by $150 million.[20] She pledged to eliminate private prisons and mandatory minimum sentences and supported ending mass incarceration, cash bail, and the death penalty. She also expressed support for a "conversation" about dangerous felons having their right to vote restored.

On immigration, Harris raised her hand during a debate in support of decriminalizing illegal border crossings, and also raised her hand in support of taxpayer-funded health care for illegal immigrants. She also used her platform to criticize ICE. "We need to probably think about starting from scratch because there's a lot that is wrong with the way that it's conducting itself," Harris told MSNBC in June 2018.

On June 28, Kamala Harris joined Democrat presidential candidates at the Homestead Migrant Children Detention Facility to protest, as the building was conveniently located near the site of the next Democratic primary debate in Florida. "It looks like any prison or jail that I have visited during the many, many years that I was prosecutor," she said. Harris spoke about how her "heart is broken" after visiting the site, blaming the Trump administration for inhumane treatment of migrants. "We're all here because we know we have to stand up for our America," she said afterward at a rally with protesters, calling it a "human rights" issue. "We are here to stand up and say that we are not going to allow this to happen. Not on our watch," she said. She vowed that when she was elected president, she would shut down facilities like Homestead and lamented the detainment of migrant children. "They are children who have fled, most of them, from murder capitals of the world, they are children who have arrived at our shore at our border, seeking safety, seeking refuge, seeking security, and we pride ourselves on the strength of our nation," she said. "Part of the strength of our nation is that we have strong arms that will embrace." During the protest, Harris stood on a ladder with other politicians and waved and put her hand on her heart and feigned profound sadness while seeing the children detained in the facility. An animated gif of her action became a meme, as the internet mocked her insincere attempt to appear heartfelt. "This Meme of Kamala Harris 'Waving Goodbye' Is So Funny I'm Wheezing," BuzzFeed senior editor Jon-Michael Poff wrote for the website, which highlighted social media users gleefully sharing the GIF.

Harris continued attacking Trump on the campaign trail on the issue of detaining unaccompanied migrant children, repeating that the president was responsible for putting "babies in cages." "You look at the fact that this is a president who has pushed policies that's been about putting babies in cages at the border in the name of security when in fact what it is, is a human rights abuse being committed by the United States government," she said during a July speech to the NAACP in Detroit.[21]

Despite her efforts to side with leftist activists, she remained elusive when asked to discuss policy details. Was it a feature or a bug that could be fixed? On July 31, 2019, Harris sat down with *New York Times* reporter Alexander Burns to discuss it.

> **Burns:** Is that why—I mean, there have obviously been times in the campaign where you've gotten these highly abstract litmus-test questions that you've, sort of, either deflected or returned to revise your initial answer. Is that just about feeling like, this is all—I mean, you can't use this word, because I can't print it, but, like this is all—
>
> **Harris:** Bullshit.
>
> **Burns:** —basically bullshit.
>
> **Harris:** Sometimes.
>
> **Burns:** Yeah.
>
> **Harris:** Sometimes, yeah. If it's—or it's, it may be that, sometimes. We could go through the questions and then figure out which is what.

Harris also tried to explain why she was vague and hesitant on the campaign trail. Why did she sound vapid and empty? Her answer:

> My orientation, again, is to really want to think through the details of how will this actually play out or impact, instead of just saying the thing that sounds good. So, sometimes I hesitate or, you

know, because I actually am running through, in my head, all the scenarios about how it would actually work, and it can be very—obviously—challenging for me as a candidate, because it can be misinterpreted, I think, as being evasive, or, "Is she sure?" or, "Is she wiffly-waffling?" or whatever. But it's just—I really do think through these things.

Harris was making the case that she thought about things too much, not too little, which is why she had a problem explaining herself. Anything else, she claimed, was "bullshit" that her opponents were not thinking through.

# BEATING UP BIDEN

*These people need to know black history. And it cannot be, as it always ends up being, that the couple of chocolate chips on the stage have to be the ones teaching everybody else about America's history.*

—KAMALA HARRIS, JULY 15, 2019

As the Democratic primary shifted into the summer, Harris was increasingly burdened by her performance in the polls. Voters were not encouraged by her public struggle to define exactly what she believed, and the results began to show. She was just one more candidate onstage competing for the hearts of the left who were either looking for the next Barack Obama or a dreamier version of Bernie Sanders. No one was fitting the bill.

Harris and her advisors were impatient. In order to break through, she needed a breakout debate performance, and for that she needed to take on Joe Biden. Biden was already agonizing the establishment figures, the media pundits, and the activists in the party. The former vice president, over a decade older than most of the candidates on the stage, was late to announce his campaign, and made gaffe after gaffe in the seemingly endless primary cycle. But Biden stood out as a candidate who not only had the experience to be the president but offered Democrat voters a more moderate approach that would compete with Donald Trump. The congressional clown candidates were only fighting with each other to win the hearts of the socialist left, most of whom were already committed to Sanders.

Harris was unsure whether to play a party peacemaker or a Biden challenger onstage. During the first debate, she tried to play the role of a peacemaker, chiding Representative Eric Swalwell, a really long-shot primary candidate trying to get noticed, for making attacks. "Hey guys, you know what?" she asked. "America does not want to witness a food fight. They want to know how we are going to put food on their table." It was a cringeworthy canned line, but the audience applauded the sentiment. Despite her call for peace, Harris soon turned against Biden to challenge his remarks about the good ol' days of his Senate career.

At a fundraiser in New York City, the former vice president started rambling about how he used to work with old-school power brokers— even some avowed segregationists—to get things done.

Biden recalled working with segregationist Democrats such as Mississippi senator James Eastland and South Carolina senator Strom Thurmond. "Things have changed, we gotta bring it back," he said. Referring to Eastland, Biden said, "He never called me 'boy,'" and imitated Eastland's southern accent. "He always called me 'son.'" Continuing his story, Biden said, "Well guess what? At least there was some civility. We got things done. We didn't agree on much of anything. We got things done. We got it finished."

The comments were immediately condemned by Democrats, but Biden was defiant. When Senator Cory Booker demanded that Biden apologize, he reacted angrily to reporters who asked him for a response. "Apologize for what?" he asked. "Cory should apologize. He knows better. There's not a racist bone in my body. I've been involved in civil rights my whole career." The young bench of the Democratic Party groaned, but their criticism did not make much of an impact. Harris, however, was ready.

Harris spent days with her team carefully strategizing her attack and she dropped a bomb on Biden during a June debate. "I do not believe you are a racist," she began—before accusing him of being a racist. "It was actually hurtful to hear you talk about the reputations of two United States senators who built their reputations and career on the segregation of race in this country," she said, turning to Biden during the debate. But her attack went further. "It was not only that, but you also worked with them to oppose busing. There was a little girl in California who was part of the second class to integrate her public schools. She was bused to school every day," she continued. Pausing for dramatic effect, Harris added, "That little girl was me."

When debate moderators offered Biden time to respond to Harris's attack, he struggled to defend his civil rights record but kept talking despite appearing rattled by the accusation. Looking up at the debate timer, he realized he could be saved by the clock. "Anyway, my time's up. I'm sorry," he said weakly. Media coverage exploded, as pundits celebrated the attack as a major moment for Harris. On social media, Biden critics cheered, viewing his "time's up" statement as a symbol for his political career and run for president.

Biden was shocked. "I was prepared for them to come after me, but I wasn't prepared for the person coming at me the way she came at me," he told CNN's Chris Cuomo afterward in an interview. Biden was also hurt. He had fresh memories of Harris and his family, particularly when she attended his son Beau's funeral in 2015. "I thought we were friends," Biden lamented during an appearance on *The Tom Joyner Morning Show* after Harris's attack. "I hope we still will be."[22] Biden also recalled when he traveled to California to nominate Harris for Senate at her state convention. Behind the scenes, Biden's family was furious. Jill Biden vented about Harris during a phone call with close supporters, arguing that her husband was not racist. "With what he cares about, what he fights for, what he's committed to, you get up there and call him a racist without basis?" Jill Biden said, according to reports. "Go f— yourself."[23] One of Beau's close friends told the *Washington Post*, "I turned to my wife and said, 'Beau's flipping in his grave.'"[24]

The Harris campaign was ecstatic. Hours later they released a T-shirt featuring an image of Kamala Harris as a young student with the slogan "That little girl was me," celebrating the viral debate moment. It looked like the campaign had set up the viral moment for maximum impact. For a moment, it had the desired effect. The campaign boasted they had raised $2 million in twenty-four hours after the debate.

Harris had a big moment, but she immediately backed down to try to dull the sting of her attack on Biden. On MSNBC's *Morning Joe* the following day, Harris tried to explain to hosts Mika Brzezinski and Joe Scarborough why she attacked Biden, a friend of the show. "I think at some point you have to draw the line, and for those people who are saying that they believe that the racists should not commingle and on the heels of a history of extreme pain and damage, not to mention death, you gotta draw the line," she said. When asked if she believed that Biden should not have worked with segregationists in the United States Senate, Harris disagreed and tried to clarify.

"I'm saying the characterization and the nostalgia of who they were I find to be misplaced and it was hurtful to me to hear that we must be nostalgic," she said. The tough, no-nonsense prosecutor was now playing to the crowd as a victim.

Harris enjoyed a polling boost from the attack, as the average of her polling numbers went from 7 percent to 15 percent. Harris also spoke about her decision to attack Biden in an interview with podcaster Jemele Hill, noting that breaking through barriers was never easy. "There's breaking involved. And when you break things it's painful. You get hurt. You may get cut and you may bleed. It will be worth it but it is not without pain," she said. Harris said she felt it was time she reminded Biden and the United States just how bad segregationists were. "They built their reputations and careers on the segregation of the races and if they had their way I would not be in the United States Senate and I would not be running for president of the United States," she said. Harris said she felt the responsibility to talk about race on the campaign debate stage but also said she did not want to be defined by it. "I have said to my team, I'm like, 'Look, I am not running for black history professor. I am running for president of the

United States,'" she explained to Hill. "These people need to know black history. And it cannot be, as it always ends up being, that the couple of chocolate chips on the stage have to be the ones teaching everybody else about America's history. It's America's history."

Given that as a child she grew up in liberal San Francisco, Harris strained credibility on the issue of public school busing, suggesting she suffered the effects of a deeply segregated society that required federal laws to integrate the schools. Harris only made things worse by appearing uncertain of her own position on federal busing, working to backtrack her position. When reporters asked her about her own views, Harris was uncertain. "If we got back to the point where governments were actively opposing integration, yes," Harris told reporters in Iowa when asked about federal legislation to make busing mandatory.[25] "I could imagine that would be when the courts would have to step in. . . . I could imagine that, but thankfully that's not where we are today." Harris, it turned out, appeared not to have thought about the issue or even what her position was, revealing she was obviously just trying to score political points. A clean political attack had initially worked, but Harris grew hesitant about the follow-up. If she had sustained the attacks with more examples of Biden's failures on issues important to black Americans, she might have further boosted her campaign. But for some reason, she and her campaign backed down.

The Bidens kept fighting. On July 8, they declared public victory over Harris's attack. "I mean, the one thing you cannot say about Joe is that he's a racist," Jill Biden said in a CNN interview. "I mean, he got into politics because of his commitment to civil rights." She reminded Harris that Biden was the vice president for the first black president. "And then to be elected with Barack Obama, and then someone is saying, you know, you're a racist?" she asked with disbelief. "The American people know Joe Biden. They know his values. They know what he stands for. And they didn't buy it," she added.

The more experienced Biden worked to demonstrate he had no hard feelings toward Harris and instead tried to soften her up. At the next Democratic primary debate, hosted by CNN on July 31, Biden approached

Harris directly for a handshake. "Go easy on me, kid," he murmured as he approached Harris before the debate, gazing at her and grasping her hand with both hands. The Harris team was outraged. "Kid?" Press secretary Ian Sams reacted on social media with incredulity. Debate moderator Jake Tapper revisited Harris's attack, noting that Biden believed that she had the same positions on federal busing mandates. Biden was right but Harris was annoyed. "That is simply false. And let's be very clear about this," Harris said, repeating that if the segregationists had their way, there would not be any black senators in the Senate. Harris ultimately went easy on Biden, after she receiving mixed reviews for her debate performance. The tables were turned just weeks later.

## TULSI GABBARD AND THE KAMALA KNOCKOUT PUNCH

Representative Tulsi Gabbard from Hawaii entered the Democrat primary in February 2019 promising to "bring the spirit of aloha" to the White House. "This is the change we need to see in the White House because the White House should be a beacon of aloha," she said in front of cheering supporters when she announced her campaign. Gabbard, a free-spirited, surfing antiwar figure who endorsed Bernie Sanders in 2016, was the exact opposite of Harris, a calculating socialite from the San Francisco political machine who endorsed Hillary Clinton in 2016. Gabbard was elected to the House of Representatives in 2012 as prominent Democrats and House Speaker Nancy Pelosi seized on her diversity as a new face for the party. A young woman with a military background, Gabbard took reporters surfing for interviews and was the topic of glowing profiles as she spoke about her love for the populist politics and aloha. But the more her profile was raised, the more she started to resist her party leaders.

Gabbard shook the Democratic Party when she resigned from the Democratic National Committee to endorse Sanders over Hillary Clinton in the 2016 presidential primary. As the establishment shook their heads sadly at what they believed was career suicide, Clinton's ultimate loss against Trump dulled the impact of her choice, shifting her into the spotlight. As a veteran, Gabbard made headlines for bucking her party as a peace maverick. When Democrats wanted to go to war in Syria to help stop the civil war there, Gabbard resisted, traveling to meet with dictator Bashar al-Assad to promote peace and repeatedly warning the United States not to get involved. The military hawks tried to whip up support for intervention as images of al-Assad torturing and gassing his citizens emerged online. But Gabbard was not moved, repeatedly warning against intervention.

Gabbard, like many supporters of Sanders, was annoyed when pundits portrayed Harris as the future of the progressive movement based on her self-professed title of a "progressive prosecutor." When it was clear that Harris was on the rise, Gabbard went for a knockout blow at a July 31 debate on CNN.

> I want to bring the conversation back to the broken criminal justice system that is disproportionately negatively impacting black and brown people all across this country today. Now Senator Harris says she's proud of her record as a prosecutor and that she'll be a prosecutor president.
>
> But I'm deeply concerned about this record. There are too many examples to cite but she put over 1,500 people in jail for marijuana violations and then laughed about it when she was asked if she ever smoked marijuana.
>
> She blocked evidence—she blocked evidence that would have freed an innocent man from death row until the courts forced her to do so. She kept people in prison beyond their sentences to use them as cheap labor for the state of California. And she fought to keep . . . [a] bail system in place that impacts poor people in the worst kind of way.

The debate audience exploded with applause. Harris responded weakly, decrying "fancy speeches" while she was actually "doing the work" of criminal justice, but the damage was done. The information Gabbard shared was not new, as progressive activists had already flagged it online. But it was the first time the information was deployed on the debate stage in such a public and devastating fashion. "I don't know why no one had the courage to ask her those questions, why I was the first person to do it. If had to guess, I would imagine it's because she's got friends in high places. I would guess it's because she's a woman of color and no one wants to be seen as the person attacking the woman of color who's running for president," Gabbard reflected afterward in an interview with podcaster Joe Rogan. (Gabbard's claim that Harris blocked evidence that would have freed an innocent man was later disproven. As attorney general, Harris blocked advanced DNA testing in the death penalty case of Kevin Cooper, which activists insisted would exonerate him after he was convicted for the stabbing deaths of four people. As a senator, Harris reversed her position in 2018 but an independent review completed in January 2023 by Governor Gavin Newsom found the evidence for Cooper's conviction "extensive and conclusive.")

After the debate, Harris tried to ignore the issue and ward off the broadside attack. "This is going to sound immodest, but I'm obviously a top-tier candidate," she said haughtily in a postdebate interview. "And so, I did expect that I would be on the stage and take hits tonight, because there are a lot of people who are trying to make the stage for the next debate." Harris had made the stage, but she was already struggling with her career as a prosecutor. The "Kamala Is a Cop" meme on social media was gleefully amplified by Gabbard's attacks. The most frequently shared image featured a photoshopped collage of a laughing Kamala Harris wearing a police uniform and putting handcuffs on a little black girl. Another video featured Harris dancing with her drum line at a school spliced together with slamming jail cell doors. Harris blamed "misinformation" for the attacks on her record as a prosecutor. "You know, I think that there has been a lot of misinformation about my background," she told leftist podcaster Jemele Hill in an interview. "And so, there is a lot of work that I need to do to just correct the record and be very clear." Harris even tried to reach out to black voters to explain her record. Her repeated assertions that she was a figure who supported justice and reform clashed with her record of identifying herself as the "top cop" in the system. "I am fully aware of that whole meme about how Kamala is a Cop and there are strategic reasons people are doing that," Harris said in an interview for Blavity TV in October.[26] Despite her awareness of the issue, the meme stuck as more voters learned about her law enforcement record.

Tulsi had drawn blood, but Harris refused to act to stop the bleeding. Instead, they tried to counterattack with hits on Gabbard. "Yo you love Assad!" her press secretary Ian Sams wrote on Twitter, calling Gabbard an "Assad apologist." Harris also tried to attack Gabbard for meeting with Assad rather than addressing the issues with substance. How could Gabbard attack her on social justice after meeting with the Syrian dictator? "I think that this coming from someone who has been an apologist for an individual, Assad, who has murdered the people of his country like cockroaches, she who has embraced and been an apologist for him in a way that she refuses to call him a war criminal, I can only take what she says and her opinion so seriously. And so, you know, I'm prepared to move on," Harris said after the debate. But the issue did not move on. Sams also tried to connect Gabbard to the Russians, as the campaign struggled to fend off the attacks. "Reporters writing their stories with eyes on the modern-day assignment desk of Twitter, read this: 'The Russian propaganda machine that tried to influence the 2016 election is now promoting the presidential aspirations of a controversial Hawaii Democrat,'" he wrote on Twitter in August. It was the same bogus playbook they tried to use against Trump.

The conflict between Harris and Gabbard made its way onto *Saturday Night Live*, as actress Cecily Strong portrayed Gabbard as a villain in a mock debate. "I want you to know that I smell your fear and it makes me stronger," she said with a deadpan voice. "I'm wearing the white suit of your fallen hero Hillary Clinton. Now fight me, cowards." Harris was played by Maya Rudolph as a "cool aunt" candidate just trying to go viral. "Tulsi, I'm going to be real with you, you scare the hell out of me. You just gave me, 'ermahgerd goosebumps,'" she said.

The skit also highlighted Harris's plunging poll numbers. "Tonight, I'm not going to worry about the polling numbers," Rudolph/Harris said in the sketch. "I'm just gonna have fun and see if I can get some viral moments," she said. "Mama needs a GIF."

# MAYOR PETE

By the summer of 2019, the Harris campaign was disappointed. Their early viral spark had faded and the dream of the nation's first black women president was not catching fire as they had hoped. Instead, Democrats were passing over Harris's moment in history to consider a new historical figure: the nation's first openly gay presidential candidate.

When South Bend, Indiana, mayor Pete Buttigieg announced his presidential campaign in April 2019, even his fellow Democrats found the idea puzzling. Who is this medium-sized midwestern mayor from a medium-sized town and why is he running for president? Buttigieg worked to wield his youth and inexperience as a strength, repeatedly telling voters that the time was right for a thirty-seven-year-old gay mayor from Middle America to make his case for president. It was not long before Buttigieg dazzled the media with unprecedented access as he spent significant time in Iowa speaking earnestly about his ideas. It felt obvious he was trying to repeat the Obama playbook.

Reporters could not resist the candidate who appeared cooked up in a lab to dazzle them for glowing profiles. Openly gay and married, he talked about his Episcopalian faith and spoke about wresting the words *freedom* and *faith* from conservatives. A veteran of the Navy Reserve, Buttigieg graduated with degrees from both Harvard and Oxford before working for McKinsey & Company consulting and running for mayor of his hometown of South Bend. Unlike Harris, Buttigieg failed to win his first statewide race when he tried to run for Indiana treasurer, losing by 20 points. If he wanted a political future, he had no choice but to run for president. It was a long shot until it wasn't.

On July 1, Buttigieg shocked the field by announcing his campaign had raised $24.8 million in the second quarter, twice as much as Kamala Harris's haul of $12 million.[27] Buttigieg even topped Harris's funding in her home state, raising $3.8 million from California donors to Harris's $3.3 million. Buttigieg's campaign was dazzling Harris's fundraising base as he scheduled multiple events with the tech elite, wealthy LGBTQ donors, and Hollywood celebrities. Prominent donors in the state who supported Harris began hosting fundraisers for Buttigieg. One of Harris's biggest supporters, Susie Tompkins Buell, announced in May they would hold three fundraisers for Buttigieg, even though they had already announced their support for Harris. Top moguls were actually fighting over who got to host fundraisers for Buttigieg as fickle elites scrambled to get access to his events.[28] As Harris started dwindling in the polls, Buttigieg was surging at just the right moment.

Buttigieg appeared more authentic in Iowa than Harris, one of many senators flying back and forth from Washington, DC, to campaign. Buttigieg was a polite product of the Midwest, while Harris was a West coast elite with the reputation of a political knife fighter. Voters liked that Buttigieg focused on policy and decency, while Harris appeared more like a consultant-driven political opportunist. The media also lost their interest in Harris as her thin-skinned campaign lashed out at perceived insults. Reporters appeared much happier riding on the bus with Buttigieg than trailing Harris.

# CHAPTER EIGHT

# RUNNING OUT OF GAS

*I'm fucking moving to Iowa.*

—KAMALA HARRIS, SEPTEMBER 18, 2019

"Look at my bus!" Harris cried out in a video her campaign released on social media in August, showing her reaction to her new bus with KA-MALA emblazoned on the side in big bold letters. "Oh my God, I love it wow. Oh wow. Look at the bus!" she continued. The video appeared performative, part of a kickoff of her five-day bus tour across Iowa. The Harris campaign was struggling in the state, despite all their early efforts to build support. Harris had already raised questions among Iowans after canceling a massive breakfast event at a church in Waterloo in February due to weather.[1] In May, Harris canceled a two-day campaign swing in the state, blaming a vote in the Senate even as other senators were doing both events.[2] One Iowa lawmaker who had planned to endorse Harris changed his mind after she canceled her trip. Harris was trying to make up for missed opportunities.

Harris also rolled out a new campaign platform on her "3 a.m. agenda." Harris used images of her mother in the ad with a soft piano soundtrack, telling voters how mom would "work all day then pour her whole heart into Maya and me when she got home. And then, after we were fed and in bed, our mother would sit up trying to figure out how to make it all work." "That's what I'm fighting for—real relief for families like yours. Not in twenty years," she continued. "Not in thirty. Starting my first day as president. Because you've waited long enough to get a good night's sleep." The Harris campaign spent six figures to run the ad in Iowa, viewing it as a way to separate her from the pack of candidates running for president. It was a consultant-driven, poll-tested nightmare. The 3 a.m. message was new for Harris's presidential campaign in Iowa, but it was familiar to California voters who heard the same message when she first ran for Senate. It appeared lazy and canned. Harris and her campaign team were trying to reboot an old idea, reeking of desperation, polling, and consultants instead of a message that Harris sincerely believed.

Harris tried to boost her "3 a.m. agenda" message with Jimmy Fallon, appearing on his *Tonight Show* to "slow-jam the news" and promote her policies. "Slow-jamming" the news with Fallon was first made "cool" for politicians by then president Barack Obama, who first participated in the comedy skit in 2012 and again in 2015. Obama voiced his talking points with a cool underlying soundtrack from Fallon's studio band the Roots. Then Fallon would follow up by interpreting Obama's remarks with a series of over-the-top smooth voice-overs. In September 2019, Harris was ready to give it a try. "At the core of my campaign is my three a.m. agenda, my plan to solve the issues that keep Americans up at night," she said, promising to give middle-class families five hundred dollars a month.

"Aw, yeah," the crooning Fallon replied. "Kamala Harris is just heatin' up. She's thinking about you late at night when you're trying to put that sweet restless body of yours to bed. Is that five hundred dollars in your pocket? Or you just happy your health care is free. With Kamala, it's both."

"Ever since Barack left we've been off track, but Kamala is trying to get us back to black," crooned the band singer, Tariq Trotter.

Other candidates tried to do the slow jam with Fallon, but the result was just the same. Following in the exact steps of Obama only reminded voters that they were not as cool as the original.

Harris's former political mentor and boyfriend Willie Brown could not keep silent in reaction to her lackluster campaign. In September 2019, he described her strategy of trying to run in the same lane as Elizabeth Warren and Bernie Sanders as an "absolutely total and complete mistake" and criticized her campaign. "You should always be yourself. Believe me, '3 a.m. in the morning' she keeps talking about . . . in the world of politics, don't be a candidate, be a person," he said.[3]

The hits kept coming. In September, Harris faced anger from disabled people after she laughed and approved of a supporter in New Hampshire who described President Trump as "mentally retarded."

"Well said, well said," Harris replied, laughing at the man's description of Trump. Deaf actor and activist Nyle DiMarco posted the video of the exchange on social media and criticized Harris. "1) R-word is unacceptable. It is a slur, an insult. 2) Kamala should have handled this better. An apology is needed," he wrote on Twitter. In response to the controversy, Harris claimed she did not even hear what the man had said but apologized. It was a rare apology from Harris, but it was inconceivable that she did not hear the words the man used, especially after it triggered her laugh.

As her polls remained low, Harris and her team continued trying to jolt her zombie campaign back to life with another viral moment. In October, Harris began calling for Twitter to suspend Donald Trump's account and used the opportunity to press Senator Elizabeth Warren on the issue of regulating big technology companies during a debate. "I urge you to join me," she said to Warren. "Here we have Donald Trump, who has 65 million Twitter followers, and is using that platform as the president of the United States to openly intimidate witnesses, to threaten witnesses, to obstruct justice, and he and his account should be taken down." Warren ignored her but Harris was not finished.

"Join me," Harris repeated.

"No," Warren responded flatly, waving her off.

"No?" Harris replied, feigning incredulity. "You can't say you're for corporate responsibility if it doesn't apply to everyone," she added. Warren brushed off the attack as Harris looked even more desperate and unserious. Former Obama speechwriter and podcast host Jon Lovett was baffled. "Kamala Harris going after Elizabeth Warren on banning Trump from Twitter is one of the more pathetic stunts I've seen in a debate," he wrote on Twitter.

As the more moderate Biden was solidifying his lead in the race, Harris behaved as if the answer was to go further left than Bernie Sanders and Elizabeth Warren. In September, Harris endorsing the idea of getting rid of the Senate filibuster to pass the Green New Deal; that would allow the Senate to pass the bill with a simple majority. "If they fail to act, as president of the United States, I am prepared to get rid of the filibuster to pass a Green New Deal," she said. Not only was the Green New Deal routinely ridiculed as an unserious vanity climate project, but few Democratic senators were serious about eliminating the filibuster.

Harris returned in September to New Hampshire, where a campaign briefing memo was accidentally left behind at a restaurant that showed her staff expected her to be grilled on her lack of presence in the state as well as her campaign's "summer slump." Primary polls in the Granite State showed her in fifth place, raising questions about why she was even campaigning there.

Low on funding and resources, the campaign decided to focus everything on Iowa. "I'm fucking moving to Iowa," Harris joked to Senator Mazie Hirono within earshot of a reporter in September 2019. Harris again went viral for the wrong reasons. True, she finally had an authentic moment on the campaign trail, but it showed her as a calculating and bitter candidate as her support was dwindling. Harris looked even more desperate, but the campaign tried to own the moment. Harris communications director Lily Adams shared a T-shirt design with Harris's line blazoned on the front.

Harris and her staff kept working to make a splash in the campaign by seeking a debate moment with attacks on Trump and pop culture references. In a September 2019 debate she compared Trump to the Wizard of Oz. When asked by moderator George Stephanopoulos about trade, Harris mocked Trump for conducing "trade by tweet" before sidetracking with a completely separate thought. "You know, he reminds me of that—

that guy in *The Wizard of Oz*, you know, when you pull back the curtain, it's a really small dude," she said, pausing for effect.

"OK, I'm not even going to take the bait," Stephanopoulos replied, himself only five feet, five inches tall.

"Oh, George. It wasn't about you!" Harris replied, bursting into laughter at the awkward moment she had created.

During an October debate on CNN, Harris tried to create another viral spark by criticizing Trump for pulling US troops out of Syria. "This is a crisis of Donald Trump's making . . . and that's why dude gotta go, and why when I am commander in chief we will stop this madness," she said. Harris had some success using the "dude gotta go" line on the campaign trail, but to deploy it on the debate stage during a discussion on foreign policy seemed whacky. Like clockwork, the campaign whipped up a new T-shirt reading "Dude gotta go" to drum up more donations.[4]

In October, Harris started blaming racism and sexism for her floundering campaign, which was still polling in the single digits. On October 3, Harris was almost despondent during a town hall in Reno, Nevada. "I'm at the stage of the campaign where I'm kind of like, you know I'm going to engage in real talk, I don't want to waste your time with anything else," she laughed. "Let's just have some real talk." Harris's "real talk" was about "electability" and her campaign for president.

"Is America ready for that?" she asked.

"No!" shouted a few people in the audience.

For once, Harris did not laugh, but replied dryly, "Well, yes they are."

In an effort to help voters envision a female president, Harris had already started referring to the president of the United States with female pronouns on the campaign trail. "The commander in chief of the United States of America has as one of her most important responsibilities the responsibility of keeping our nation secure," Harris said in a speech. She explained it was important to use female pronouns to talk about the presidency so that voters could "see what they've not seen before."[5] "Especially in light of the whole discussion about 'electability,' which drives me bananas," she added. "It's important for people to understand that they have to really check how they're thinking about these things. But we have to help along the way, and part of it is about how we use language." Harris also gave a nod to transgender activists by announcing her pronouns during a CNN town hall on LGBTQ issues. "How are you? And uh, thank you guys, and my pronouns are *she, her,* and *hers*," Harris said as she was introduced by CNN's Chris Cuomo.[6] Despite her best efforts, though, the use of pronouns was not helping her poll numbers.

Harris grew more despondent. During an October interview with Axios, Harris spoke about "electability," openly suggesting that her low polling numbers were the result of racism and sexism. "I have also started to perhaps be more candid, talking about what I describe and what I believe to be the elephant in the room about my campaign," she said in an interview with reporter Margaret Talev. Harris was no longer unburdened by what had been, but burdened by what could not be. "Is America ready for a woman, and a woman of color to be president of the United States?" she asked glumly. Talev reminded her that America elected Obama, which was itself a historic moment and a symbol of change, but Harris was not convinced. "There is a lack of ability or a difficulty in imagining that someone who we have never seen can do a job that has been done, you know, forty-five times by someone who is not that person," she said. At a time when Democrats were looking for a political movement to challenge Trump's unique coalition, Harris was paralyzed with self-imposed limitations based on her identity.

It was easy to see why Harris grew frustrated. The aging Biden continued to lead in the polls, despite gaffe after gaffe piling up. After Harris's attack on his civil rights record bounced off without any follow-up attack, he continued boasting of his efforts within the African American community. "I have more people supporting me in the black community that have announced for me because they know me. They know who I am. Three former chairs of the black caucus, the only African American woman who has ever been elected to the United States Senate," Biden said in a November debate. The incredulous Harris, a black woman serving in the United States Senate, replied, "Nope, that's not true. The other one is here," and burst out laughing. It was one more sign that Biden was stuck in the past, referring to Carol Moseley Braun, who had served as a US senator from Illinois a decade earlier.

Running out of momentum and campaign cash, Harris and her team began looking for ways to break through online, and into Iowans' hearts. In order to show voters the "real" Kamala Harris, the campaign started featuring her in the kitchen. "Bacon is a spice as far as I'm concerned," Harris said in an October video, specifically pointing out her decision to use "beautiful Iowa apples" and "Iowa bacon" for one of her favorite family recipes. "Pancakes are meant to be stacked," she told the audience before taking two pancakes for her plate before talking about politics. "Some of the best conversations happen over a batch of cookies" was the caption of one of her November videos of Harris baking "Monster Cookies" with one of her supporters. She also visited actress Mindy Kaling to cook an Indian dish, masala dosa, in her kitchen in Los Angeles, marveling that Mindy kept her spices in Taster's Choice instant coffee jars. The hard-nosed lawyer ready to prosecute the case now looked like she was auditioning for the Food Network.

As Harris traveled the country looking for supporters, she took an edgier approach with an October visit to a California gay bar. During the event, Harris met with drag queen superstar Shangela, a character from the television show *RuPaul's Drag Race*. Shangela showed Harris how to "clack a fan" like the drag queens on the show and enthusiastically endorsed her on Instagram.

"I feel like she's stood by our community for a long time—it's nothing new. So I definitely trust her. Right now, I'm just so happy to finally meet her in person—and she knew me! I said 'Halle-loo!'" the drag queen wrote.[7]

By November, Harris tried to put a brave face on the future of her campaign and political career. "You know, I have in my career been told many times, 'It's not your time. It's not your turn,'" she said in a video posted to social media. "And let me just tell you, I eat 'no' for breakfast, so I would recommend the same. It's a hearty breakfast."[8]

As the campaign limped along, Harris decided the answer was to spend Thanksgiving in Iowa. It was an unusual strategy, but Harris tried to rally staffers who were already running on fumes. "I know it's a great sacrifice," she told them. "I know many of you will not be home for Thanksgiving. I know that Thanksgiving is one of those holidays where you really like to be around your family and the people you have grown up with. So many of you have longstanding traditions around Thanksgiving, but you're spending it here in Iowa."[9] The life of a campaign staffer is not always glamorous, but this was a new low.

Harris temporarily moved into an empty home in Des Moines after making sure the kitchen was big enough for the press to join Harris in the kitchen as she boiled chicken stock and chopped celery. When local TV reporters asked Harris what she was thankful for, Harris replied, "You know, I'm thankful to be an American, imperfect though we may be."

There was little to be thankful for. On November 15, *Politico* reported that Harris's campaign was "careening toward a crackup." "No discipline. No plan. No strategy," one staffer said, pointing to campaign chair Maya Harris, campaign manager Juan Rodriguez, and ultimately Kamala Harris herself for the mess. Staffers complained of weak leadership and lack of vision and began openly questioning their campaign strategy as funding dwindled. Harris was portrayed as clueless.

"I don't think anybody wanted to tell her," one former aide said, adding, "I still don't think she knows the severity."[10] Harris soon learned what everyone else was talking about behind her back. The day after Thanksgiving, the *New York Times* published a devastating account of Harris's doomed campaign. Disgruntled staffers were bailing and leaking to reporters just how bad things were. Reports claimed that Rodriguez refused to challenge or cross Maya, who in turn was accusing Rodriguez of critical missteps. The campaign was rudderless as Harris was unable to make a decision about the future. The campaign's state operations manager, Kelly Mehlenbacher, went on the record with her resignation letter, which she shared with the *Times*. "This is my third presidential campaign and I have never seen an organization treat its staff so poorly," Mehlenbacher wrote in a letter dated weeks before the story. "With less than 90 days until Iowa we still do not have a real plan to win." "Our campaign For the People is made up of diverse talent which is being squandered by indecision and a lack of 'leaders who will lead.' That is unacceptable," she wrote, adding that "morale has never been lower." Campaign leadership, she said, "refused to confront our mistakes" and continued "making the same unforced errors over and over." More than fifty current and former campaign staff members and allies of the campaign spoke to the *Times* about the horrors they experienced on the campaign trail. "Many of her own advisers are now pointing a finger directly at Ms. Harris," the report read, noting she was uncertain and inconsistent. Senior campaign advisor Jim Margolis told donors in November they were going to "let Kamala be Kamala" and take a less scripted approach to the campaign. But fundraising was drying up as donors lost interest.[11] Campaign advisors found Harris unapproachable and her circle of trust extremely tight.

Harris later revealed that distance was an intentional defense mechanism for her. "It's really important for all of us, as women, to create safe spaces and be conscious about who is in your tight circle," she said in an interview after her campaign. "I have girlfriends who are sisters to me. My best friend from kindergarten is one of my closest friends. Choose to surround yourself with people who will applaud you, and who will encourage you."[12] Harris was looking for cheerleaders, not truth-tellers.

The embarrassing *New York Times* story effectively killed Harris's campaign. Buttigieg was flourishing in Iowa and boosting his numbers in New Hampshire to compete with Sanders. Biden was leading comfortably in South Carolina. In most polls, Harris's support was in single digits, coming in at a distant fourth place, even in her home state California. On December 3, Harris announced her decision to end the campaign, preventing an embarrassing loss in Iowa but also before getting embarrassed in her home state. Harris's failed campaign wasted $40.1 million before she called it quits—before Democrat voters even got to vote. In her announcement, Harris blamed a lack of funding for her failure. "I'm not a billionaire," she said. "I can't fund my own campaign." Funding was the least of her problems.

# CHAPTER NINE

# THE VEEP PRIMARY

*Joe, in selecting a woman of color, a woman of color to be his vice president, what an audacious move. The audacity of Joe Biden to actually just make that decision, and then follow through on it.*

—KAMALA HARRIS, AUGUST 23, 2020

Kamala Harris finished off 2019 at the lowest point of her political career, but she still had a job that she was elected to do in the Senate. Plus, there was always the hope that a failed presidential candidate could one day be selected as a running mate. But that decision was still months away, and there was still a lot of work to do. Democrats were still on the war path against President Donald Trump. On January 15, 2020, the House voted to send impeachment articles to the Senate, kicking off a weeks-long trial accusing him of abusing his power for political gain after a congratulatory phone call with Ukrainian president Volodymyr Zelensky. It was no ordinary phone call, as he suggested to Zelensky that he investigate former vice president Joe Biden and his son Hunter, who received hundreds of thousands of dollars as a board member of energy firm Burisma—at the same time Joe Biden was leading the Obama administration's policy on Ukraine. Harris was not featured in the impeachment effort, despite her role as a prosecutor, and her experience in political theater. Democrats wanted a more serious approach to the charges. California media commented that Harris was "virtually invisible" as the trial went to the Senate and it was no surprise when she announced her decision to vote to convict the president.[1]

While Democrats spent months trying to impeach the president, they were ignoring a looming threat from the East. It came from China, a respiratory coronavirus that was identified in Wuhan in late 2019, prompting government officials to lock down the city in order to stop the spread of the virus. Chinese officials also tried to block the truth about the virus from spreading. The Trump administration tried to slow the virus from entering the United States with a travel ban on flights from China. The virus came anyway and started spreading in the United States, sending federal health officials into crisis mode. By February 26, Trump put Vice President Mike Pence in charge of the government response to the coronavirus. On March 16, Trump, Pence, and a host of government officials announced restrictions for the American people for fifteen days to try to slow the spread of the virus. The director of the National Institute of Allergy and Infectious Diseases, Dr. Anthony Fauci, detailed instructions for Americans to avoid social gatherings of more than ten people and avoid restaurants and bars as well as discretionary travel. Teachers and children were forced to stay home from school and "nonessential" workers were advised to stay home from work. On March 29, Trump announced his decision to extend the "social distancing" order for an additional thirty days, plunging the nation into full crisis mode. Democrats took political advantage, attacking Trump at every turn for failing to do enough to fight the virus. There were not enough ventilators, masks, or tests, and they blamed Trump for not acting fast enough to acquire the materials. Harris used her platform to focus on more government assistance and rent forgiveness, but also prioritized racial issues within the virus response from the government. In May 2020, she introduced the COVID-19 Racial and Ethnic Disparities Task Force Act of 2020 and in July she introduced the COVID-19 Bias and Anti-Racism Training Act of 2020. Harris also sponsored the Black Maternal Health Momnibus Act of 2020 to address the high black maternal mortality rate. The big problem, she argued, was the racist health care system in America.

"Black folks are not receiving the same kind of treatment that others receive," she said in an interview, criticizing "systemic racism" in the health care system.

Harris also united her cause to that of climate activists, promoting the idea of "environmental racism." In August 2020, she and Representative Alexandria Ocasio-Cortez introduced the Climate Equity Act of 2020, a more woke version of the Green New Deal. The legislation promised to fight "systemic socioeconomic disparities." Harris wrote, "We need a Green New Deal based in climate and environmental justice, which means building a clean economy that protects communities that have been neglected by policymakers for far too long."[2] Why was Harris spending so much time in 2020 on racial issues? "I feel a great sense of responsibility as the only black woman in the United States Senate to ensure that all of those people who lifted me up so I could be in this place that their voices are in that room with me every day of the week," she said.[3] It also looked like a calculated play to win the hearts of racial justice advocates and to lift her into the vice presidential conversation.

Harris was not immediately thought of as a front-runner for a running mate, after her humiliating primary campaign, but as Biden tried to close the primary race against Senator Bernie Sanders, he made a promise to Democrats. "I commit that I will in fact appoint a woman to be vice president," Biden said during one of the final primary debates in March 2020. "There are a number of women who would be qualified to be president tomorrow."[4] Maybe there was a chance.

The Biden family, however, still held a grudge against Harris. When it became likely that Biden would pull off a primary victory, Democrat donors predictably started asking questions about his running mate. In March 2020, Jill Biden admitted to fundraiser attendees in Chicago that Harris's debate attack on Biden was like a "punch to the gut."[5] It was a warning shot not to expect the Biden family to forget any transgressions. In her 2019 memoir, Jill revealed she was the grudge holder of the family. "Joe has an incredible capacity to forgive, and he's incapable of holding a grudge. But that means I end up being the holder of the grudges. I remember every slight committed against the people I love," she continued. "I can forgive, sure—but I don't believe in rewarding bad behavior." [6]

# SUMMER OF RAGE

An incident in Minneapolis changed everything. "I can't breathe!" George Floyd pleaded repeatedly with police officers as he was pinned down and placed into a chokehold for resisting arrest on May 25. Video of Floyd's arrest and death at the hands of Minneapolis police officers fueled three days and nights of protests that grew violent as businesses in the Twin Cities were looted and burned to the ground and police officers abandoned a precinct building beset by rioters.

Harris seized the opportunity to boost her profile. Suddenly the failed presidential candidate was everywhere promoting herself as a superhero for the long-suffering black community—and also floating her political resume. The senator hit the interview circuit with black media figures such as Roland Martin, Al Sharpton, and Don Lemon to share her outrage. The former top cop in the United States was now playing a public prosecutor of the country's police force. "I'm sick of it," Harris told Martin in a Skype interview. "This has been going on for decades and generations, which is that the enforcement of American law is applied differently depending on the color of the skin of the person to whom it is being served." She invoked the Los Angeles riots that took place in 1992 in reaction to the acquittal of police officers who had been charged in the death of Rodney King, claiming that Americans had learned nothing from the incident. "Folks are in pain and have been in pain for a long time because of the injustices," she continued. "There is black blood staining the sidewalks of America."

On Saturday, May 30, Harris marched with Black Lives Matter protesters in Washington, DC, who gathered in Lafayette Park across from the White House. "People are in pain. We must listen," Harris wrote on social media, sharing a video she took of the protesting crowds. The night before, the protests outside the White House grew violent as Park Police and Secret Service battled with rioters to push them back from the complex. Violence came the night after as well. Rioters set fires, looted businesses, torched cars, and assaulted police officers. Although Harris tried to separate the violent actions from angry protesters storming the White House, she started making excuses for the destruction. "I will never condone vandalism and violence in these protests. But you need to recognize and appreciate the fact that people have a right to feel pain and to feel anger about the fact that this is still happening this many years later," Harris said in an interview on CNN that night.[7] The following night was worse. CVS stores and commercial buildings were looted and vandalized. A National Park Service building in Lafayette Square was set ablaze and even national monuments were vandalized. A fire was also started in the basement of the historic St. John's Episcopal Church, across from the White House, but the building was saved by fire crews. Over 150 law enforcement officers were injured during the so-called peaceful protests in Washington, DC, which Harris failed to condemn.[8]

Historically, "Kamala the Cop" supported more police officers on the street, but the new version of Harris appeared open to defunding the police. "Well, it's a concept," she said diplomatically when asked about the idea. "We do have to reimagine what public safety looks like." Sidestepping her old assertion that more police meant more safety, Harris argued against it. "It is status quo thinking to believe that putting more police on the streets creates more safety. That's wrong. It's just wrong."[9]

Harris made one of her most aggressive plays for the vice presidential slot in an interview with Sharpton on May 31. "I'm a United States senator. I represent one in eleven Americans. I'm the second black woman elected to the United States, history of the United States Senate. I was one of the first black woman ever elected attorney general of any state of the nation. And I ran the second-largest department of justice in the United States," she boasted, adding that she was "a child of the civil rights movement, my parents marched and shouted for justice." Harris challenged all potential vice presidential picks on their records on the civil rights issue. "Whether or not anybody is thinking about running for vice president of the United States, they should be held accountable. What is their history of taking on this issue versus sitting by the sidelines and watching it happen without rolling up their sleeves and actually do something about it?" she asked. At a time of national crisis, Harris was shamelessly pitching herself as the solution to the problem—despite her record.

Harris also took action to prove she was on the side of jailed protesters. As Minneapolis police continued arresting criminals for looting and burning businesses, Harris promoted the far-left Minnesota Freedom Fund, which helped bail out individuals thrown in jail by law enforcement. "If you're able to, chip in now to the @MNFreedomFund to help post bail for those protesting on the ground in Minnesota," she wrote on social media on June 1. Harris's support for the organization continues to haunt her political career. The fund bailed out multiple criminals, some of whom were later accused of horrific crimes, including rape, sexual assault, child molestation, strangling women, domestic violence, and murder.[10]

Biden and his team knew that the Black Lives Matter protests had changed the narrative of the election, but he was also suffering criticism in the black community for a series of boneheaded comments about race. On May 22, Biden reacted poorly in a virtual interview from his basement with black radio host Charlemagne Tha God. After a contentious interview, Biden tried to cut off the host and end it, claiming he was pressed for time, but Charlamagne replied, "You can't do that to black media!"

"I do that to white media and black media because my wife has to go on at six o'clock," Biden snapped back.[11] Charlamagne replied that he had more questions for Biden. "You've got more questions?" Biden replied sharply. "Well, I tell you what, if you have a problem figuring out whether you're for me or Trump, then you ain't black." The comment was one more embarrassing tone-deaf comment from the vice president that triggered more criticism from the black community. It was no surprise that his aides believed a black running mate might help smooth over some of the tensions.

Harris was busy, but it was clear the vice presidency was still in the front of her mind. In May, Harris took time to send a public message to the Biden family about their deceased son, Beau Biden. "You couldn't find a man with more principle and courage who cared deeply about his family and the nation he served," Harris wrote, sharing a photo of her and their late son together on social media. "Joe Biden and Dr. Biden, thinking of you and the entire Biden family today." The desperation was apparent.

As Biden continued his search for a running mate, Harris kept up her media blitz to fuel ongoing Black Lives Matter protests. On June 18, she appeared virtually with CBS late-night host Stephen Colbert to talk about Black Lives Matter and the ongoing protests. Colbert was puzzled there was no news coverage about ongoing Black Lives Matter protests.

"Are they gone?" he asked Harris. "Are we just not going to talk about them anymore?" Despite the ongoing rioting, looting, and violence in the name of the Black Lives Matter movement, Harris praised the "intensity and brilliance" of it, describing it as a "counter-force" that would bring about change:

> But they're not going to stop. They're not going to stop. They're not. This is a movement. I'm telling you. They're not going to stop, and everyone, beware. Because they're not going to stop. They're not going to stop before election day in November, and they are not going to stop after election day. And everyone should take note of that on both levels. That they're not going to let up. And they should not, and we should not.[12]

It was no surprise that Harris was cheerleading the protests—the trajectory of the movement affected her political future.

Team Biden was in a bind. In order to "heal the nation," as Biden promised, they would need to narrow his focus for a running mate even further to pick a woman of color to help him meet the moment. Some on Biden's short list of vice presidential candidates saw the writing on the wall. Senator Amy Klobuchar, one of Biden's potential picks, took herself out of consideration, urging him to choose a woman of color. Klobuchar could sense the momentum shift against a strong "law and order" candidate in the Democratic Party, and she had her own history to think about. As a county attorney in Minnesota, Klobuchar had come under attack from activists for her role in sending Myon Burrell, a black teenager, to prison for life after an eleven-year-old girl was killed by a stray bullet.

Michigan governor Gretchen Whitmer also felt like dropping out and spoke with Biden, urging him to pick a black woman as his running mate instead.[13] But Biden called her and urged her to remain in the mix as he weighed his options. Biden liked Whitmer's populist style. Her winning campaign promise to "fix the damn roads" in her state delighted the infrastructure-focused Biden and he appreciated her willingness to hold fast on draconian coronavirus policies, despite anger in her state from the Republican right and President Trump. During the search, Biden invited Whitmer out to meet him, proof that she was on the top of his short list. That triggered backlash from black Democrats and activists, who publicly vocalized their disappointment. "The backlash is very real, and it will be felt all across this country," said Democratic strategist Karen Finney. "Black women are sick and tired of being considered the backbone of the Democratic Party. We want to be recognized as leaders. We want all the things. We're due."[14] The fact that Biden was considering Whitmer felt like a betrayal to black Democrats after they helped save his political campaign in South Carolina. The pressure continued. Black activists were empowered after the failed 2016 campaign, when it was apparent that Hillary Clinton failed to inspire black voters to show up. Only 59 percent of black voters voted in 2016, down from 66 percent in 2012 and 65 percent in 2008 for Barack Obama.[15] Even though Biden captured the majority of the black vote in the Democrat primary, his team believed the best way to motivate black voters was with a woman of color on the ticket.

As the only woman of color who ran for president in 2020, Harris was already in the conversation of whether she could be a good candidate for vice president. As early as May 2019, members of the Congressional Black Caucus, Harris's allies, began floating the idea of a Biden-Harris ticket to the media. At the time Harris was unimpressed and even insulted. "I think that Joe Biden would be a great running mate," she said dismissively to reporters who asked her about the idea. "As vice president he's proven he knows how to do the job."[16] Harris was annoyed by the idea that she was somehow running for the number two slot. Her husband sent the message. "She's running for President. Period," Emhoff wrote tersely on Twitter, sharing a *Washington Post* article denouncing the idea as racist. Of course, the sentiment was premature. Harris's campaign failed spectacularly before voters even had a chance to cast a ballot, while Biden survived the entire primary process to earn the nomination.

Sharpton had already publicly pressured Biden about the importance of choosing a black woman on the ticket, including on his MSNBC show. "I really do understand that, Al, for real," Biden replied during an interview, reassuring him that there was "significantly more than one black woman that's going to be considered."[17] Biden knew that Sharpton preferred failed candidate for Georgia governor Stacey Abrams, who delighted activists after she followed up her campaign with accusations of voter suppression while refusing to admit defeat. In April, the *New York Times* reported that Sharpton was preparing to announce his support for Abrams as his preferred choice for Biden but backed down. In his book *Battle for the Soul*, Edward-Isaac Dovere reported that Kamala's sister, Maya Harris, called Sharpton and pressured him to rethink his position, reminding him that Abrams was not a front-runner with Biden. By picking a losing option, Maya warned, Sharpton could do damage to both himself and Biden.

Abrams had already vexed the Biden team in March after she reacted negatively to early reports that he was considering choosing her as a possible running mate. Biden met with Abrams before announcing his campaign for president, followed by rumors that he was actually considering her as a possible vice presidential candidate. It was an early signal to black voters that he was listening. Axios reported in March 2019 that Biden was considering Abrams as a vice presidential candidate, even before announcing his own campaign. The report noted that Biden and his team were even thinking about announcing his vice presidential preference early to bring "diversity and excitement to the ticket" and show voters that he "isn't just another old white guy." Abrams did not respond well to the reports. "I think you don't run for second place," she said during an appearance on *The View*, suggesting that Biden would make a good running mate for her.

By 2020, however, Abrams had already ruled out a presidential run and was ready to play. "As a young black girl growing up in Mississippi, I learned that if I didn't speak up for myself, no one else would, so . . . my mission is to say out loud if I'm asked the question, 'Yes, I would be willing to serve,'" Abrams said on NBC's *Meet the Press* in April. It was amazing how explicit she was on TV, after she first seemed insulted by the idea, but Biden had already moved on.

When the vice presidential search team narrowed in on Harris, members of Biden's family and even some of his advisors were not happy with the idea. Why would the campaign choose the woman who accused Joe Biden of being a racist? Harris had also attacked Biden for reported misconduct with women. In April 2019, Harris backed four women who alleged that Biden had inappropriately touched or kissed them. "I believe them, and I respect them being able to tell their story and having the courage to do it," she told reporters at an early presidential campaign event in Nevada. What frustrated them most was that Harris never expressed contrition for her attacks on Biden during the campaign, particularly on issues of race. When asked by Stephen Colbert in June about her savage attacks against Biden during the Democratic primary, Harris began laughing.

"It was a debate!" she replied.

"Not everybody landed punches like you did though," Colbert replied with a grin.

"It was a debate!" Harris repeated, laughing again.

"So, you don't mean it," Colbert continued.

"It was a debate. The whole reason. Literally, it was a debate," Harris continued, laughing out loud in response to Colbert's bewildered reaction. "It was called a debate. Everyone traveled to the debate. There were journalists there covering the debate where there would be a debate."

Her response was unsettling to anyone looking for an apology. Biden's wife, Jill Biden, and his sister, Valerie Biden Owens, were still holding grudges from the campaign. Former senator Chris Dodd, part of Biden's search team, was also not impressed with Harris's response when he asked her about her attacks during the presidential campaign.

"She laughed and said, 'that's politics.' She had no remorse," Dodd said, according to a donor who had a conversation with him as the search continued.[18] Despite concerns about Harris, there was belief among some on Biden's staff that she could adjust to the role.

While Kamala Harris was publicly laughing in interviews, her political allies behind the scenes were working to savage her biggest rivals. Biden seemed eager for options other than Harris, and other black women such as California congresswoman Karen Bass and former top Obama official Susan Rice soon emerged as serious contenders.

It was not long before damaging information about their past began recirculating in the press. Bass was scrutinized for her past praise of Cuban dictator Fidel Castro and her admiration for the socialist government in Cuba. In 2016, Bass reacted to Castro's death by referring to him as the "comandante en jefe," a title of honor, and mourned "a great loss to the people of Cuba." In the 1970s, Bass joined groups of leftist college-aged activists who teamed up with Castro's Venceremos Brigade to visit and work in Cuba. During the trip she heard Castro speak and described him as "extremely charismatic." As a congresswoman, Bass visited Cuba several times as well as when President Barack Obama visited the island in 2016.[19] Castro was anathema to many Floridian voters, especially among Cuban exiles. It was unclear whether Biden could win Florida in 2020, but choosing Bass would be an unwelcome headache for the campaign. But Bass had powerful allies behind the scenes: California members of Congress such as House Speaker Nancy Pelosi and Senator Dianne Feinstein leaned in favor of Bass, who actually had a substantial record in Congress, instead of Harris, who had arrived more recently.

Rice had baggage from the Obama administration, in which she served as ambassador to the United Nations and as national security advisor, especially regarding the 2012 terrorist attack on the American compound in Benghazi, Libya, which she falsely described as a protest gone wrong. Questions about Rice's son Jake, a Trump supporter and a College Republican at Stanford University, also posed a liability to Biden's campaign. Rice also had the reputation of being toxic behind the scenes of government and dropping f-bombs in the office—hardly the right choice for Biden to restore the soul of America. The volume of negative information surfacing in the media alarmed Bass and Rice, who complained to the Biden campaign; they believed Harris's political team was stabbing them in the back. Although Harris remained mostly quiet about the process in public, the ruthless campaign network was back and playing dirty behind the scenes.[20] The fact that Rice was a serious candidate surprised many Democrats, who were well aware of her contentious history in the Obama administration. But Biden had a familiar relationship with Obama's national security advisor when he was vice president. She also had an ally in the Biden family. A former White House official confirmed to me that Rice was Jill Biden's favorite during the selection process.

While Harris waited for Biden to make a choice, an old voice from her past emerged to offer her some advice. "If Joe Biden offers the vice presidential slot to Sen. Kamala Harris, my advice to her would be to politely decline," Willie Brown wrote in the *San Francisco Chronicle* on August 7. Brown wrote that he understood the historic nature of a Vice President Harris but warned that it could be a "dead end" for her career, because the position had "no real power and little chance to accomplish anything independent of the president." Those words proved prophetic.

As Biden remained indecisive, a key Harris ally tried to reassure him about the idea of Vice President Harris: his former boss, President Barack Obama, who was already a fan. Behind the scenes, Obama patiently reminded Biden to let go of the past when making his decision. One of Obama's political advisors assured me the former president held off endorsing her entirely, making sure that the choice would be Biden's to make. But Biden still hesitated. He blew past his first personal deadline of August 1 to name a running mate, and then skipped over his promise to choose a running mate in the first week of August. Donors anxiously watched Biden stall his decision while the Democrat convention was scheduled for August 17. The *New York Times* reported that Biden had "a habit of extending deadlines in a way that leaves some Democrats anxious and annoyed."[21] When Biden finally made his decision on August 11, his campaign staff helped him put in a video call to the California senator.

"You ready to go to work?" Biden asked.

"Oh my God. I'm so ready to go to work," Harris replied in a video that was later published online by the campaign.

Obama was thrilled with Biden's choice. "Joe Biden nailed this decision," he wrote in a statement praising his former vice president. Obama said that Biden's choice proved "his own judgment and character," which were "requirements of the job" of president. "I've known Senator Harris for a long time. She is more than prepared for the job," Obama said. It was certainly an overenthusiastic and optimistic appraisal of the situation.

The pick was in. Harris's political career was single-handedly resurrected by an aging white dinosaur politician who was over twenty years her senior. The new version of Kamala Harris was introduced by Biden on a stage in an empty room in Wilmington, Delaware, due to coronavirus pandemic protocols. "After the most competitive primary in history, the country received a resounding message that Joe was the person to lead us forward and Joe, I'm so proud to stand with you," Harris said in her introduction speech. The campaign glossed over the hard feelings between Harris and Jill Biden. "Jill, I know you'll be an incredible First Lady, and my husband Doug and I are so grateful to become a part of your extended family," she said. Harris continued her saccharine speech, gushing over the Biden family and remembering her relationship with his deceased son, Beau. "Joe and I, yes, we are cut from the same cloth. Family is everything to me too," she said. The campaign tried to emphasize Harris's softer side in her speech. "'Cause whether I'm cheering in the bleachers in a swim meet or setting up a college room dorm or helping my goddaughter prepping for her school debate, or building Legos with my godson, or hugging my two baby nieces or cooking dinner, Sunday dinner, my family means everything to me," she said, reaching for any feminine identity that voters could identify with. Harris even adjusted the story of her history of marching in the civil rights movement, "strapped tightly in my stroller" with her parents. (Her earlier version told the story of how her parents did not realize she had fallen out of the stroller.) Abandoning her attacks during the primary, Harris spoke proudly of Biden's history of fighting for civil rights. "Today he takes his place in the ongoing story of America's march towards equality and justice as the only—as the only, as the only one who has served alongside the first black president and has chosen the first black woman as his running mate," she said.

Trump and his campaign team could not believe it. Biden had selected the most unlikable, radical left candidate as his running mate. "She was my number one draft pick, and we'll see how she works out," Trump told reporters after the decision was announced. "She did very, very poorly in the primaries, as you know. She was expected to do well. And she ended up right around two percent and spent a lot of money," he added. "I was a little surprised that he picked her, I've been watching her a long time."[22] The Trump campaign immediately published a video reminding the world that Democrat voters had already rejected the radically left Harris because they saw her as a "phony."

"Slow Joe and Phony Kamala: Perfect together, wrong for America," the video concluded.

At campaign rallies, Trump was more emphatic about the danger Harris posed to the country. "How about Kamala?" Trump asked as the audience booed. "I don't think so. That's not going to be your first woman president. That's not gonna happen. She's further left than Crazy Bernie. He's like a conservative compared to her." Trump repeatedly brought up Harris's attack on Biden, reminding the crowd that "nobody was meaner to Joe Biden than Kamala," mocking him for choosing the one presidential candidate who accused him of being a "racist" who mistreated women. Trump also warned that Biden would soon get "tired" of the presidency and turn it over to Harris, who could not even get enough support to make it to the primary elections. "That's no way to get into the office because we're going to have a woman president someday, but you know what, it can't be Kamala," he said.

Trump also made fun of the vice president and her staff getting notoriously picky about people pronouncing her name correctly, especially after Fox News host Tucker Carlson was accused of being a racist for pronouncing her name as "Cam-a-la" instead of "Comma-la."

"How about Harris? How about Harris?" Trump would ask on the campaign trail. "Kamala. Kamala. You have to pronounce her name right. It's Kamala, like a comma, Kamala. And yet she pronounces her name differently than that, doesn't she, huh?" At an October rally in Georgia with Trump, Republican senator David Perdue also mispronounced her name. "Ka-mal-a, Comma-la, Ka-Mala-mala-mala," he said. "Whatever." The Harris campaign and multiple journalists reacted by sharing their outrage at Perdue's remarks. "Well that is incredibly racist," Harris's press secretary, Sabrina Singh, wrote on Twitter. They ignored the fact that Biden was also on tape mispronouncing Harris's name, with zero outrage from the left. On the campaign trail, Trump frequently referred to Harris as a "mad woman," "disrespectful," "nasty," and "angry." Trump's descriptions of Harris only triggered more accusations from journalists and Democrats that Harris was a history-making hero and Trump and his allies were sexist and racist for criticizing her performance.

The Biden team proved prescient for choosing a woman of color who would help them respond as more racial justice protests and riots that swept the nation. Harris's first solo speech as the Democrat vice presidential nominee addressed the protests surrounding the police shooting of Jacob Blake in Kenosha, Wisconsin, on August 23, 2020. Blake, who already had a warrant for his arrest for domestic violence and sexual assault, struggled against police officers who unsuccessfully tried to tase him. Police officers said Blake was armed with a knife and refused to comply with orders to drop it, prompting them to open fire and shoot him seven times. Protests ensued, which ultimately turned into violent riots as people started breaking windows, setting fires, and looting businesses for three nights straight. President Trump rallied for law and order, but the Biden campaign set up Harris to call for justice. "Justice: let's talk about that because the reality is that the life of a black person in America has never been treated as fully human, and we have yet to fulfill that promise of equal justice under law," Harris said during a speech at George Washington University.

As the first woman of color chosen as a running mate, Harris was also used to help defend Biden from criticism from black voters. She was asked about Biden's controversial comments with Charlamagne Tha God on black voters during an interview with ABC's Robin Roberts on August 23. "So, when you have a running mate who makes a comment like, 'You ain't

Black,' and leads some people to say, 'He just doesn't get it.' Have you been able to speak truth to him about that?" Roberts asked. Harris dismissed the question as well as questions about her own attack on Biden's civil rights record during the campaign as a "distraction."

"He has been outspoken on those issues and, and continues to talk about disparities, and I know where his heart is. I know where his heart is," Harris replied glowingly, an abrupt turnaround from the contentious presidential primary campaign. "Joe speaks the words and actually knows how to say the words 'Black Lives Matter.'" She also praised Biden for his "audacious move" of choosing a woman of color of his running mate, branding him as one of the civil rights heroes of his generation despite his long history of racially awkward statements. "Joe really walks the talk," she said before launching into a spiraling soliloquy on the "audacity" of Joe Biden.

> Joe, in selecting a woman of color, a woman of color to be his vice president, what an audacious move. The audacity of Joe Biden to actually just make that decision, and then follow through on it. And in that way, advance something that might have taken many, many, many years otherwise. And I think that's a very important aspect of Joe's selection of me. To run with him to be on the ticket with him, and God willing to serve with him. And, and that's one of the things that really makes me so respect and have affection for Joe Biden, because those are the kinds of things he does, and he doesn't seek permission to do it. He doesn't look to whether or not it's popular. He said I'm going to select a woman, and then he selected a woman of color. Right? It says a lot.

It said a lot that Biden's pick for vice president could not answer simple questions without burdening her sentences with over a dozen dependent clauses.

Harris continued struggling in news interviews, proving unable to take hard questions. When reporters questioned Harris about her political beliefs, she laughed. "I promised Joe that I will give him that perspective and always be honest with him," Harris said in an interview with CBS reporter Norah O'Donnell for *60 Minutes* after she asked Harris how she identified politically.

"And is that a socialist or progressive perspective?" O'Donnell asked.

"No! No!" Harris replied, laughing awkwardly, reminding O'Donnell she had a number of perspectives in life, including those of a black woman who liked hip-hop.

"Like, what do you wanna know?" she added, continuing to laugh. Harris tried to laugh off all of her uncomfortable moments in the interview, but she was not prepared for prime time.

Trump noticed. At a campaign rally, he singled out Harris's laughing during the *60 Minutes* interview as problematic. "Did you see his performance on that show?" Trump asked about Biden. "The only thing almost as bad was Kamala with the laugh. 'Haha that's so funny, hahaha,'" Trump said, imitating Harris. "She kept laughing. I said, 'Is there something wrong with her too?' . . . She kept laughing at very serious questions."

Trump seized on something that more people were noticing about Harris after Biden selected her as vice president. Whenever she was surprised, caught off guard, or found herself in an awkward moment, she burst out laughing no matter what the topic. Her AKA sorority sisters were familiar with her laugh, describing it in interviews as "that belly laugh, where her whole body shakes" or "a hearty laugh" or "that full, mouth-open laugh," and "just a full-on party laugh."[23,24] In 2013, Hollywood producer J. J. Abrams wrote for *Vanity Fair* that Harris deserved "the Best Belly Laugh in Politics award."[25] While shaking hands with voters on the campaign trail, her laugh could be disarming, but on the debate stage, at a press conference, during an interview, or at the podium, it frequently made her appear awkward, unserious, and unprepared. Sometimes she laughed to mask surprise or genuine fury; other times she laughed when events spiraled out of her control. Political enemies dubbed it the "Kamala cackle" and spliced together highlight reels of awkward laughing moments to demonstrate she was not suited for the seriousness of the job.

Harris further embarrassed Biden's team after she apparently fell for a hoax by a pair of Russian comedians. On August 21, a tape was released of a recorded conversation between Harris and Russian comedians Vovan and Lexus, who called Harris and impersonated young Swedish climate activist Greta Thunberg and her father. The over-the-top characterization of the young activist, who was tormented with nightmares of President Trump, did not ring any alarm bells as Harris only tried to encourage her. "Greta, do not be discouraged, you have the ability to see what is possible in a way that many do not and there will be people who are going to work against progress," Harris replied. She urged the fake Greta to keep fighting, reminding her that she was a historical figure. "You have been a great leader, do not be deterred," she said. The woman who was running as second in command of the United States had been duped by two-bit Russian comedians.

Harris was running with Biden, but some of her social media content leaned further left than the campaign was used to. In November 2020, Harris's team released a controversial video on "equity," a campaign buzzword arguing for the government intervention to help people of color get more opportunities. Harris delivered the following remarks as an animated campaign video explainer about the true meaning of equity:

> So there's a big difference between equality and equity. Equality suggests, "oh everyone should get the same amount." The problem with that, not everybody's starting out from the same place. So, if we're all getting the same amount, but you started out back there and I started out over here, we could get the same amount, but you're still going to be that far back behind me. It's about giving people the resources and the support they need, so that everyone can be on equal footing, and then compete on equal footing. Equitable treatment means we all end up in the same place.

Something about the argument was familiar. "That's equality of *outcomes* enforced by the government," wrote journalist Andrew Sullivan on Twitter. "They used to call that communism."

# RETURN TO THE DEBATE STAGE

Fans of Harris anticipated she would mop the floor with Vice President Mike Pence in the one and only vice presidential debate, eagerly expecting her to eviscerate the mild-mannered vice president from the Midwest as she had done with Trump officials in the Senate. Harris and her team only added drama before the debate by demanding the vice president be separated from Harris by a Plexiglas barrier due to the coronavirus pandemic. Pence tested negative for the virus, but the Harris team raised fears that the vice president could easily contract the virus by coming into contact with Trump aides, who, the Harris team argued, were not taking the virus serious enough. Pence's staff criticized the idea of Plexiglas, viewing it as a political stunt. "We don't think it's needed," Pence's chief of staff, Marc Short, said. "There's no science to support it. The tables are twelve feet apart, and each participant is tested. It's important for the American people that the debate go forward." But Harris and her team used the moment to accuse the Trump administration of not being serious about the virus. "If the Trump administration's war on masks has now become a war on safety shields, that tells you everything you need to know about why their Covid response is a failure," Harris's spokeswoman Sabrina Singh said to the press. Pence ultimately acquiesced to Harris's request, even though he continued to test negative for the virus.[26]

At the beginning of the debate, Harris utilized one of her familiar strategies of appearing deeply offended every time a man interrupted her. Only this time, Harris was interrupted by debate moderator Susan Page, an editor of *USA Today*. "Well, let's . . ." Page began before Harris talked over her. Pence took the interruption as an opportunity to also insert a comment, but Harris was not having it. "Mr. Vice President, I'm speaking," she stated flatly. "I'm speaking."

At another moment, Harris shot Pence an annoyed glance when he interrupted her, which prompted him to pause. Pence also interjected to remind her during a denunciation of Trump's tax cuts that they saved the average working family two thousand dollars a year. Harris was not amused. "If you don't mind letting me finish, we can then have a conversation, okay?" she replied icily. Most of the debate focused on the administration's handling of the coronavirus, and Pence labored to reassure the American people that the administration was responding competently. Pence tried to tie Harris to the radical left agenda that clashed with the opinions of the majority of the American public, reminding her that she ran on the idea of banning fracking. "Senator Harris, you're entitled to your own opinion, but you're not entitled to your own facts," he said, repeating an old quote from the late senator Daniel Patrick Moynihan. Pence was polite but professional, and Harris was not delivering a knockout blow that her supporters expected. Harris was ultimately upstaged by the viral buzz created online after a fly flew around and landed on Pence's head for two solid minutes. The fly, not Harris, was the headline of the evening.

Pence was polite with Harris, but the following morning, Trump phoned into the Fox Business network to bury her debate performance. "This monster that was onstage with Mike Pence, who destroyed her last night, by the way, but this monster," Trump said. He described Harris as "terrible" and "totally unlikable," declaring that the debate was not even a contest. "She's a communist," Trump added for good measure. Once again, Democrats excoriated Trump's attacks as "racist" and "sexist" particularly because had called her a monster. "Calling the first Black woman to ever take the Vice Presidential debate stage a 'monster' tells you all you need to know about President Trump's respect for women and people of color," Pennsylvania senator Bob Casey wrote on Twitter.

# VIRTUALLY AWKWARD

With the pandemic limiting the number of events, Harris and her team began doing Instagram and YouTube interviews with celebrities like Lizzo, Jaden Smith, Miley Cyrus, and Selena Gomez to introduce Harris to more voters. The playbook was familiar as the campaign worked to boost her ID and sell voters her running narrative: I'm Kamala Harris. I was raised in a family marching and shouting for Justice. I went into the system to fix the system from the inside. I am making history. I love Joe

Biden. Vote for me and Joe Biden. When Lizzo questioned Harris about her political record, Harris suggested her choice to be a prosecutor was not only difficult, but the bravest thing she could do. "We really oughta know the power that we have in every place and never decide that anyone place is excluded from us being there to get the kind of change we want. So I made the decision to go up the rough side of the mountain to go inside the system," Harris explained during an Instagram event to celebrate National Black Voter Day.

At times, however, Harris struggled to connect in more informal Zoom settings. In October, she appeared in a Zoom event with Marvel superhero actors Chris Evans, Paul Rudd, Zoe Saldana, Scarlett Johansson, Don Cheadle, and Mark Ruffalo. The goal of the event was to encourage Marvel fans to vote, but Harris could not help politicizing the moment by comparing the president of the United States to Thanos, the genocidal villain in the Avengers series who wipes out half of Earth's population. Harris recalled speaking to her political team about the great story of the Avengers and using their story to encourage her team to discover their powers and rally against the forces of evil (that is, Trump). "I often will talk to my team about the Avengers, by the way, they just think I am like, walking out on this . . . but the special powers right? Everyone brings their own power and are appreciated for that, and then all those superpowers in particular coming together at the end, right? To deal with Thanos," Harris said. Harris struggled to make her point, but ultimately she explained to the audience that Trump was like Thanos because he was skeptical about the doomsday predictions surrounding global warming. "I just think there is such symmetry around that in this moment," she said laughing. "Because of course that was about the fate of the universe and he held the fate of the universe in his hand, and right now we're looking at someone who is denying science." When asked by Johansson about which superpower she would like to have, Harris fell apart more spectacularly than a New York City skyscraper in the path of the Hulk.

You know I mean I think lots of superpowers I would love to have, that you all have, but I think that you know when we think of the princess of Wakanda, that incredible sister, Shuri, I think that you know, the ability to come together and develop new technologies and tackle climate change and invest in—you know, I often say the ability that we should all have to be able to see what can be unburdened by what has been. Right? Um. I think that's such an incredible superpower if you will, it's an incredible talent and it's part of what we need which is all of us to be able to see a world and imagine a world where we have peace and where we have equity and where we cherish this God-given planet and value education of our children and imagine that and then work to get that. I think that's an incredible quality that's actually a superpower when people have it.

It was a simple question, but her answer was so confusing some of her cohosts looked as if they had forgotten the question she was answering.

If livestreams were difficult, edited videos for social media were easier for Harris. The campaign was using Harris to try to enhance Biden's image online. In one edited video, Harris spoke with President Barack Obama to discuss his vice president's love of ice cream and pasta and red sauce. Other videos featured Harris reacting to old photographs on an iPad featuring a soft soundtrack. Looking fondly at an old photo of Joe Biden, Harris recalled when she spotted the vice president on the street and jumped out of her car to take a picture with him. "We hugged and we talked and we took a photograph. And here it is. Looks so great. I love Joe Biden. Very much," she said flatly.[27] She was not winning any Oscars.

The modified campaign trail because of the pandemic also kept Harris out of the spotlight. Instead of delivering speeches at crowded events and shaking hands with real people at restaurants and arenas, Harris frequently found herself shouting a script at parking lots of people in their cars, honking enthusiastically in response to whatever she had to say. Other campaign events featured a masked Harris sitting on a stage in the middle of a circle speaking to activists. Reporters also lacked access to the vice presidential candidate, thanks to social distancing regulations. There was a lot less room for error and a lot less time left to campaign.

# THE LOSS OF RBG

On the evening of September 18, 2020, the left experienced their worst nightmare. Their champion on the Supreme Court, Justice Ruth Bader Ginsburg, died at the age of eighty-seven, despite every effort to keep her alive until after a new president was elected. Harris was set up by the campaign to recognize the legacy of Ginsburg, who had achieved celebrity status with the young radical left. The kids had begun referring to the legendary justice as "The Notorious RBG," using her initials to put her on the same level of pop culture stardom as the Notorious B.I.G., a nickname used by the late rapper Biggie Smalls, born Christopher Wallace. The campaign tried to lean into the meme by including a mention of it in Harris's prepared remarks. "She was part of our culture. Yes, we wear those Notorious B.I.G. T-shirts with a lot of pride, but since she passed, there are parents reminding their children that she helped their lives," Harris said, botching the nickname by referring to Ginsburg as the famous rapper. The press noticed. "FWIW, Harris's prepared remarks did say 'Notorious RBG' and for anyone not in the loop, that's a reference to shirts like this that use the Notorious BIG aesthetic," reporter Emily Larsen explained on social media afterward. It was an amateur mistake, proof that Harris could screw up even though she had a teleprompter.[28]

Biden, Harris, and Democrats pleaded with Republicans to wait to fill the empty Supreme Court seat until after the election, but they ignored it. Senator Mitch McConnell famously angered the left in May when asked if he would fill a Supreme Court nominee in 2020—even though he refused to allow Obama in 2016 to fill the late justice Antonin Scalia's seat, saying it needed to wait until the next president was elected. "Oh, we'd fill it," he said of Ginsburg's seat in a speaking appearance in Kentucky, smiling broadly and triggering laughter in the crowd. Republicans soon confirmed that Trump would nominate a replacement for Ginsburg with a superstar female judicial mind of their own: Amy Coney Barrett. The confirmation hearings were rushed forward in October, just three weeks from the election. It was time for Senator Kamala Harris, now the Democrat nominee for vice president, to step up and prosecute the case.

The Biden team, however, played it safe. Prior to the hearings, CNN reported that "close allies of the California senator cautioned that viewers tuning in shouldn't expect those kind of fireworks from the vice presidential candidate," noting her "complex duel role" during the campaign. It turned out that Democrats were concerned about appearing as outrageous and unhinged as they were during the Kavanaugh confirmation hearings and made a pointed effort to play it safe. When it became time to question Amy Coney Barrett, Harris took a different strategy. Instead of marching into the Senate to fire up the viral clip machine, she retreated to her office. Harris's team insisted it was not safe to appear in person with Barrett due to the coronavirus pandemic, prompting speculation from Senate staffers she was not ready to go toe-to-toe with Barrett and her sharp legal mind. The last thing the Biden campaign wanted was Barrett making Harris look foolish in the same room.

Harris participated in the hearing via video, reading her notes dutifully from a script in front of her, the tinny audio confirming the campaign was phoning it in. She began her opening remarks raising the alarm about the coronavirus pandemic, preaching a gospel message about the need to take care of the American people and not overturn Obamacare. Barrett listened patiently as she droned on. Leftists anticipating a show were left disappointed and the New York Times explained why it was different this time. "After all, being vice president means checking your ego at the Oval Office door," the paper noted, reminding readers that Harris had to be a "loyal soldier."

Harris did play the loyal soldier. She worked earnestly to win the respect from the vice president's team, including longtime loyalists who still did not trust her. Harris was comfortable in the campaign role, finally lifted up out the primary struggle and put on stage as a number two. No longer was she struggling in states like Iowa and New Hampshire to win a slice of the electorate with her own campaign. The majority of her critics and her former rivals faded away and instead rallied behind her and Biden in the hope they could finally defeat Trump in November.

# CHAPTER TEN

# MADAM VICE PRESIDENT

*And I'm vice president, and my name is Kamala Harris.*

— KAMALA HARRIS, DECEMBER 18, 2021

All vice presidents receive some level of ridicule from the press as part of the job. Mike Pence was dismissed as the square, a Boy Scout, and the mild-mannered Christian compared to the more volatile and controversial Donald Trump. When he was vice president, Joe Biden was seen as the bumbling, out-of-touch, overeager uncle to the more serious and intellectual Barack Obama. Al Gore was the hapless monotone nerd compared to Bill Clinton's gregarious, glad-handing persona. The most powerful vice president in recent memory was Dick Cheney for President George W. Bush, and the weakest was Dan Quayle, who was thoroughly mocked by the media as an idiot while serving Bush's father, George H. W. Bush.

A vice president's existence is inherently political during the election, but ultimately an awkward sideshow when they are in office. They are the number two, but never in charge. Any political success they achieve is attributed to the president. Positioned in the executive branch, they are stuck across the street in the Eisenhower Executive Office Building. When they leave the residence, they are usually attending public events to fill in for the president. The White House controls their messaging, their schedule, and even has the power to veto staff choices. Their number one job? Do not embarrass the president. Harris successfully navigated the campaign trail as a running mate, and despite a few hiccups, and after working with Biden's cautious and close-knit team, brought home a victory against Trump. Moving into power, however, would prove to be a different set of circumstances.

"We did it. We did it, Joe. You're gonna be the next president of the United States," Harris said in a patronizing tone while she was on the phone with President-elect Joe Biden just after Election Day 2020. Harris was out for a jog when she received a call from the president-elect as her husband, Doug Emhoff, filmed the conversation on his phone. Her team shared the video on social media as a message to the world that the contentious presidential election was over and, more importantly, Harris would make history as the first black woman as vice president of the United States. What was left unclear, however, was what kind of vice president she would be.

Biden and Harris barely knew each other. Due to the pandemic, they had limited time on the campaign trail as Biden spent most of his time campaigning virtually from his basement. Their lack of rapport was evident after the election as they started doing interviews together, preparing for their next step as political partners. At the beginning, Harris sought approval from Biden and his team, carefully crafting an image of her future role as vice president that would satisfy the president-elect. A glowing CNN article in December emphasized sources who insisted that Harris was a team player: "Harris has told people close to her that she wants to shape her vice presidency after the way Biden worked with President Barack Obama over eight years: testing and pushing the administration in private, while in public remaining a dedicated and loyal lieutenant." The article also cited a source asserting that Harris was "trying to prove that she is capable of being a second. For her, there is as much learning and watching as there is participation." The article added that Harris "worked to get to know the President-elect by talking on the phone nearly every day, something Harris believes will help her better understand the kind of partner Biden wants her to be." The press office was working overtime to sell the idea to the West Wing.

When they started, Harris and Biden appeared eager to demonstrate the beginning of a buddy relationship. Biden wanted someone he could work with, joke with, and bounce ideas off of, just as he believed that he and Obama had, but neither one of them knew what to expect. Biden made a point of demonstrating his full commitment to his political partnership with Harris, appearing on CNN with her in an interview with anchor Jake Tapper in December. Harris was careful to appear deferential to Biden, having little to say about what she expected from the president, instead comfortable watching him define her role.

"How do you plan on working with your new boss?" Tapper asked Harris, noting that current vice president Mike Pence was leading the government's coronavirus response and a host of other issues. "What will your specific portfolio be? And how do you plan on working with your new boss? Will you have weekly lunches? Will you be the last one he speaks to before he makes a decision, as then Vice President Biden did with then President Obama? How do you see your role?"

"Yes," Harris replied with her signature laugh at the long list of questions posed by a somber Tapper. But she immediately shifted to a more patronizing tone. "We are full partners in in this process," she said, noting that Biden had asked her to "be the first and last in the room." She added, "I will be there to support him and support the American people." When Tapper asked Harris again about her portfolio, Biden interrupted her and said, "Let me take this one."

"Sure. Sure," Harris replied, deferring to her new boss. It was not a normal reflex for Harris, but one that she would have to get used to as number two. As a former vice president, Biden explained he wanted a vice president that was just like he was for Obama—willing to take on tough positions no matter what the political cost. "Whatever the most urgent need is that I'm not able to attend to, I have confidence to be turning over to her," he said. Biden pointedly recalled he was extremely loyal to President Obama, and promised him that "I'll do whatever the urgent need at the moment." Looking at Harris, Biden said, "And that's how it's going to work." Harris smiled and nodded wordlessly.

Biden declared that he and Harris were "simpatico" politically despite their limited time together and had put the awkwardness of the presidential campaign behind them. Biden reassured Democrats that he had forgiven Harris for the blindsided attacks during the campaign—but left unsaid was that Harris never apologized. "First of all, I understand how campaigns can sometimes get a little out of whack a little bit. And as I told her, you know, because you asked the question, I don't hold grudges," Biden said.

Tapper recalled that Biden's wife, Jill, was the grudge holder of the family. But Biden insisted it no longer mattered.

"She and Kamala have become friends," he volunteered.

"Yes," Harris agreed.

Biden was so caught up with the idea of how he served as a vice president, he recalled telling Obama that he would resign if he had any major disagreements with the president. "Like I told Barack, if I reach something where there's a fundamental disagreement we have based on a moral principle, I'll develop some disease and say I have to resign," he joked.[1] The joke did not land. It wasn't clear whether Biden would resign if he disagreed with Harris or expected Harris to resign if she disagreed with Biden. The two were hardly "simpatico" at the moment and it was a sign of things to come.

# DECLARING WAR ON *VOGUE*

Harris made it clear, even before taking her oath of office, that she had specific requirements from the media on how she was perceived in her new job. On January 10, 2021, just days before her inauguration, *Vogue* magazine released their cover photo for an issue profiling the future vice president. The photo showed Harris smiling in a casual black Donald Deal jacket and wearing black Converse sneakers in front of a pink and green background. Emblazoned across it were the words MADAM VICE PRESIDENT: KAMALA HARRIS. Harris was furious. Her communications team went to work, letting reporters know that she was very displeased with the cover photo. She wanted something more elegant after posing in a powder blue suit during the photo shoot and indicated that *Vogue* had betrayed them.

It was the vice president–elect's first crisis. "Blindsided" is how reports cited the reaction from Harris and her team in response to the *Vogue* cover. Magazine staffers were puzzled at the backlash. They had allowed Harris to pick the outfits and the backdrop settings. Throughout her political career, Harris made a big deal about her love of Converse sneakers, a symbol of how casual and cool she was. "I have a whole collection of Chuck Taylors: a black leather pair, a white pair, I have the kind that don't lace, the kind that do lace, the kind I wear in the hot weather, the kind I wear in the cold weather, and the platform kind for when I'm wearing a pantsuit," she said to *New York* magazine in a 2018 interview on "How I Get It Done." Harris's husband, Doug Emhoff, told CBS News that her Chuck Taylors proved that she was "down-to-earth" and "shockingly normal."

Harris was not happy, however, when the Chucks were featured on the cover of *Vogue*, which had hired black photographer, Tyler Mitchell, for the shoot.

"The team at *Vogue* loved the images Tyler Mitchell shot and felt the more informal image captured Vice President–elect Harris's authentic, approachable nature—which we feel is one of the hallmarks of the Biden/ Harris administration," *Vogue* said in a statement.

The vice president's team wanted *Vogue* to pick a new cover but it was too late. In response to the criticism, they offered a new "digital" cover of the vice president–elect's preferred photo. The very public squabble over the cover concerned members of Biden's staff, who cringed at the tone coming from Harris's office over what they viewed to be a "first world" problem, according to reporters Jonathan Martin and Alexander Burns in their book *This Will Not Pass.*[2]

The early tone of Harris's relationship with the press was not a surprise to those covering her presidential campaign. Already, news editors and reporters had been on the receiving end of complaints of sexism and racism from Harris's team when it came to news coverage. Reports emerged that Harris herself was keeping an "enemies" list, tracking political players and reporters who she thinks "don't fully understand her or appreciate her life experience."

"She particularly doesn't like the word 'cautious,' and aides look out for synonyms too," Edward-Isaac Dovere wrote for the *Atlantic*. "'Careful,' 'guarded,' and 'hesitant' don't go over well."[3] During her presidential campaign, Harris called out the entire media industry, accusing them of covert racism. "We still have a lot of work to do on cultural awareness in our country because there are a lot of people who are journalists who have the power of the pen who are not familiar with the cultures of the people they are covering . . . there's still a lot of work to do in journalism," Harris complained in an interview.[4]

Despite Harris's early struggles, she still enjoyed experienced glowing coverage of her historic inauguration as America's first black woman vice president. Even a stumble on the Capitol Hill stairs in her high heels on her way to the ceremony earned her sympathetic media coverage after she recovered and flashed a thumbs-up sign. "Social media users celebrate Kamala Harris's relatability after brief stumble heading to inauguration" read a headline from *The Hill* news website.[5] The oath of office was again taken on two Bibles, one the Shelton family Bible and the other the Bible of Supreme Court justice Thurgood Marshall. Justice Sonia Sotomayor administered the ceremony, and pronounced Harris's first name wrong, but no one decried her as a racist after the mistake.

# LET'S GET TO WORK

When Joe Biden and Kamala Harris were first elected, Biden's first chief of staff, Ron Klain, revealed to author Chris Whipple that he offered two models of the vice presidency to Harris—that of Vice President Al Gore or Vice President Joe Biden. Gore, he explained was given the chance by Clinton to carve out five issues to permanently spend his time on. Biden, on the other hand, was allowed by Obama to be a more general number two, serving wherever he was needed. For whatever reason Harris chose the Biden model, even though she had no idea of what was in store.[6] How could Harris shine with her lack of experience, new and unfamiliar staff, and issues she had never faced as a prosecutor and attorney general? How would she fare with the historic narrative of serving as the first woman vice president aligned with the nearly prehistoric establishment Joe Biden, who was himself controlled by his tight-knit circle of staff?

In the beginning, Americans wondered if Harris would be secretly controlling Biden from behind the scenes, but the opposite was true. Harris was essentially frozen out from the president's inner circle. Biden and his team had already achieved their goal of winning, using Harris's identity to "make history" and inspire voters to pull the aging presidential hopeful across the finish line. But when they took office, Harris was sidelined. Despite Biden's promise to make Harris a full partner in everything, Harris began the job literally standing behind Biden. At event after event at the White House, Harris stood masked in the back of the room while the president detailed his agenda to fight the pandemic, promoting vaccines, wearing masks, and his massive coronavirus spending package. The vice president was rarely asked to deliver remarks ahead of Biden, remaining literally masked (due to the pandemic) and silent as the president repeated his pleas for Americans to mask up and get vaccinated.

Harris looked as if she was either being silenced by the president or quietly plotting her ascension to power. Or acting as babysitter. On occasion Harris would remind the president to put his mask back on when the forgetful Biden would walk away from the podium without it and start shaking people's hands. At one event, as Biden approached her to greet Harris, the vice president looked at him and asked, "Where's your mask?"

"My mask," Biden remembered, walking back to the podium to retrieve his mask and put it on. "My mask. My mask." Putting Harris next to Biden grew distracting for audiences, who watched Harris for any kind of reaction while the president was speaking. The results did not make Biden look competent.

Going into the administration, Harris and her team did not have a plan for action. With HBO cameras in tow, Axios reporter Mike Allen appeared on the White House grounds with Harris in the first month of office to discuss her vice presidency. When asked what her signature issue would be, Harris replied, "Making sure Joe Biden is a success." When asked how it was going, Harris replied with a laugh, "It's three weeks in, Mike, give me a break!"[7]

## HOMELESS IN DC

Harris spent the first three months of her vice presidency living in Blair House, the guest quarters across the street from the White House, while renovations for the vice president's home at the Naval Observatory were still under way. She grew frustrated as she waited weeks for the renovations to be completed, living out of a suitcase while staring across the street at the White House, where the Bidens were residing comfortably. Was it an intentional slight? After two months in office, Harris and her husband were still stuck at Blair House. Reports that Harris was frustrated with the slow process emerged in public. It was revealed that she had requested updates to the kitchen before moving in, which explained some of the delay.[8] The vice president's office vigorously contested the notion, but Harris's love of cooking was already known; indeed, it was therapeutic.

"You know when you gotta work stuff out, you gotta chop, chop, chop, chop, chop," Harris said during a podcast interview with *Marie Claire* magazine, describing the soothing task of chopping up ingredients with a large knife.[9] She certainly seemed to enjoy wielding one.

## FROM VACCINE SKEPTIC TO AMBASSADOR

Harris was unprepared to help the fight against the coronavirus as she unraveled during interviews, and reversed previous positions, even while spreading misinformation and hypocrisy about the virus. Harris never wanted to be sidelined as the "woman of color" in the administration, but the West Wing pointedly asked her to help sell the coronavirus vaccine to black Americans. She faced an immediate lack of credibility on the issue after expressing her own fears of the vaccine developed by the Trump administration during the presidential campaign. "Let's not let COVID get us," Harris said with a chuckle to black Americans during an interview with Sharpton to celebrate Black History Month (and sell the vaccines). "Let's get the vaccine instead, right?"

If the black community was hesitant to get the vaccine, it might have been because Harris herself raised doubts about it during the presidential campaign, since it was developed under the leadership of President Trump. During a September 2020 interview with CNN's Dana Bash, Harris demurred when she was asked if she would get the vaccine.

"Well, I think that's going to be an issue for all of us," Harris replied. "I will say that I would not trust Donald Trump. And it would have to be a credible source of information that talks about the efficacy and the reliability of whatever he's talking about. I will not take his word for it. He wants us to inject bleach. I—no, I will not take his word." During the vice presidential debate with then–vice president Mike Pence, Harris again raised questions about the vaccine. She said that if Dr. Anthony Fauci endorsed the vaccine she would get it. "But if Donald Trump tells us that we should take it, I'm not taking it."

Now, with Biden in charge, Harris changed her tune, warning black people to get the vaccine or suffer severe consequences. "She explained to Al Sharpton: "The point, Rev, is this. I got vaccinated. I can tell you first of all that these vaccines are safe. It will save your life." Sharpton claimed he was initially hesitant to get the vaccine but Harris had convinced him. During the interview, Harris also urged Americans to wear masks. "Wear your mask. I have my mask right here," she added, raising her own black cloth one. "Wear your mask all the time when you are in front of other people. Six feet of distance. Wash your hands with warm or hot water with soap." Harris and Biden repeatedly demanded that Americans wear a mask to help prevent the spread of the coronavirus but were repeatedly criticized for hypocrisy when they showed up at events without one. On April 4, Harris visited a school in Washington, DC, without a mask, while the rest of the students were masked for the entire event, prompting mockery from political opponents. "Kamala Harris: Rules for thee but not for me," wrote Senator Ted Cruz on social media, mocking her hypocrisy. The masking theater only increased as the Biden administration tried to enforce masking mandates across the country. In May 2021, Harris and her husband were ridiculed after they kissed goodbye while wearing their masks on the airport tarmac before a flight. Both of them were vaccinated and outdoors for the masked kiss. They repeated the masked kiss in October as they held Harris's fifty-seventh birthday party indoors.[10]

Harris's talking points on the coronavirus pandemic were repeatedly contradicted by government scientists such as Dr. Anthony Fauci. Harris parroted the White House line in February that the administration was "starting from scratch" on the vaccination strategy, just as the vaccines were starting to roll out. Her assertion clashed with Fauci, who told reporters at the White House that there was already a vaccination plan. "We certainly are not starting from scratch because there is activity going on in the distribution," he said.

After a year of fighting the coronavirus, the Biden administration struggled with the rise of the Delta and Omicron variants that were still infecting even people who were masked and vaccinated. Americans struggled with a shortage of available tests and wondered if the vaccinations were already outdated. Harris admitted to the *Los Angeles Times* that the administration had failed to anticipate the gravity of the variants. "We didn't see Delta coming. I think most scientists did not—upon whose advice and direction we have relied—didn't see Delta coming," she said. "We didn't see Omicron coming. And that's the nature of what this, this awful virus has been, which as it turns out, has mutations and variants." But Fauci publicly disagreed with the vice president. "We definitely saw variants coming," he said defensively, although he conceded that the extent of the mutations was "unprecedented." Biden and Harris had run for office promising to bring expertise and competence to the White House to fight the coronavirus based on science. There was little Harris could do to help the administration succeed. Her public blunders, hypocrisy, and reversals on key issues surrounding the pandemic further damaged the administration's credibility with the American public. By the end of

2021, more Americans had died from the coronavirus under the Biden administration than in 2020 under Donald Trump.[11]

## BUILDING BACK BETTER

In the first year, Biden and Harris struggled to get their enormous agenda through the Senate, frustrating activists as the administration continued making concessions at the behest of more moderate Democrat senators like Kyrsten Sinema and Joe Manchin. Biden's promises of free college, higher subsidies for health care, and free child care were getting picked off one by one even though his spending agenda was still in the trillions.

The idea that Harris was going to use her powers of persuasion to help get Biden's agenda through Congress was a joke to Biden's team. Biden was a veteran senator who spent decades on Capitol Hill, frequently traveling overseas with his Republican colleagues. He knew how to make a deal, despite the odds they were facing. He valued the old-school negotiations of what appeared to be a bygone era and valued compromise to bring Republicans to the table. Harris, however, had barely even had time to make any friends on the Hill. The unserious pursuit of her personal political rise alienated her Senate Democrat colleagues, even as she was hoisted up by Biden into the vice presidency. But Harris tried anyway, at one point trying to bully Manchin into submission by speaking directly to the voters of West Virginia. Harris did an interview with a local TV station and pointedly told the local audience that Democrats should "work with a sense of urgency" on the coronavirus rescue package. Manchin was furious, telling reporters that no one from the White House had told him about the interview. Harris appeared to be stabbing him in the back.[12] As a result, someone from the West Wing had to reach out to Manchin to address the controversy and sooth tensions with his office.[13] Manchin's office never responded to questions about whether Harris ever contacted him personally to smooth things over.

As the administration continued struggling with Manchin and Sinema, supporters of Harris began voicing their disappointment. Charlamagne Tha God again interviewed Harris in December 2021 to talk about the ongoing struggle to move their agenda forward. As the virtual interview drew to a close, Charlamagne dropped a bomb. "I want to know who's the real president of this country, is it Joe Biden or Joe Manchin?" he asked. Harris flipped her hair back and prepared to respond, but her press secretary, Symone Sanders, interrupted and suggested the vice president could not hear him and so they had to wrap up the interview.

"She can hear me . . . they're acting like they can't hear me," Charlamagne scoffed, turning to his crew.

They were caught.

"I can hear you," Harris responded coldly.

When Charlamagne repeated his question about who the real president of the country was, Harris grew angry.

"C'mon, Charlamagne. C'mon. It's Joe Biden," she replied, unable to contain her disappointment with the host.

When Charlamagne tried to defend his question, Harris shut him down.

"No. No. No. No. No," Harris said, raising both hands to stop him from speaking. "No. No. No. No." Raising her finger and jabbing it toward Charlamagne, Harris continued.

"It's Joe Biden. It's Joe Biden. And don't start talking like a Republican about asking whether or not he's president. It's Joe Biden." She then reminded Charlamagne of her own position. "And I'm vice president, and my name is Kamala Harris," she said before listing accomplishments of the Biden administration and the messages they were sending to the black community simply by being in office. Charlamagne appeared modestly impressed at the level of heat she brought against him. "I just want you to know, Madam Vice President: that Kamala Harris? That's the one I like," he said. "That's the one that was putting the pressure on people in Senate hearings. That's the one I'd like to see more often out here in these streets."[14]

But that Kamala Harris retreated and by the summer the spark had faded. Charlamagne appeared on *The View* in July 2022 to talk about the moment. "What did she say?" cohost Joy Behar asked, after revisiting the incident. "Nothin'," he replied shortly, prompting laughter from the hosts and audience. "She didn't really give an answer." Charlamagne said he was still disappointed with Biden and Harris. "I feel like Democrats have tried every political strategy except for courage," he said.

# YOUTUBE DISASTER

Even the most monumental efforts to boost Harris's global image and profile came up short as the vice president struggled with basic communications projects. In October 2021, the vice president's office debuted a new YouTube series, *Get Curious with Vice President Harris*. The debut video, posted by NASA, featured Harris interacting enthusiastically with a group of children from across America about the excitement of space exploration. Each child was introduced in the video, which showed their arrival to film the video with Harris at the vice president's residence: There was Emily from New Jersey; Derek from St. Louis; Zorielle from Lafayette, Louisiana; Trevor from California; and Sydney from Iowa City, Iowa. Harris tried to emphasize her excitement in the video, speaking earnestly to the children gathered around her. "You guys are going to see, you're gonna literally see the craters on the moon with your own eyes!" she said to the group of children, gesturing with her hands and pointing at her eyes. "With your own eyes, I'm telling you. It is going to be unbelievable, so that's one of the things we can do here too which makes it so exciting." The launch of the video generated all of the wrong headlines. Critics mocked the vice president's overacting tone and exaggerated excitement. The vice president of the United States appeared to be auditioning for *Sesame Street*. It got worse. The seemingly random group of excited children surrounding Harris turned out to be paid child actors. The company that produced the video was named Sinking Ship Entertainment, and was based in Canada, not the United States.[15] It was also revealed that Harris filmed the video in August while the Biden administration was struggling to contain the political fallout from the botched Afghanistan withdrawal. Harris and her staff planned for an entire YouTube series featuring the vice president, but it promptly flopped. Despite drawing from a talented pool of Washington expert consultants, it became immediately obvious they could not help her as she struggled to manage even the most basic job of a highly produced and pre-taped video.

# THE BORDER CZAR ABDICATES

*You know, to use a phrase from an old television show,* Cheers, *you know, "where everybody knows your name." Most people don't want to leave home.*

—KAMALA HARRIS ON THE MIGRANT CRISIS,
APRIL 14, 2021

Just three months after taking office, the Biden administration had a full-scale migration crisis on their hands. "We are on pace to encounter more individuals on the southwest border than we have in the last 20 years," Secretary of Homeland Security Alejandro Mayorkas said on March 16.

He was right. Thousands of unaccompanied minors, families, and single adults continued pouring across the border as patrol agents took 172,331 migrants into custody in the month of March alone.[16] It was the highest number of detainments at the border since March 2001. Images of children in overstuffed detainment centers emerged and Republicans pointed directly at Biden's failed leadership.

The crisis was the predictable result of Biden's campaign rhetoric promising open borders. On the campaign trail, Biden rarely made a distinction between illegal and legal immigrants, comparing them to his ancestral family from Ireland who traveled aboard coffin ships and risked everything for a chance to build a better life. Biden also vowed during the presidential campaign to overturn President Donald Trump's efforts to secure the border and vowed "there will not be another foot of wall" constructed along the border with Mexico if he was elected president. On Inauguration Day, Biden made a public spectacle of signing five executive orders on immigration. He also ordered a hundred-day moratorium on deportations by ICE and promoted his plan to offer amnesty to illegal immigrants. For all of Biden's rhetoric about "humane" immigration policy, he was only making conditions for migrants worse.

In early March, the Biden administration reached a record number of detained unaccompanied migrant children, many of them detained longer than the seventy-two-hour limit. Reports noted that 3,200 children were in custody, far above the total number detained by Trump. What was worse is that some were being held in jail cells meant for adults. Harris, who was once famous for denouncing President Trump for putting "babies in cages" and for her heartfelt waving to detained migrant children, was now on the team of throwing a record number of children into a jail cell. When reporters questioned Harris about the news ahead of trip, she refused to comment. "I haven't been briefed on anything today about it, but I will when I get on the plane," she said awkwardly. She did not follow up.

Harris had promised to step up and help the president when she was needed the most, but when Biden looked to her to take a contentious issue off his plate, she froze. On March 24, 2021, Biden announced his decision to appoint the vice president to help him handle the migrant crisis, even as White House press secretary Jen Psaki and the rest of the West Wing tried mightily to not call it a crisis. Appearing with Harris in the State Dining Room of the White House, Biden announced, "I've asked her, the VP, today—because she's the most qualified person to do it—to lead our efforts with Mexico and the Northern Triangle [El Salvador, Guatemala, and Honduras] and the countries that help—are going to need help in stemming the movement of so many folks, stemming the migration to our southern border." It was a familiar playbook. Biden recalled he had been asked by Obama to perform a similar task when he was vice president, explaining that one of the reasons migrants were leaving was the lack of economic opportunities in Central American countries. He also cited Harris's record as a former prosecutor. "I can think of nobody who—who is better qualified to do this than a former—this is a woman who ran the second-largest attorney general's office in America—after the US—after the United States attorney general—in the state of California, and has done a great deal upholding human rights, but also fighting organized crime in the process."

Harris had little experience as the leader of controlling immigration and border security, as San Francisco was one of the oldest and proudest sanctuary cites in the nation and the state of California continued making it easier for illegal immigrants to remain. Biden mentioned the importance of Harris handling the "root causes" of the crisis, but felt comfortable shifting the entire narrative to her, putting her on a pedestal as a smart and capable leader. "[S]he's leading the effort because I think the best thing to do is to put someone who, when he or she speaks, they don't have to wonder about is that where the president is. When she speaks, she speaks for me. Doesn't have to check with me. She knows what she's doing, and I hope we can move this along. But—so, Madam Vice President, thank you. I gave you a tough job, and you're smiling, but there's no one better capable of trying to organize this for us."

On the surface, Harris was smiling, while her allies were furious. Was the West Wing trying to single-handedly sabotage her political future? Republicans couldn't believe it. Joe Biden had branded his rookie vice president as the "border czar." It wasn't long before Republicans displayed at a press conference a picture of Kamala Harris on a milk carton reading, "Missing at the border." Harris was quick to react, trying to wriggle out of the political millstone that had been tied around her neck. Aides tried to clarify her role, as Harris insisted she was not a "border czar" and wasn't even supposed to focus on the US border itself, but instead on the causes of migration in the home countries on the Northern Triangle. She wasn't going to let anyone tell her otherwise—not even President Biden. In April, Biden and Harris met with the Congressional Black Caucus behind closed doors. Biden praised the vice president and said she would do "a hell of a job" handling the migration crisis. But Harris corrected the president in front of everybody, according to reports, reminding him she was only handling the Northern Triangle portion of the immigration crisis.[17]

Harris began her new assignment cautiously, as her staff assembled a roundtable of experts to talk about the migrant crisis. On April 14, Harris tried to explain how she could help fix the migration crisis by promoting economic development in migrants' home countries by invoking the theme song to a famous sitcom set in Boston. "You know, to use a phrase from an old television show, *Cheers*, you know, 'where everybody knows your name,'" she said in her opening remarks, reciting words from the show's theme song. "Most people don't want to leave home."

As her early remarks on the issue failed to impress, Harris and her staff planned a trip to Guatemala in June to demonstrate to everyone exactly what she was focusing on and what she was not. But controversy followed before she even landed. As Harris and her team took off aboard Air Force Two, staff passed around cookies made in the vice president's image to celebrate their first foreign trip. The cookies were decorated like an obvious profile of the vice president, completely with pearl earrings, a necklace, and carefully styled hair. But there was no sketched-out face on the cookies, just blank brown frosting. But Harris was delighted with the gesture and went back to the plane to show them to reporters. "VP made an OTR [off-the-record] visit to the back of the plane and delivered cookies decorated with the shape of her likeness as well as AF2," *USA Today* White House correspondent Courtney Subramanian wrote on social media, sharing a photo of the cookies. Republicans immediately took shots at what appeared to be an obvious vanity project. "Handing out cookies with her face on them as the border crisis rages . . . ," Republican National Committee chairwoman Ronna McDaniel wrote on social media. "The modern-day equivalent of 'let them eat cake.'" The National Republican Congressional Committee also jumped on the issue. "Instead of trying to fix the Democrat-made Biden border crisis that's wreaking havoc on our southern border, Kamala Harris is commissioning cookies in her likeness," the organization wrote on social media. "Dems don't take the border crisis seriously and refuse to fix it." The controversy exploded on social media, prompting the vice president's office to clarify. A statement released to reporters insisted the cookies were a "gift" from a staff member and that Harris was only sharing. "The vice president wanted to make sure the cookies were shared with everyone," the statement read. The result was far beyond what anyone could have imagined as images of the embarrassing cookies were shared around the world.

As the vice president's motorcade drove through Guatemala City, Guatemala, a group of protesters made it clear she was not welcome. "Mind your own business," one sign read. Another large group stood in front of a "Kamala Trump Won" sign. Harris spoke about the importance of Guatemala citizens to "find hope at home" despite pointing out the corruption, security, and economic failures to leaders in the region. Harris was also embarrassed during her press conference when her press secretary called on "Maria Fernanda of Univision," who began her question by telling the vice president that she voted for her. "Thank you, Madam Vice President. For me, it's an honor because I was able to vote for the first time as a nationalized citizen and I voted for you," the woman began. She asked Harris what her message was to "women of color" who were looking for hope. "That's a great question, and thank you," Harris said with a smile. It turned out that the woman, Maria Fernanda Reyes, was not a reporter connected to Univision, but rather a businesswoman from San Francisco. The vice president's staff appeared to have failed to properly vet their list of "approved" reporters for Harris's press conference.

"Let it be clear to everyone that Ms. Maria Fernanda Reyes is not part of this media organization," Univision News president Daniel Coronell announced on Twitter, after the question was ridiculed on social media.

Harris also tried to dissuade migrants from making the trip to the United States. "I want to be clear to folks in the region who are thinking about making that dangerous trek to the United States–Mexico border: Do not come. Do not come. I believe if you come to our border, you will be turned back," she said during her press conference. It was a far cry from Harris's heartfelt position during her presidential campaign and her hypocrisy triggered anger from the left. Representative Alexandria Ocasio-Cortez said Harris's comments were "disappointing to see." "[T]he US spent decades contributing to regime change and destabilization in Latin America. We can't help set someone's house on fire and then blame them for fleeing," Ocasio-Cortez wrote on Twitter. Despite Harris's best efforts to discourage migrants from coming into the United States, they didn't listen. By the end of the fiscal year, arrests at the border had hit their highest levels.

During her trip to Guatemala, Harris sat down for an interview with NBC's Lester Holt to talk about the crisis. The veteran news anchor noted twice that Harris had not visited the border and asked if she had plans to do so. "At some point, you know, we are going to the border," Harris said, fumbling for the right words. "We've been to the border. So this whole thing about the border. We've been to the border. We've been to the border."

"You haven't been to the border," Holt noted.

"And I haven't been to Europe," Harris replied with a laugh. "And I mean, I don't understand the point that you're making. I'm not discounting the importance of the border."

Harris was shockingly unprepared for a question that Republicans and reporters had been asking her for months. What alarmed staffers further was that she had recently received comprehensive media training, according to reports, including a prepared answer in case she was asked why she had not visited the border.[18] It was not the first time she had been asked the question either. When asked by reporters in March if she would visit the southern border, Harris burst into laughter. "Not today," she replied, laughing and adding, "I have before and I'm sure I will again." The vice president was literally receiving on-the-job training and failing miserably.

The border problem did not go away, and it was clear that Biden was not going to address it ahead of the 2022 midterms. Republicans continued hammering the president and vice president for failing on the issue, demanding that Harris or Biden visit the border. As the problems got worse, former president Donald Trump decided to visit the border himself to highlight the Biden administration's failures. In response to Trump, the White House argued that a trip to the border was not necessary and merely a political stunt. But after Trump announced his plan, Harris suddenly agreed to make the trip herself, ninety-three days after Biden appointed her to lead on the crisis. Harris's move was a bit of a surprise, as she claimed it was "always part of the plan" despite weeks of resisting the idea. Trump declared victory. "After months of ignoring the crisis at the Southern Border, it is great that we got Kamala Harris to finally go and see the tremendous destruction and death that they've created," Trump wrote in a statement sent to reporters.

Harris later angered border-state Republicans including Texas governor Greg Abbott by declaring the border "secure." On September 11, during an interview on NBC's *Meet the Press,* Harris said: "The border is secure, but we also have a broken immigration system, in particular, over the last four years before we came in, and it needs to be fixed. . . . We have a secure border that is a priority for any nation, including ours and our administration." Abbott reacted by sending buses of migrants from Texas to Washington, DC, some of them dropped off near Harris's official residence at the Naval Observatory, in Northwest Washington. "We're sending migrants to her backyard to call on the Biden Administration to do its job & secure the border," Abbott wrote in a statement announcing the transports. At first Harris had no reaction, trying to avoid the subject altogether. But after days of silence she spoke out. "I think it is the height of irresponsibility . . . frankly, a dereliction of duty, when you are an elected leader, to play those kinds of games with human life and human beings," she said in an interview with *Vice.* Her scolding of the Republican governors did not make a difference. The busloads of migrants from Texas kept coming—on September 15, September 17, October 6, November 18, and on Christmas Eve.

The "border czar" also started treating border enforcement agents like garbage. After a group of agents on horseback were falsely accused of "whipping" migrants from Haiti who were trying to cross into the United States, Harris sided with the activists, who were whipping up lies and misinformation about what actually happened. "What I saw depicted, those individuals on horseback treating human beings the way they were was horrible," Harris said to reporters as the controversy escalated. "I fully support what is happening right now, which is a thorough investigation into what is going on there. But human beings should never be treated that way, and I'm deeply troubled about it." Four days later, on ABC's *The View,* Harris expanded her thoughts, comparing the border agents to slave owners. "I was outraged by it, it was horrible, and deeply troubling," she said, again calling for an investigation. "Human beings should not be treated that way and as we all know it also evoked images of some of the worst moments of our history where that kind of behavior has been used against the indigenous people of our country, has been used against African Americans during times of slavery," she added. Harris was throwing law enforcement agents to the wolves at a time when they needed the most political support.

After Harris's failure on the border, Biden and his team realized they would have to address the issue themselves. The vice president did fewer public events on the border crisis as record numbers of migrants continued crossing the border. Biden was loath to give in to Republican demands for him to visit the border, but the immigration narrative had to be reset. In January 2023, Biden personally visited the border and even spoke with border officials. He also appeared with Harris at the White House to deliver remarks on the crisis. "Today, I'd like to—the vice president and I would like to talk you about how my administration is dealing with our situation in the southwest border," he said. Harris stood behind the president as he spoke, but she did not deliver any remarks.

In May 2023, the administration braced for an influx of migrants into the United States as Title 42, a Trump-era provision allowing migrants to be expelled at the border, expired. Kamala Harris was nowhere to be seen. Governor Abbott used the occasion to send more busloads of migrants to Harris's home in Washington, DC, reminding everyone how she was failing on the issue of immigration. Rather than relying on Harris, the West Wing took the lead, deploying 1,500 troops to the border to handle the crisis. The vice president, however, was deployed to Atlanta for a fundraiser. On May 11, two more busloads of migrants from Texas arrived outside her home.[19] It did not stop Harris from ignoring the problem. When asked about the crisis in a local TV interview, Harris dismissed the crisis and punted the question to Congress. "You know, I hear that everything in the last couple days is going rather smoothly, given what the concerns were," Harris said. "The bottom line, however, is that this issue of immigration falls squarely within the responsibility of the United States Congress."

# CHAPTER ELEVEN

# STAFF EXODUS

*We are not making rainbows and bunnies all day.*

—KAMALA HARRIS SPOKESPERSON SYMONE SANDERS,
JUNE 30, 2021

When it comes to a political office in Washington, DC, nothing matters more than your staff. It's the sign of great leadership. Inspire your staff, and they will offer you their best work and make you look good. Mistreat them, and they will become monotone yes-people and dodge responsibility for critical errors and eventually stop caring. If the boss is not getting better, it's time to bail and look for another job. The executive branch is considered a coveted position for staffers on Capitol Hill, who immediately start shopping their resumes when their party takes power in the White House. But working for Harris was an entirely different experience.

With a boss who was thin-skinned, uncooperative, and impatient during her first year in office, staff exits from the vice president's team mounted as reports of a nightmarish working environment piled up in the press, while DC insiders marveled at the wreckage. Reports cited "an abusive" office environment under an unpredictable boss who berated staffers who failed to fulfill her erratic demands, or even for handing her the wrong type of pen. A June 30 *Politico* story made public the months of behind-the-scenes chaos as even the most experienced employees were looking for a way out. "It's not a healthy environment and people often feel mistreated. It's not a place where people feel supported but a place where people feel treated like s—," one person revealed.[1]

Harris demanded Pilot Precise V7 Roller Ball pens in her office, according to former aides. "You had to always have one on your desk in case she ever asked for a pen," a former aide said. If you didn't, "you'd have to go get her one. She'd be, like, 'Not this one.'" The pens are "seared into everyone's brain."[2] Former staffers who worked for Harris before she became vice president also shared their stories of a manager who easily threw staff under the bus for her own mistakes. Staffers said that interns and low-level staffers frequently were reduced to tears as she berated them when she felt they were unprepared and hung up abruptly during phone conversations. In her Senate office, Harris was ranked No. 9 among senators for highest staff turnover from 2017 to 2020. Several administration officials used the word *shitshow* when describing Harris's office, Axios reported.[3]

Harris tried to stem the bleeding by hosting an all-staff barbecue at the vice president's residence in July, hoping to generate social media posts to send the message that everything was fine. One post from Harris's personal aide featured a group photo of smiles and team unity along with a quotation from the vice president's speech to staff: "You're having an impact on people you may never meet, people who may never know your names but because of the work you do their lives forever will be uplifted and better." But the bleeding did not stop.

Just like in the early aftermath of a massive battle or natural disaster or the sinking of a ship at sea, the casualty list was constantly updated. It started with the director of advance, Karly Satkowiak, and deputy director of advance, Gabrielle DeFranceschi, both resigning in June 2021. Satkowiak was a five-year veteran of advance travel at the Obama White House who had joined the Harris team to help get operations off the ground. News of the executives' departure broke after Harris's disastrous trip to Guatemala and right before she visited the southern border. For DeFranceschi, the deputy director of advance, the departure came down to a "difference in opinion on how things should run," according to reports, as sources said that Harris's office is run "very different" from the Obama operation, where DeFranceschi previously worked. "If you have an opinion about how things should run and it's not listened to, that can be frustrating," a source told *Politico*. Rajan Kaur, the director of digital strategy, also resigned in June after six months working for Harris.

Harris's speechwriting team was also bailing. It was clear the vice president was not a charismatic figure no matter how good a script she had in front of her. Deputy director of speechwriting Sarah Gouda, no stranger to controversy after serving as a speechwriter to the then president of Planned Parenthood, Cecile Richards, resigned in November 2021. Chief speechwriter Kate Childs Graham resigned in February 2022. She was familiar with tough political bosses, having served as communications director for Senator Amy Klobuchar, another political figure with a reputation for mistreating staff.[4] Director of speechwriting Meghan Groob announced her departure in July 2022, after just four months in the job. Communications chief Ashley Etienne, a former senior advisor to Obama and Biden's presidential campaign, resigned in November 2021. Etienne had worked three and a half years for House Speaker Nancy Pelosi but called it quits after a year with Harris.

In response to the flood of reports, Harris's senior advisor and chief spokesperson, Symone Sanders, tried to assure Washington, DC, that it was a normal part of working for a top executive in the executive branch. "We are not making rainbows and bunnies all day. What I hear is that people have hard jobs and I'm like 'welcome to the club,'" Sanders said. Sanders was no stranger to tough jobs, a campaign veteran who worked as a press secretary during the 2016 campaign for Senator Bernie Sanders, a famously demanding and cantankerous political figure.[5] She joined Joe Biden's presidential campaign during the 2020 Democratic primary as a senior advisor, putting up with criticism from some of her former Bernie colleagues as she worked to prop up the aging former vice president, who was struggling mightily in the primary. In March 2020, Symone Sanders burst on the stage and tackled an anti-dairy protester who tried to confront Biden during a campaign event in Los Angeles. Despite her loyalty on the campaign trail, Biden opted against bringing in Sanders to the West Wing to serve as his press secretary, choosing longtime Democratic spokeswoman Jen Psaki instead. Sanders took a consolation prize and went to work for Harris. But after a year working in the "club" taking on hits for the vice president, she wanted out. "I'm so grateful to the VP for her vote of confidence from the very beginning and the opportunity to see what can be unburdened by what has been," Sanders wrote in an all-staff email announcing her exit on December 1, 2021.

The departures continued into Harris's second year. Senior advisor Adam Frankel left the team in January 2022. Frankel was brought into Harris's office along with Lorraine Voles, a former director of communications for Vice President Al Gore, in August. An Obama veteran, Frankel began his speechwriting career when Obama was a senator and worked two years in the West Wing. (He also married Stephanie Psaki, the sister of White House press secretary Jen Psaki.) Frankel and Voles were brought in as shock troops, temporary positions to focus on organizational development, strategic communications, and long-term planning.[6] After six months, Frankel left, but Voles stayed. Deputy press secretary Sabrina Singh resigned in March 2022, shifting her career to the Department of Defense after just one year with Harris. Singh had also seen enough, as she was a press secretary for Harris on the campaign trail and one of her senior advisors.

The biggest shift came after Harris's chief of staff, Tina Flournoy, announced her departure in April 2022. Flournoy, a respected veteran of Washington, DC, had worked for President Bill Clinton and Vice President Al Gore, but after a year with Harris, she was ready to leave. Deputy chief of staff Michael Fuchs announced his decision to leave in April 2022. Fuchs was also a veteran in Democratic politics, serving as a foreign policy advisor to Clinton and at the State Department under Obama.

The reports of staff dysfunction continued. What was going on? Biden senior advisor Cedric Richmond, a fierce defender of Harris, suspected something nefarious. He told one news outlet that the stories stemmed from a "whisper campaign designed to sabotage her." Staffers began to wonder. Was the West Wing quietly leaking damaging information about

Harris? Biden wanted to reassure Harris that she had his support. In June, reports surfaced that the president himself brought staffers into the Oval Office and warned them they would be fired if he found out any of them were behind the negative stories. It appeared to be a cover, as no one on his team was fired.

The chaos was not a surprise to some of Harris's staff who opted to take lower positions in the West Wing rather than a job with the vice president's office. Ian Sam, who had worked for Harris as her national press secretary during her failed presidential campaign, chose a modest position as a spokesman for the White House counsel's office instead of a job with Harris. Karine Jean-Pierre worked with Harris as her chief of staff after Biden selected her as her running mate but opted to work as a deputy press secretary on the Biden communications team, rather than take a senior position with Harris.

The resignations kept coming. Deputy director of public engagement and intergovernmental affairs Vincent Evans resigned in January 2022, opting out of Harris's office to go back to Congress as the executive director of the Congressional Black Caucus. Director of press operations Peter Velz, also a longtime Obama veteran, resigned in January 2022. National security advisor Nancy McEldowney resigned in March 2022. One of Harris's longest-serving aides, domestic policy advisor Rohini Kosoglu, exited the vice president's team in July 2022. Kosoglu had served with Harris as a chief of staff and a deputy chief of staff when she was a senator, shifting to senior advisor for her campaign and staying on to work with Harris in the vice president's office. Director of public engagement and intergovernmental affairs Michael Collins, a well-respected Democrat aide who spent twenty-three years working for civil rights icon Representative John Lewis, left in July 2022 after sixteen months working for Harris. Harris rounded out her second year with the departure of communications director Jamal Simmons, who had agreed to help the vice president's team manage the chaos after the first year. The departure of Simmons meant that Harris still needed someone who could keep her on track. Bad news stories continued trickling out as more and more staffers left Harris's office and spoke to reporters about what was really going on. "With Kamala you have to put up with a constant amount of soul-destroying criticism and also her own lack of confidence," a former staffer told the *Washington Post* in December. "So, you're constantly sort of propping up a bully, and it's not really clear why."[7] The impact showed. By the end of the first eighteen months, at least thirteen staffers had called it quits.

The number of anonymous complaints about Harris from disgruntled staff was unprecedented. I reached out to her former staffers to ask about their experience in the vice president's office. Some offered off-the-record thoughts and clarified their roles in the administration—especially if they viewed their roles as temporary to begin with. Others ignored requests for comments. No one would go on the record to defend or praise Harris. Some of them, however, are still loyal to the vice president. Not long after I reached out to former staffers, I received word from Harris's office. Deputy Communications Director Rachel Palermo revealed the Harris team had heard I was writing a book about the vice president and wanted to participate. We talked on the phone, and she agreed to look at some written questions for the book. I never heard back from Palermo, but in October 2023, she announced her decision to quit.

# CHAPTER TWELVE

# WORD SALADS

*It's time for us to do what we have been doing, and that time is
every day.*

— KAMALA HARRIS, JANUARY 13, 2022

"Turn on HBO and watch *Veep*." That's how one former aide to Kamala
Harris reportedly described what it was like to work in the vice president's
office.[1] HBO's *Veep* is a comedy series that stars Julia Louis-Dreyfus as
Selina Meyer, a sociopathic, egocentric vice president plucked from the
Senate after a failed presidential campaign, struggling with her lack of
power and influence. (Sound familiar?) "Did the president call?" Meyer
asks her staff repeatedly. "No," they reply patiently. The fictional show reveals the comedy behind life in Washington, DC, as staffers and politicians claw, manipulate, and fake their way through their daily routines,
putting on their best face on events that frequently spiral out of their control. Meyer earns ridicule for her personal obsession with her image and
her use of empty political talking points to escape embarrassing situations. The show is a favorite in Washington, DC, as fans say it is far more
accurate than political shows like *House of Cards* or *The West Wing*. In one
scene, the fictional vice president records an apology video in a desperate

attempt to clarify an embarrassing political gaffe. "My fellow Americans, words have many meanings and sometimes instead of conveying our meaning they can suggest other meanings," the fictional vice president says in a sincere voice. It was not lost on fans of the show when the tone of Kamala Harris's vice presidency grew more and more like the fictional comedy about America's first female vice president. When it was clear Harris was no longer speaking for herself but for Joe Biden, it became obvious that she had difficulty speaking at all. Moments of Harris devolving into confusing circular remarks with overstuffed platitudes quickly went viral on social media, with people marveling at the latest "word salad" from the vice president.

Harris demonstrated her inability to connect with audiences with some of her jokes. In April 2021, Harris laughed aloud at a canned line about the construction industry while promoting the administration's record of job creation. "Because there's an interesting fact in case you didn't know, hard hats are actually unisex," she said. "Everybody's laughing!" she continued, pointing and laughing at her own joke even as it was evident that few if any people in the audience were genuinely amused.

In August 2021, Harris appeared at a community health center in Washington, DC, to discuss the importance of health care. "We also must work together to call on Congress to advance other components of our Build Back Better agenda: to expand Medicaid in every state—to expand Medicaid in every state," she began. "People live in every state; that's the logic," she added, bursting into laughter.

In November 2021, Harris undertook a high-profile visit to Paris to speak about the importance of the alliance between the United States and France. In her remarks, she said, "And in then this moment, for nations who are partners and allies, we must together, work together, to see where we are, where we are headed, where we are going and our vision for where we should be, but also see it as a moment, yes, to together address the challenges and to work on the opportunities that are presented by this moment."

In a May 2022 speech to the United Nations, Harris spoke to the world about working "together" to combat climate change: "Our world is more interconnected and interdependent. That is especially true when it comes to the climate crisis, which is why we will work together, and continue to work together, to address these issues, to tackle these challenges, and to work together as we continue to work operating from the new norms, rules, and agreements, that we will convene to work together on to galvanize global action. With that I thank you all. This is a matter of urgent priority for all of us and I know we will work on this together."

Americans soon realized how bad Harris was in interviews, even with friendly news networks. In January 2022, NBC's Craig Melvin interviewed Harris and raised a question about an open letter from former Biden officials urging the administration to change their coronavirus strategy. "Does the administration say, 'You know what, this strategy isn't working. We're going to change strategies.' Is it time?" he asked.

"It's time for us to do what we have been doing, and that time is every day," Harris replied. "Every day it is time for us to agree that there are things and tools that are available to us to slow this thing down."

During a visit to Louisiana in March 2022, Harris again spoke about time: "We were all touring the library here and talking about the significance of the passage of time, right? The significance of the passage of time, so when you think about it, there is great significance to the passage of time in terms of what we need to do to lay these wires, what we need to do to create these jobs. And there is such great significance to the passage of time when we think about the day of the life of our children."

Harris tangled up her words during even the simplest events with sympathetic audiences. During an event with Jamaican prime minister Andrew Holness in March 2022, Harris struggled to explain the importance of sending economic aid to the island. "We also recognize just as it has been in the United States, for Jamaica, one of the issues that has been presented as an issue that is economic in the way of its impact has been the pandemic. So to that end, we are announcing today also that we will assist Jamaica in COVID recovery by assisting in terms of the recovery efforts in Jamaica that have been essential to, I believe, what is necessary to strengthen not only the issue of public health but also the economy."

At a May 2022 event at Children's National Hospital in Washington,

DC, Harris spoke about the importance of children. "When we talk about the children of the community, they are children of the community," she said. During a speech at the scene of a mass shooting in Highland Park, Illinois, near Chicago in July 2022, Harris missed the moment to genuinely empathize with grieving residents: "We've got to take this stuff seriously, as seriously as you are because you have been forced to take this seriously. The whole nation should understand and have a level of empathy to understand that this could happen anywhere any people in any community. And we should stand together and speak out about why it's got to stop."

In September 2022, Harris spoke about the importance of community banks during a roundtable discussion at Claflin University in Orangeburg, South Carolina. "We invested an additional $12 billion into community banks, because we know community banks are in the community, and understand the needs and desires of that community as well as the talent and capacity of community," she said.

Harris was also ridiculed for frequently referring to Venn diagrams, using them as a crutch while trying to use her words to paint an image for the audience as she struggled to make a point.

"Let me just say, I love Venn diagrams. I really love Venn diagrams. You know, the circles, right?" she said to an audience in October 2022. Speaking to an audience in Michigan in January 2023, Harris again tried the rhetorical flourish to make a point about climate change as she used her hands to demonstrate what a Venn diagram looks like. "Think of the movement through the lens of something I love, which is to always think about complex issues through the frame of a Venn diagram. I love Venn diagrams. I do. I love Venn diagrams. So, the three circles—and you can do more! Nobody says a Venn diagram has to only be three circles, right?"

Harris also drew mockery for a January 2023 speech at a White House ceremony to award the Congressional Space Medal of Honor after she explained space exploration to astronauts Colonel Douglas Hurley and Colonel Robert Behnken and their families as if they were children. "Bob and Doug returned to the Kennedy Space Center. They suited up, they waved to their families, and they rode an elevator up nearly twenty stories. They strapped into their seats and waited as the tanks beneath them filled with tens of thousands of gallons of fuel. And then, they launched," she said, trying to emphasize her wonder and awe to the audience. "Yeah, they did," she added, laughing awkwardly.

During a White House reception marking Women's History Month in March 2023, Harris made her own historic word salad. "So, during Women's History Month, we celebrate and we honor the women who made history throughout history, who saw what could be unburdened by what had been," she said.

At a March 2023 roundtable event in Florida about climate change, Harris recalled coming home from school one day and asking her mother, "Why are conservatives bad, Mommy? Because, I thought we were supposed to conserve." Then she burst into laughter. "I couldn't reconcile it." She added ominously, "Now I can." Her story was too much for some conservatives to believe. "I can't tell if she laughs because she believes the content is funny or because she knows there are a few suckers dumb enough to believe this actually happened," the Daily Wire's Virginia Kruta wrote on Twitter.

Once celebrated as a future Democratic star, Harris was going viral for all the wrong reasons. Even comedians on the left couldn't ignore it. *The Daily Show*, a comedy newscast, spliced together some of the most viral Kamala Harris moments with clips of fictional Selina Meyer's own vapid speeches in a video. "The *Veep* reboot looks amazing," the show's account wrote on Twitter. The video quickly earned over a million views across multiple social media platforms, cementing the perception of awkward similarities between Harris's public persona and the fictional paranoid politician.

Harris has even referred to the show despite growing online chatter about the similarities between Meyer and Harris. "I know you love *Veep*," Harris said with a grin to Stephen Colbert during a March 15, 2023, appearance on his CBS late-night show. "There are bits of it that are quite accurate," she added, sharing a story of her aide lighting a fire in her office without opening the chimney flue and smoking out the office. Colbert smiled awkwardly, pointing out that the show was primarily about the struggle for a vice president to find her place in the administration. Harris pivoted. "Well, I have the great privilege of serving with Joe Biden, who is president of the United States," she said as she sat back to appreciate the applause from the studio audience. "Right! Right! Exactly right. Exactly right," she said as she smiled and nodded. "And was vice president," she added.

"Does he understand what it's like to be vice president?" Colbert asked.

"He does. He does. And he really is a true partner, and he understands the job," Harris replied. She added cloyingly, "[H]e's an extraordinary leader and I wish people could see what I see. Because there's only one person who sits behind that Resolute Desk. And the decisions that person has to make are the decisions that nobody else in the country can make and he's an extraordinary leader."

"That's an excellent answer," Colbert replied with a wry grin. "And the question was, what is the job of the vice president? And your answer is part of the job, I'm guessing." Outside the studio, a group of environmental protesters were condemning Biden's decision to approve the Willow oil-drilling project in Alaska. For Colbert, it seemed like an easy question for Harris, who likely saw the protesters as she entered the building. But when Colbert asked Harris to respond, she unleashed another awkward collection of words that made little sense. "The concerns are based on what we should all be concerned about, but the solutions have to be and include what we are doing in terms of going forward, in terms of investments," she replied.

The vice president's latest word salad went viral again. Even supporters of Harris could not believe their ears. "Don't come @ my neck I voted for her," wrote MSNBC TikTok producer Manny Fidel, who pulled together a social media video of Harris's most cringeworthy moments, including the recent one from the Colbert interview.[2] "Kamala Harris used to be a super sharp prosecutor and senator who could eviscerate any witness that came her way, but ever since she became Vice President, she has been media trained to an extent to where she is constantly putting out the most baffling statements," he lamented.

During a speech on abortion rights at her alma mater, Howard University, in April 2023, Harris could not prevent herself from spiraling into another circular moment in her speech in front of a friendly audience, as she was speaking from notes instead of using a teleprompter. "So, I think it's very important, as you have heard from so many incredible leaders for us at every moment in time and certainly this one, to see the moment in time in which we exist and are present, and to be able to contextualize it, to understand where we exist in the history and in the moment as it relates not only to the past but the future." As Harris prepared to return to the campaign trail, even supportive journalists acknowledged there was a problem in how she spoke to audiences. "It is true that she often burdens her sentences with more dependent clauses than they can bear, and verbatim transcripts of her extemporaneous remarks can sometimes be hard to follow," *Washington Post* columnist Eugene Robinson wrote in April 2023. "But she also connects powerfully with audiences and communicates her message, even if it might be hard to diagram."

But the hits kept coming. In May 2023, Harris riffed extensively on the Cajun dish of gumbo in an interview with YouTube personality Lynae Vanee when asked about her favorite food. "One of my favorite dishes probably is gumbo. I love gumbo," she said, recalling her connection with her "second mother," Regina Shelton. "She made the best gumbo and I have been a lifelong gumbo apprentice. Learning how to make gumbo my whole life."[3] On July 1, 2023, Harris participated in a roundtable conversation about abortion rights during the Essence Festival in New Orleans with *The View*'s Sunny Hostin and queer activist Monica Simpson. During the conversation, Simpson reminded Harris about the importance of using culture to shift hearts and minds toward abortion and asked her to share her thoughts.

"Well, I think culture is—it is a reflection of our moment in our time, right?" Harris began. "And—and present culture is the way we express how we're feeling about the moment. And—and we should always find times to express how we feel about the moment that is a reflection of joy, because every—you know, it comes in the morning," she said, then started laughing before continuing. "We have to find ways to also express the way we feel about the moment in terms of just having language and a connection to how people are experiencing life. And I think about it in that way, too." It was stunning. Harris had arrived to speak at a culture festival without being prepared to talk about culture. Video of Harris's remarks shot across the internet as the latest word salad went viral over the Fourth of July holiday weekend. "Anytime Kamala Harris starts riffing on time and moments, it's gonna get good," wrote Ryan Grim, the Washington, DC, bureau chief of left-wing news website the Intercept on social media.

Harris's team was stung by the mockery but blamed racism for any criticism of the vice president. In response to conservative news anchor Eric Bolling's mockery, press secretary Kirsten Allen posted an old video clip of Harris criticizing journalists during the presidential campaign for their lack of "cultural awareness" when covering black candidates. Allen did not recognize the irony of the clip, as her boss was struggling with awareness of culture.

Harris again triggered ridicule on July 12, 2023, after she held a meeting in her office to discuss the challenges of artificial intelligence, or AI. "AI is kind of a fancy thing," Harris said in her opening remarks. "First of all, it's two letters. It means artificial intelligence, but ultimately what it is, is it's about machine learning." Although the beginning of her remarks appeared as if she were speaking to a kindergarten class, Harris continued, "And so, the machine is taught—and part of the issue here is what information is going into the machine that will then determine—and we can predict then, if we think about what information is going in, what then will be produced in terms of decisions and opinions that may be made through that process. So to reduce it down to its most simple point, this is part of the issue that we have here is thinking about what is going into a decision, and then whether that decision is actually legitimate and reflective of the needs and the life experiences of all the people."

Then, two days later, Harris inadvertently called for the world to "reduce population" in order to improve the environment. "When we invest in clean energy and electric vehicles and reduce population, more of our children can breathe clean air and drink clean water," she said during a speech at Coppin State University in Baltimore. Harris did not correct herself, and the audience applauded, sparking immediate shock and confusion about what she was talking about. "Reducing population is [nuts]," wrote billionaire Elon Musk on Twitter, sharing an emoji of a peanut in response to Harris's remarks. "We need to increase population." Harris and her team did not publicly admit the mistake. The release of the official White House transcript, however, revealed she was expected to say "reduce pollution" instead of "reduce population."

On July 28, Harris appeared with former Democrat operative Jennifer Palmieri to discuss abortion rights and started a circular discussion about democracy: "I do worry a great deal about what this means in terms of the strength of our democracy. And so, here's how I think about that. The nature of democracy is it's—there are two sides to it, in terms of the nature of it. There's a duality. On the one hand, when democracy is intact, it is incredibly strong in terms of the strength it bestows on the individuals, in terms of their rights and their freedoms—incredibly strong, in terms of what it does for its people. On the other hand, it's very fragile."

Harris's word salads provided endless content and entertainment for comedians and conservative media organizations, but her inability to communicate quietly sparked a crisis of confidence in the Democratic Party. The ability to speak well is one of the most crucial skills of a political candidate, particularly in the sphere of traditional and social media. As more people watched, they realized that Harris was never that good at speaking or answering questions and was only getting worse. No one wanted to talk about it publicly, as criticism of Harris was immediately branded as racist and sexist by her defenders. "Well, I do think sexism and racism are part of the problem, no question about it," White House chief of staff Ron Klain said in an interview with Kara Swisher on the podcast *On with Kara Swisher* after leaving the administration in 2023. Few Biden advisors had more reason to prop up Harris than Klain, who had been an enthusiastic cheerleader for her selection as vice president. Try as they might, Harris continued to career from reboot to reboot, with few substantial returns. Democrats quietly gave up on the notion that Harris would take over for Biden in 2024 as she lacked one of the most basic political skills for the executive branch.

## VAMPING WITH VEEP

When actress Julia Louis-Dreyfus, who portrayed Selina Meyer on *Veep*, appeared at the White House in March 2023 to receive a National Medal of Arts from Biden, Harris bumped into the actress at the reception and cried, "*Veep!*" as she moved in for a hug.

"Veep!" Louis-Dreyfus responded, hugging the real vice president.

Biden watched the exchange and remarked, "By the way, she left as president. Remember that."

The president did not mention that the ending of the show (spoiler alert) features the fictional vice president finally getting elected president after abandoning all of her principles in her selfish pursuit of power and burning through all of her most loyal staff to win. It was not a happy ending.

# CHAPTER THIRTEEN

# THE REACH FOR RELEVANCE

*I mean, listen, guys, we're talking about the potential for war in Europe.*

—KAMALA HARRIS, FEBRUARY 20, 2022

As vice president of the United States, Kamala Harris sought out opportunities to flaunt her growing profile, but her record of achievement was sadly lacking. Sometimes she would appear eager to pile up specific issues on her plate; at other times she cautiously sidestepped thorny issues that might damage her political future. But ultimately she was fading further and further into the background. *Los Angeles Times* columnist Mark Z. Barabak declared in November 2021 that Harris was "the incredible disappearing vice president."

The character of the modern vice presidency has only expanded its significance in foreign policy. Under President George W. Bush, Vice President Dick Cheney almost single-handedly influenced the president's approach to foreign policy. One of the reasons President Barack Obama selected Biden as vice president was to bring his decades of foreign policy experience to bolster his presidential ticket. But Harris only had a few years studying foreign policy in her role as a US senator and had little to show for it. Despite her lack of experience, Harris appeared eager to perform on a global stage, but her efforts were peppered with awkward moments, gaffes, and critical mistakes. But that did not stop Harris from bragging about her foreign policy experience on top of her international travel. "As vice president of the United States, I have now, twenty months in, met with and directly talked, by phone or in person, with one hundred world leaders. Presidents, prime ministers, chancellors, kings," Harris boasted at an October 2022 fundraiser with wealthy Democrat supporters. Harris was ahead of herself. It takes more than a few meetings to impress on the national stage.

# HARRIS DISAPPEARS AS AFGHANISTAN GOES TO HELL

In April 2021, Kamala Harris asserted in an interview with CNN's Dana Bash that she was the last person in the room with Biden before he made the decision to withdraw from Afghanistan and that she was comfortable with it. That was in April, but by August, as the withdrawal from Afghanistan grew catastrophic, Harris was nowhere to be found. Typically, a vice president steps up when others in the administration back down, leading the defense of the president's actions and urging the American people to trust his leadership. Harris went missing for several days following the disastrous exit from Afghanistan and the subsequent death of thirteen members of the armed forces in a terrorist suicide bombing attack in Kabul. She vanished from public view for a week when the president needed defending the most. (Her only public engagement was through sharing preapproved statements on social media together with official White House photos of her and the president.) White House reporters were told that Harris would attend an August 16 speech by Biden defending his actions in Afghanistan, but when the speech began, Harris was nowhere to be seen. White House officials later noted that Harris had watched it from a separate room. It seemed she had no interest in being on camera with Biden during his moment of crisis.[1] Harris looked like she wanted little to do with the devastating results of the administration's decision.

Harris reemerged on August 20 to leave for her previously scheduled trip to Vietnam. As reporters shouted questions about Afghanistan at the airport, she approached the cameras and started laughing. "Hold on, hold on, slow down, everybody," she said, bursting into laughter. The optics were terrible. At a press conference in Singapore, Harris finally spoke about the chaotic exit, over a week after the Afghan government fell to the Taliban. Harris pointed to Biden's "great emotion" over the horrific events that occurred during the exit from Afghanistan and suggested that any criticism of Biden was a "distraction." She tried to prop up Biden, who was struggling in real time to respond to the chaos, but also trying to maintain his August vacation schedule. "But there's no question that what many of us have seen on television, as the president has said—I mean, the president has, I think, shown great emotion in expressing sadness about some of the images we have seen," she said. Americans later witnessed the lack of Biden's "great emotion" when they saw him check his watch during the dignified transfer ceremony at Dover Air Force Base of the thirteen service members slain in Afghanistan. At least Biden was visible. It seemed that Harris's goal was to evade the crippling political aftermath for their administration as much as possible.

## PUTIN INVADES UKRAINE

Harris's first major foreign policy moment was her appearance at the Munich Security Conference in February 2022, as Russian president Vladimir Putin continued accelerating the drumbeat of a likely invasion in Ukraine. It almost felt like a setup by Biden's advisors. They could not have Biden arrive and issue threats to Putin only to have the Russian leader ignore them as soon as the president of the United States left the region. It was another "opportunity" for Harris to build her foreign policy experience, but she did not go alone. The White House made sure that the vice president was not the only one at Munich to reassure America's allies. Secretary of State Antony Blinken was also there to strengthen American diplomacy. Longtime American diplomats were not impressed. "You could argue it's a divide-and-conquer strategy, but that's far-fetched," an American official told the *Washington Post*. "The Harris stop is about burnishing her political credentials as a leader in the middle of a crisis."[2] It was a rare moment of honesty.

The United States government and President Biden had concluded that Putin had already decided to invade Ukraine, but they needed to send one last warning. Who better to send the message (that they expected to be ignored) than Vice President Harris? Harris arrived in Munich with some very scripted tough talk for Putin in her speech. "We have clearly articulated the consequences we have in store, and they will be severe and swift," Harris warned. Off script, however, Harris struggled rhetorically in front of reporters during a press gaggle as she tried to emphasize the importance of her trip. "We are looking at a moment that is a very decisive moment," she said, fumbling for the right words. Harris even said she admired Ukrainian president Volodymyr Zelensky's desire to join NATO, poking the Russian bear into further provocation. She also stumbled when trying explain to reporters what NATO was. "NATO is a membership. It is about nations coming together as a group, making decisions collectively around, again, principles and what will be, then, the conditions and—and the standards of membership. And so that is the process," she said. The vice president hardly impressed world leaders with her grasp of foreign policy and world affairs as she earnestly tried to explain the gravity of the moment to reporters. "I mean, listen, guys, we're talking about the potential for war in Europe," she said. "I mean, let's really take a moment to understand the significance of what we're talking about. It's been over seventy years. And through those seventy years, as I mentioned yesterday, there has been peace and security. We are talking about the real possibility of war in Europe."

Harris's remarks on foreign policy were simplistic. Her comments about seventy years of "peace and security" in Europe ignored the forty-year Soviet occupation of Eastern Europe, the violent breakup of Yugoslavia in the 1990s, Russia's invasion of Georgia in 2008, and its annexation of Crimea in 2014.

Despite the vice president's best efforts in Europe, Putin ignored the warnings. On February 24, he announced his decision to invade Ukraine.

Back in the United States, Harris's remarks about the conflict in Ukraine were patronizing, especially when she tried to simplify her descriptions of political events. "Ukraine is a country in Europe. It exists next to another country called Russia. Russia is a bigger country. Russia is a powerful country. Russia decided to invade a smaller country called Ukraine. So basically, that's wrong," she said to a radio audience in March 2022 when asked to explain to listeners why the Biden administration was acting in Ukraine.[3] The host had asked Harris to simplify the issue for his listeners, but not to the intellectual level of a toddler.

In March 2022, Harris again flew to Europe to reassure allies as the war in Ukraine continued. But the day before she left, she found herself in an awkward position. The Department of Defense had pointedly shot down a Polish government proposal that the US would support sending fighter jets to Ukraine. The conflict made her trip more difficult as she tried to wave off any suggestion that the United States was not fully supportive of Poland. The trip got more uncomfortable during a joint press conference with Polish president Andrzej Duda. Harris insisted there was nothing wrong. "I want to be very clear. The United States and Poland are united in what we have done and are prepared to help Ukraine and the people of Ukraine; full stop," she said, even though the United States had already made it clear the two countries were not on the same page. The press conference grew more awkward as Harris was asked a question by a reporter about Ukrainian refugees and Duda was asked a question whether he had requested the United States to accept more refugees. Harris was supposed to answer first, but she turned expectantly to Duda, who motioned for her to answer.

"Okay," Harris replied awkwardly. Bursting into her signature laugh, she replied, "A friend in need is a friend indeed!"

Duda did not understand what she meant.

"Go ahead. You first," he said, motioning to Harris.

Harris kept laughing and again motioned to Duda to answer first.

A puzzled Duda ultimately took his question first, throwing a lifeline for Harris.

## CONFUSION IN THE DMZ

Despite her confident pursuit of foreign policy, Harris was still making her own critical mistakes. On the way home from Asia in September 2022, she took a trip to the demilitarized zone dividing North Korea and South Korea. An American leader visiting the region makes for one of the most significant optics in Asia. Harris, wearing sunglasses, stood at a podium in front of a military helicopter and announced to South Korean leaders, "So the United States shares a very important relationship, which is an alliance with the Republic of North Korea and it is an alliance that is strong and enduring." It was an inexcusable gaffe that she did not correct or apologize for.[4]

Harris frequently appeared unprepared for the international stage, at a time when America needed to project strength and competent leadership. When the going got tough, she got nervous and tried to laugh off awkward exchanges. Harris and her staff would frequently ignore criticisms or obvious mistakes, which suggested she was not taking the job seriously. Although she was Biden's "number two," Democrats felt increasingly uneasy about her ability to lead the party into the next political cycle.

## KAMALA'S DAY OF INFAMY

Harris had kicked off 2022 by angering Americans when she marked the first anniversary of the January 6th riot at the US Capitol. The Biden administration used the occasion to raise fears of "Ultra MAGA" Republicans who were a danger to the very fabric of American democracy. Harris went further, comparing the violent protests to the deadly Japanese attack on Pearl Harbor and the 9/11 terrorist attacks. "Certain dates echo throughout history, including dates that instantly remind all who have lived through them—where they were and what they were doing when our democracy came under assault," she said stoically. "Dates that occupy not only a place on our calendars, but a place in our collective memory. December 7th, 1941. September 11th, 2001. And January 6th, 2021." It was an outrageous notion. The death toll for Pearl Harbor was 2,403

196

Americans; the death toll for the 9/11 attacks was 2,977 Americans. On January 6, 2021, only one American was killed, a protester supporting Trump who was shot and killed by Capitol Police. It was absurd for the vice president to compare a riot of American citizens on Capitol Hill to the terrorist attacks on American soil by foreign enemies where thousands of Americans were killed and which sparked horrific foreign wars.

# VOTING RIGHTS

In the summer of 2021, Harris personally asked Biden for a lead role on voting rights—an issue that was front and center in Democrat voters' minds ahead of the midterm elections. She was eager to move beyond her failures as immigration czar and wanted something she felt was more suited to her strengths. Biden agreed, announcing Harris's new assignment during a June speech in Tulsa, Oklahoma. "With her leadership and your support, we're going to overcome again, I promise you, but it's going to take a hell of a lot of work," Biden said. For Harris, it looked easy. She already knew and had the support of civil rights activists, and it was a perfect way for her to burnish her law enforcement credentials. Harris began by boosting her media profile on the issue, holding roundtables with activists and giving them a seat at the table to make their voices heard. Some of the activists, however, did not even want a seat at the table, as they were frustrated with inaction. As the president and vice president traveled to Atlanta in January 2022 to deliver a speech on the issue, a coalition of local voting rights groups boycotted the event. "We don't need even more photo ops. We need action," Cliff Albright, the cofounder of Black Voters Matter, told reporters before Biden and Harris visited.

Despite adding voting rights to her profile, Harris did not have command of the issue, as demonstrated in an interview with BET News host Soledad O'Brien in July. O'Brien surprised Harris with a question about whether it was time to compromise with Republicans on voter ID laws. Harris argued it was "almost impossible" for rural voters to photocopy their IDs. "I don't think we should underestimate what that should mean because in some people's mind, that means, well, you're going to have to

Xerox or photocopy your ID to send it in to prove who you are. Well, there are a whole lot of people, especially people who live in rural communities, who don't—there's no Kinkos, there's no OfficeMax near them," she said. Harris's statement proved how clueless she was about Americans in rural communities. She also appeared ignorant about the popularity of voter ID. In 2021, new polling showed that voter ID laws were actually quite popular with Americans. One poll showed 80 percent in support of the idea—even with 62 percent of Democrats.[5] But Harris expressed hesitation over the proposal, spiraling through the struggle of what it would take for voters to identify themselves with their ID.

Harris was also caught spreading false information about the new voting security laws passed in Georgia. "They are punishing people for standing in line to vote," she told O'Brien. "They are saying 'Well, if you are going to be standing in that line for all those hours, you can't have any water or any food.'"[6] Harris was wrong. The new law banned giveaways for free food and water but specifically allowed poll workers to set up a water stations for voters, and no one could stop voters from eating or drinking while standing in line.

The vice president's efforts did not have the desired effect in Washington, DC. On January 19, both Senators Joe Manchin and Kyrsten Sinema voted against a Senate bill that would change the filibuster rule to pass the voting rights bill. Harris had used her bully pulpit, but the effort failed again.

## THE BABY FORMULA DISASTER

Every presidential administration experiences a domestic crisis that no one could have seen coming. But the Biden administration's failure to act in time to prevent the baby formula shortages could have been avoided if anyone was paying attention. President Biden was forced to take the blame, while Harris tried to take the credit for fixing the crisis. "I'll answer the baby formula question because, all of a sudden, it's on the front page of every newspaper," Biden grumbled to reporters after an event on May 13, 2022. It was true. The closure of a baby formula factory in Michigan by order of the Food and Drug Administration was having a devastating effect in stores; photos and videos of empty shelves flooded across traditional and social media. Biden resisted weighing in on the crisis, until it was too big to ignore. Asked if he failed to act soon enough, he was defiant. "If we had been better mind readers, I guess we could've, but we moved as the problem became apparent to us," Biden said. But he did not need to acquire psychic powers to know that the country was about to experience a shortage. Business executives had been warning of shortages for weeks. The president was painfully slow in addressing the crisis but ultimately started doing what he could to alleviate it.

Harris, however, tried to reassure parents with a word salad. "You know, when we talk about our children, and I know for this group we all believe that when we talk about the children of the community, they are a children of the community," she said awkwardly in an attempt to show parents she cared deeply about their starving babies. Behind the scenes, Harris was asked by the White House to meet a cargo plane of baby formula from overseas as evidence they were working to combat the shortage. She declined, which forced First Lady Jill Biden to go instead. When the heat of the controversy dissipated, Harris finally agreed to meet a shipment a month later.[7] "Let's be clear, this really is about what should be one of the highest purposes for any one of us, which is to ensure that we are meeting the needs of our children, the children of our country," she said. It should have been, but it seemed to be an afterthought for Harris, who was trying to escape blame for the crisis. Despite the Biden administration's efforts to bring in more baby formula from overseas, the crisis continued into the summer, and Harris kept her distance.

## LOSING POLITICAL STEAM

On the fundraising circuit for the midterm elections, the vice president's difficult year continued as reports revealed that the Democratic National Committee started slashing prices for a fundraiser and photo with Harris after not enough tickets were sold for $15,000. The event was later postponed. The bad news did not let up. In Virginia, she angered the entire Jewish community in September 2021 when she nodded along as a college student accused Israel of "ethnic genocide," and commended the student for "your voice, your perspective, your experience, your truth."[8] On October 1, 2022, speaking in the wake of Hurricane Ian's assault on Florida, she declared that federal disaster aid should be allocated "based on equity"—sparking concerns of racial preferences superseding communities' individual needs. By the end of the summer, Harris had angered or disappointed nearly every political force in the Democratic Party.

## PRONOUNS AND TRANS RIGHTS

Kamala Harris began her vice presidency with a public show of support for the LGBTQ community even as Republicans publicly voiced their dissatisfaction with what they described as the transgender agenda. As vice president, Harris continued introducing herself by indicating her pronouns at select events where she believed it would make an impact. "My pronouns are *she* and *her*," Harris said as she opened up a teleconference with gay activists in June 2021. In July 2022, Harris again specified her pronouns during a roundtable meeting with disability advocates about the importance of abortion. "I am Kamala Harris. My pronouns are *she* and *her*," she said before adding a message to the visually impaired that she was the "woman in the blue suit."

The vice president made a point of celebrating Pride Month every year she was in office, a stark change from her predecessor, Mike Pence, a committed Christian and an opponent of gay marriage and gender reassignment surgery. She routinely marched in Pride parades and hosted Pride receptions at the vice president's mansion with transgender activists and drag queens. In 2023, Harris excoriated Republican leaders for passing laws banning gender-changing surgery for minors. That June she celebrated Pride Month at the vice president's residence and intentionally edited the signage on the bathrooms to be more inclusive. One bathroom was specifically labeled "gender neutral" and the other featured the traditional man figure and woman figure but also a figure with half pants, half dress as a nod to gender-fluid guests. "Pride is patriotism," Harris proclaimed in a speech as LGBTQ activists and drag queens partied late into the evening. But when support for LGBTQ Americans grew controversial, she quietly stepped back.

# DROPPING DYLAN MULVANEY

In March 2023, the vice president joined a number of corporate brands celebrating transgender activist and influencer Dylan Mulvaney's 365th day living as a woman, a journey that was chronicled on social media. "I am grateful for your dedication and courage, and I hope you continue to use your platform to spread positivity and create change," Harris wrote in a signed letter to Mulvaney. "I look forward to seeing all that you will accomplish in the future." The future got real controversial real fast.

Harris was not the only one celebrating Mulvaney's transition from male to female. Marketers for Anheuser-Busch's Bud Light beer gave the social media influencer a commemorative can celebrating the anniversary of the social media project. Mulvaney posted a video of the special can, which angered beer drinkers, who responded to the advertising push by boycotting the brand. Musician Kid Rock posted a video of himself shooting cases of Bud Light in protest, using his MP5 machine gun. "Fuck Bud Light, and fuck Anheuser-Busch," he concluded while flipping off the camera. Sales of Bud Light across the US cratered and it was dethroned as America's bestselling beer. Mulvaney complained afterward that Anheuser-Busch failed to stand by the marketing project. "For a company to hire a trans person and then not publicly stand by them is worse in my opinion than not hiring a trans person at all because it gives customers permission to be as transphobic and hateful as they want," Mulvaney said. Budweiser was not alone in trying to distance their brand from Mulvaney. Despite her earlier support, Harris remained silent as the Mulvaney faced ongoing backlash. The vice president and her team were more than willing to support Mulvaney when it appeared trendy to do so but ignored the activist when it turned controversial. In June 2023, Harris threw another LGBTQ party at the vice president's residence to celebrate Pride Month.

An invitation to the party could have been a perfect opportunity for the vice president to stand with Mulvaney amid the ongoing controversy, but the influencer was not there.

## POLICE REFORM STALLED

Harris also struggled to make an impact on the issue of police reform, despite the Biden campaign's significant emphasis on the issue during the summer of riots and protests in 2020. The issue was deadlocked in the Senate. A bipartisan effort to pass legislation collapsed in 2020 after Democrats insisted on lifting qualified immunity for police officers, protecting them from getting sued in civil courts. Even a more limited reform effort led by Republican senator Tim Scott of South Carolina collapsed in 2021 as Democrats walked away from months of bipartisan negotiations. Ultimately, Harris and Biden demanded the passage of the Democrat-led bill, the George Floyd Justice in Policing Act, and Democrats refused to compromise.

In February 2023, Kamala Harris attended a funeral for Tyre Nichols, a young man who died three days after he was beaten by members of the Memphis, Tennessee, police department. After Al Sharpton took the pulpit, he surprised the audience by inviting Harris to preach. It was a moment for Harris to make an impact on the grieving community, but she gave a scripted speech that also got sharply political by demanding the passage of the George Floyd Justice in Policing Act, She vowed to "speak truth," calling the bill "nonnegotiable." She concluded her five-minute speech by quoting "one of my favorite verses in scripture," Luke 1:79, "which tells us God will help us to shine a light 'upon those who sit in darkness and in the shadow of death, to guide our feet in the way of peace. . . .'"

Some in the black community were not impressed. *Daily Show* guest host and comic D. L. Hughley joked that it was "the very first time in history" that a vice president had attended the funeral of a black person slain by the police. "I'm very proud and I'm happy she's showing up in Black mode, not in cop mode, because. I mean, she was a district attorney and that could have been a sting operation," Hughley joked, referring to

Harris's background in law enforcement. "But seriously, there is a good reason to have a Black vice president," he added. "If you're not going to do anything about police reform, at least you can have somebody that goes to those funerals."[9]

## BASKETBALL DIPLOMACY

Harris struggled with bad political optics wherever she went, triggering more awkward moments. In March, Harris appeared with her husband, Doug Emhoff, at a basketball game in Iowa to watch Howard University play in the March Madness tournament against Kansas. The Associated Press, not a news outlet that typically exaggerates facts, reported that Harris was booed when she was shown on the video screen, drowning out any clapping and cheering that might have occurred. The game did not go much better. The University of Kansas Jayhawks team trounced the Bison with a score of 96–68, but Harris appeared in the locker room afterward to offer some words of encouragement. "You made all us Bison so, so proud," she said in a patronizing voice. "You keep playing with chin up and shoulders back, because you showed the world who Bison are. Right? I mean literally what you have done is in historic proportion," she added urgently, trying to improve the mood of the team. Typically, champion sports teams get a full White House welcome from the president of the United States as a reward for their hard-earned victory. Harris told the losing team that she would give them a White House tour, even though they lost the game. She earned polite applause from the team of athletes as she concluded her speech, but there appeared to be zero interest in her offer.

President Biden also used Harris to help him combat anger over his decision to free WNBA star Brittney Griner, who was detained in Russia after a marijuana vape pen was discovered in her luggage and was sentenced to nine years in prison. Many Americans were upset after Biden announced a deal with the Russians to swap Griner's freedom for notorious Russian warlord Viktor Bout, known as the "Merchant of Death" for spreading weapons, war, and destruction around the world. What made it worse was that Biden chose to deal for Griner and not former

U.S. Marine Paul Whelan, who had been languishing in Russian prison since 2018. When the athlete returned to the basketball court for a game, activists and supporters of the WNBA demanded more attention for her return. If the president had attended, it would have drawn unprecedented levels of attention and a firm commitment to standing by his decision. Instead, the West Wing sent Harris. During her remarks to the team, Harris claimed that world leaders would often speak to her about the WNBA. "It makes me so proud as vice president of the United States to go around the world talking to folks about a variety of issues, and one of the subjects that does come up is the WNBA. [The world] is watching what you guys are doing, lifting up the excellence of the finest athletes in the world," she said. The few WNBA fans in the United States may have appreciated the patronizing remarks but it was hardly the truth. Her inspirational speech did not lead the team to victory either. Griner's team lost to the Los Angeles Sparks by 23 points.

# ABORTION CRUSADER

The first two years were tough for Harris as she struggled through a series of mistakes and awkward moments on a host of issues. If she ever had a positive streak, it was when nobody noticed anything she was doing and failed to make any headlines. The mainstream media narrative on Harris is that she finally found her political stride on the issue of abortion in the summer of 2022. But the truth is more complicated, as Harris made a number of missteps in her early response to that issue and even angered activists ahead of an important election.

In May 2022, Democrats and abortion activists were stunned by a leaked draft of a Supreme Court decision to overturn *Roe v. Wade*. For decades, Republicans and pro-life activists had marched, prayed, and campaigned for the moment, to send decisions about abortion back to the states. For pro-choice advocates like EMILY's List, NARAL, and Planned Parenthood, it was a five-alarm fire. On the issue of abortion, President Joe Biden was an uncertain ally, hesitant to use the word in speeches and disinterested in making it a priority. Abortion rights activists turned instead to their superhero Kamala Harris. She delivered a speech that matched the fury of the movement. "How dare they!" Harris repeated in a May speech to the pro-abortion group EMILY's List after the leaked draft went public. "How dare they tell a woman what she can do and can not do with her own body! How dare they! How dare they try to stop her from determining her future!" The room cheered.

The final ruling, *Dobbs v. Jackson Women's Health Organization*, was passed down by the Supreme Court in June, triggering pro-abortion activists across the country. The Biden administration appeared to be caught flat-footed and Harris made some early blunders that angered supporters. In an interview with CNN's Dana Bash, Harris expressed her shock about a ruling she knew had been coming for months. "I was shocked. You know it's one thing when you know something happens it's another thing when it actually happens," she said. "I couldn't believe it. Because they actually did it." Bash asked Harris why Democrats had failed to act on the issue despite having control of the White House and majorities in both the House and the Senate.

"Do what now? What now?" Harris asked. "I mean we need, listen, what we did, we extended the child tax credit for first year. . . ." Viewers were surprised that Harris seemed to have forgotten the topic of the interview. But they were even more discouraged when they realized that she did not have any action items lined up. When Bash asked Harris about whether the administration would consider making abortions available on federal land, she responded with a word salad. "I think that is what is most important right now is that we ensure that the restrictions that the states are trying to put up that would prohibit a woman from exercising, what we still maintain is her right, that we do everything we can to empower women to not only seek but to receive the care where it is available," she said. When Bash asked for specific answers to pro-abortion activists' concerns, Harris pointed to the upcoming midterm elections as the solution. The meandering interview confirmed to abortion activists that the administration had no plans for a legislative response to an issue they knew was coming for months. Instead, Harris tried to empathize with everyone's struggle. "I thought about it as a parent, we have two children who are in their twenties, I thought about it as a godparent of teenagers, I thought about it as an aunt of preschool children . . . and a woman myself, and the daughter of a woman, the granddaughter of a woman," she said. The Biden administration's preferred response was a double dose of identity politics.

During one speech on the issue of abortion, Harris cited the Declaration of Independence to defend the "unalienable Rights" enshrined in the documents. "A promise we made in the Declaration of Independence that we are each endowed with the right to liberty and the pursuit of happiness," she cried, leaving out the third specific right to "life" mentioned in the document. Pro-life activists could not believe their ears. Harris was convinced there was no middle ground or compromise on the issue of abortion. She even tried to convince Americans opposing abortion on moral grounds that there was actually a strong faith-based argument to support it. "I say this: One does not have to abandon their faith or their beliefs to agree that the government should not be making that decision for her. It's literally that basic," she said about the right for a woman to choose an abortion. It was an insulting assertion to make to pro-life activists who believe that abortion is murder.

Harris also inexplicably compared what she believed was the Supreme Court's ruling against a constitutional right to abortion to America's history of slavery, during a speech to the National Association for the Advancement of Colored People in July. "We know, NAACP, that our country has a history of claiming ownership over human bodies. Today, extremist so-called leaders are criminalizing doctors and punishing women from making health care decisions for themselves," she said. At the White House, even press secretary Karine Jean-Pierre was unsure of mounting a defense of Harris's radical statement. "I need to actually see exactly what was said and in what complete context, that's what I need to do as a spokesperson for the administration," she told reporters.

Harris also insisted the issue of abortion was "settled" even though Democrats failed to get a bill passed making it into federal law. In May, the Democrat-led Senate pushed forward a bill expanding abortion rights that was so expansive, even pro-choice Republicans did not support it. Democratic senator Joe Manchin joined with Republicans in voting against it, ensuring it was not even close to meeting the sixty-vote threshold to avoid a filibuster. It failed to pass. In July, Harris was caught off guard during an interview with CBS News reporter Robert Costa when he asked why Democrats in Congress had not codified *Roe v. Wade* into federal law. "I think that, to be very honest with you, I do believe that we should have rightly believed, but we certainly believe that certain issues are just settled. Certain issues are just settled," Harris responded.

"Clearly we're not," Costa replied.

"No, that's right," Harris said. "And that's why I do believe that we are living, sadly, in real unsettled times." The Senate did not revisit their attempt to enshrine the right to abortion into federal law, even after Democrats maintained their Senate majority in the midterms. Harris had failed to build momentum on the issue. The cynical message to voters was asking them to elect more Democrats so that something could be done.

A year later, Harris delivered a speech in North Carolina marking the first-year anniversary of the *Dobbs* decision, but the message had not changed. She blamed Congress. "The United States Congress must pass legislation to restore the protections of *Roe v. Wade*, and when they do, President Joe Biden will sign it," she cried. Harris delivered her same message from a year ago: go out to the polls and elect more Democrats. *The View*'s Joy Behar was not impressed, noting that for decades Democrats failed to codify abortion rights into federal law. "What makes her think this is going to happen now?" she scoffed in response to Harris. Ultimately, however, the pro-abortion lobby appreciated Harris for vocally siding with them—no nuance on the issue, no limits on abortion, no concessions to the pro-life argument.

# LOADED PORTFOLIO

Harris struggled to make progress on several issues on her plate, but that did not stop her from pursuing new opportunities. Nothing seemed too big for her portfolio, as she volunteered for new roles in the administration, while leaving failed projects in the dust. In her short time as vice president, Harris had either volunteered or had been assigned to lead on immigration, "disinformation," abortion rights, broadband access, black maternal mortality, racial inequality, women in the workforce, infrastructure, voting rights, artificial intelligence, and the Space Council.

"I've always multitasked and certainly there's a lot to get done. Maybe I don't say 'no' enough," she said with a laugh in a BET interview with Soledad O'Brien, when asked how she got it all done. The American public, however, failed to see that she got anything done.

# CHAPTER FOURTEEN

# STRUGGLING RELATIONSHIPS

*She's making me look good.*

—JOE BIDEN ON KAMALA HARRIS, OCTOBER 28, 2022

Joe Biden had substantial legislative successes in his first two years as president, passing trillions in spending on coronavirus recovery, infrastructure, and green energy in an evenly divided split Senate. These legislative successes were widely considered to be separate from his vice president's efforts, although Biden always tried to give her some credit. But as Biden patiently wore down thorns in his side like Senators Joe Manchin and Kyrsten Sinema, it became more apparent that Biden was succeeding despite Harris, not because of her. The White House noticeably spent less time defending Harris as time went on. The personal relationship between Harris and Biden was not only stagnant but wearing thin, despite the president's initial promise to have lunch with her every week. By April 2022, the president's and vice president's public schedules only showed two lunches in four months of that year. White House aides insisted the president and vice president didn't have to have lunch every week to remain in "constant touch" with each other. It was a far cry from the warm relationship that Biden promoted in the beginning.

Democrats began talking publicly about replacing Harris on the 2024 ticket. Liberal comedian Bill Maher was not joking when he criticized Harris during an October 2022 panel discussion about the upcoming election. "What I could see is replacing the vice president," he said, eliciting enthusiastic applause from his studio audience. "Because she's not very popular anywhere. And it didn't seem to work out." "I just think she's a bad politician," he continued. "I think she's a very bright person. But I can see them doing that because a lot of the problem with Biden being old is, 'Oh, if he dies then, you know, you're gonna get this person.'"

In public, Biden referred to Harris in glowing terms, but in private, he had his own doubts. "She's making me look good," Biden said during a Pennsylvania Democratic Party reception just days before the 2022 midterm elections, prompting laughter from the audience. "And God love her. She's more like my buddy and my sister, but I trust her with my life. I trust her completely." Behind the scenes, Biden admitted frustrations with his vice president, who he believed was struggling in the job. She was not stepping up to the plate and appeared too cautious about her political future. Harris herself was telling people close to her that she felt constrained in the job.[1] The president was displeased by the details surrounding Harris's dissatisfaction, but he kept trying. In one reported conversation, Biden described her as a "work in progress."[2] The events of the first two years proved Harris was not ready to be a number two, let alone a number one. She was too interested in her own political career to think about Biden and was overly cautious about getting dragged down by his failures. The West Wing gradually accepted that Harris would not offer much assistance and let her figure it out herself. A former administration official told me that Biden was essentially trapped. "Her success and her failures is a reflection on him," the official said, noting that "the political consequences would be far worse" if she was replaced. Other aides agreed. "You cannot replace your first Black woman vice president and think that Black people and women are going to just vote for you," a former White House official said to Reuters. "He needs her."[3]

# KAMALA AND JILL

In May 2021, the story of Jill Biden's expletive-laden reaction to then-candidate Harris's 2019 debate attack on Biden on the issue of civil rights emerged in public for the first time. When asked about the report, the First Lady's spokesperson, Michael LaRosa, issued a famous nondenial statement. "Many books will be written on the 2020 campaign, with countless retellings of events—some accurate, some inaccurate," he said. "The First Lady and her team do not plan to comment on any of them." The story was a hot one. The *Daily Mail*'s Emily Goodin asked the First Lady about it during an event she held with Dr. Anthony Fauci to promote coronavirus vaccines. She did not deny it either. "That was two years ago. We've moved on from that," Biden said cryptically. Other reports fleshed out Jill Biden's dissatisfaction about her husband selecting Harris as his running mate, part of the reason he spent so much time considering other black women to add to the ticket. But when Harris was the choice, Jill Biden dutifully welcomed Harris and Emhoff to her home, offering them homemade chocolate chip cookies.

Tensions between Kamala Harris and Jill Biden emerged, despite their outward attempt to appear united behind the president. As the war in Ukraine continued, Western leaders flocked to the area to demonstrate their support for the war effort and President Volodymyr Zelensky. The First Lady's team began planning a trip to Poland that would align with her spring break from her job teaching at the local community college. But Harris stepped in with her own planned trip to Poland in the spring, clearly trying to emphasize the impact of her own foreign policy presence. That scuttled the first lady's plans, but she was not about to play second fiddle to Harris. In May, the first lady surprised the world by making an unannounced trip to Ukraine itself and meeting personally with Ukrainian First Lady Olena Zelenska on Mother's Day.

Zelenska praised Jill Biden for her "very courageous act" in visiting and thanked her for her support. Harris may have upstaged Jill Biden, but the First Lady outshone her months later.

In public, the First Lady's relationship with Harris was cordial, but the pair did not spend time together outside of official events. Even the public relationship was still awkward, however, as both Jill and Joe Biden mistakenly referred Harris as "the president" on multiple occasions. Joe Biden even accidentally referred to Harris as the "First Lady," at one event, sparking laughter from the audience. Despite her love of cooking, Harris has yet to host the Bidens at her home for dinner.

"We have a plan to do it, but we have to get a date," Harris told the *Atlantic* in October 2023. "But he and I have a plan, we have a plan to do it. And yeah, no, we actually have a plan to do it." The Bidens have not welcomed Harris and her husband to the White House for a personal dinner either.

## "DOUGIE" THE SECOND GENTLEMAN

In public, the nation's first second gentleman, Doug Emhoff, or "Dougie" as Harris affectionately calls him, appears gregarious and easygoing—a supportive husband to his wife's political career. "My main job is to be a loving husband and to support her," he said during an interview with Symone Sanders in March 2023 for an SXSW conference panel. When asked what he wanted his legacy to be, Emhoff replied easily, "More Kamala Harrises." Emhoff admitted struggling with how his wife is talked about in public, recalling a conversation he had with President Barack Obama about the difficulties of being a spouse in the public eye. "He literally said, 'Hey man, don't read the tweets, don't read the comments,'" Emhoff recalled. He admitted that he initially did not listen to the former president's advice, but after getting a taste of the nasty comments about his wife, he did stop reading. Behind the scenes, however, Emhoff was a bit more vocal about how his wife was being treated. Reports emerged that Harris's husband Doug complained of the West Wing's handling of her political portfolio and was also quietly telling Democrats that the party should rally around Harris if Biden decided against running in 2024.[4]

The comments annoyed Biden and his team, one more sign of the lack of loyalty from the vice president's family. When Harris was inaugurated, Emhoff had left his law firm, DLA Piper, which had a Washington lobbying branch, and kicked off his position as Second Gentleman. In public, Emhoff was dubbed by political observers as "the happiest man in Washington" as he willingly participated in political events with a cheesy smile and an eager demeanor. Emhoff also easily slipped into Washington academia. Before Harris even took office, Georgetown University announced that Emhoff would join the law school to teach classes on entertainment law disputes and become a distinguished fellow at the Institute for Technology Law and Policy. Life was good for Emhoff, and he looked like he was feeling guilty. In an interview with MSNBC's Jonathan Capehart, he specifically criticized men as one of the biggest problems. "There's too much of toxicity—masculine toxicity out there, and we've kind of confused what it means to be a man, what it means to be masculine," he said. "You've got this trope out there where you have to be tough, and angry, and lash out to be strong." The message was clear: blame "toxic masculinity" for the vice president's problems and promise to use your platform to combat it.

While Harris and Jill Biden's relationship remained frosty, the First Lady's relationship with Harris's husband only improved. The pair were already close during the campaign, having in common the role of supportive spouse. "Doug and Jill already were buddies, for real," Joe Biden told *People* magazine in a 2020 interview.[5] In Las Vegas, Jill Biden and Emhoff teamed up for a gay pride parade on the campaign trail and were frequently spotted sitting together during debates laughing and talking. When Harris dropped out of the race, a source told me that Jill Biden called Doug to sympathize with her fellow political spouse, despite the resentment she harbored against Harris. The pair also sparked headlines after they both kissed on the lips on camera prior to President Biden's State of the Union address in March 2023. Video of the kiss went viral online, making it just newsworthy enough to prompt Univision reporter Edwin Pitti to ask Harris about the moment during a Spanish-language interview. "What is your reaction to the video, which many say they have to gossip about?" he asked in a translation of the question. Harris appeared dumbfounded, but swiftly dodged the question. "No, I haven't watched the video," she replied, before pivoting to another topic. The awkward public moment did not disrupt the friendly relationship between Doug and Jill. In May 2023, Biden and Emhoff were spotted at the same place during a themed Harry Stiles–versus-Lizzo workout session in Georgetown.[6]

# PETE'S PROGRESS

As Harris continued struggling, one member of the administration was continuing to enjoy relatively positive feedback from the Washington elites. Biden had ultimately plucked Senator Kamala Harris out of the pile of discarded Democratic presidential candidates to serve as his running mate, but he chose Pete Buttigieg to join his cabinet as secretary the Department of Transportation. Buttigieg and his husband, Chasten, drew fawning coverage in the press after arriving in Washington, DC, as the former presidential candidate impressed the city with his "cognitive powers" and "cathedral mind," as chronicled in *Wired* magazine.[7]

While Harris continued to suffer withering criticism, Buttigieg's future appeared bright, as he took several weeks of paternity leave to welcome new baby twins into his home. Team Harris appeared jealous of Buttigieg's success, as the vice president's office noticed that the West Wing was more willing to defend Buttigieg than they were the vice president. The speculation even took a racial turn. "It's hard to miss the specific energy that the White House brings to defend a White man, knowing that Kamala Harris has spent almost a year taking a lot of the hits that the West Wing didn't want to take themselves," a former Harris aide told reporters. Rumors began buzzing of a political rivalry between the two—as Washington, DC, chattered about which one of them actually had a political future.

Buttigieg tried to tamp down the rumors. "There's no room to get caught up in the parlor games, and I'm proud to be part of the Biden-Harris team," he said to NBC for a story about the tensions between the two Biden officials. Buttigieg repeated that the only job he was focused on was his job as secretary of transportation.[8] It was the perfect thing to say for someone considering a future run for office. Amid the controversy, Harris invited Buttigieg to travel to an infrastructure event with her in Charlotte, North Carolina, in December 2022. The pair exchanged niceties during the trip, as Buttigieg lavished unwarranted praise on Harris. "It's my honor to be here today with somebody who did so much to make this infrastructure law possible, and that's Vice President Harris," Buttigieg said during his speech. If his goal was to kill with kindness, he was succeeding.

# GAVIN NEWSOM FLEXES

As Biden and Harris labored through their first two years, an old character from Harris's past emerged to test the political environment: California governor Gavin Newsom. Newsom and Kamala Harris came up into California politics together, both part of the Willie Brown political machine, both suspiciously watching each other's political ambitions and carefully choosing their battles. When both politicians were eyeing a potential run for governor, Harris chose to run for the Senate, after Barbara Boxer's retirement opened up a spot. When asked if she had ever thought about facing Newsom in the governor's race, Harris replied, "I would have won—wasn't it obvious?" and burst into laughter. It was actually not so obvious. As governor, Newsom smashed the attempt to recall him as in 2021 after his draconian coronavirus policies and easily won reelection in 2022, which led him to test his appeal on the national stage. In June 2022, Newsom challenged Democrats for failing to defend their positions more aggressively on issues like immigration and abortion. "Where the hell is my party? Where's the Democratic Party?" he asked. "Why aren't we calling this out? This is a concerted, coordinated effort. And, yes, they're winning." It was not lost on grassroots activists that Newsom voiced his criticism about his party just as Harris was leading the administration's lackluster response to the abortion fight.

Newsom also started picking fights with Republican governors. He bought ads in Florida over the Fourth of July weekend in 2022, attacking Republicans like Florida governor Ron DeSantis for restricting abortion. Newsom's attack on a popular Republican governor who was preparing a presidential run sparked interest from Democrats, who were still unsure whether Biden would run. Newsom enjoyed taunting DeSantis and repeatedly challenged him to a debate. The path to a Newsom run for president was clear. If Democrats lost big in the midterms, Biden's brand would be mired in failure and Harris would be tied to it. Biden's team was very sensitive to Newsom's rising profile, and they were not happy about him boosting his political prospects when Biden had already said he intended to run for reelection. Team Harris was livid.

After Democrats survived the midterm elections with minimal losses, Newsom reassured Harris and Biden that he would stand down. He also endorsed Biden for reelection. "He not only beat Trump once, I think he can beat him again," Newsom said after visiting with Biden's team. "I hope he runs, I'll enthusiastically support him."[9] The California governor reassured the president by piling on the flattery. At a California fundraiser in June 2023, Newsom offered Biden the highest praise for his legislative accomplishments. "I am here, Mr. President, as a proud American, as a proud Californian, mesmerized by not just your faith and devotion to this country, and the world we're trying to build, but by your results, by your action, by your passion, by your capacity to deliver," he gushed. Newsom was doing a better job defending Biden than his vice president was. His ongoing political presence intrigued Democrat donors looking for another choice for 2024. Harris allies were offended, describing Newsom's political activity as "disrespectful" to the vice president. Once again, Newsom's and Harris's political ambitions appeared close to an ugly collision, but this time on the national stage.

Democrat donors kept asking but Newsom finally put the idea of a 2024 campaign to rest, telling his cheerleaders in a *Meet the Press* interview in September that it was "time to move on" and support Biden. Newsom also suggested that Harris would be considered Biden's successor in 2024 if the president was unable to run. "I think the vice president is naturally the one lined up and the filing deadlines are quickly coming to pass," he said, neatly tying Harris to the lackluster Biden administration. When host Chuck Todd asked him if he could imagine running against Harris, he denied it. "Of course not. By definition. Won't happen," he said. Newsom had sufficiently ruled out 2024, but he never revealed what his plans were for 2028.

On September 29, 2023, California Senator Dianne Feinstein died in office at the age of ninety, requiring Newsom to select her successor. Newsom had previously promised he would select a black woman to fill Feinstein's seat until the 2024 election, but he surprised Californians when he selected one of Harris's biggest political allies, Laphonza Butler, the president of the pro-choice political action committee EMILY's List, to fill the seat. Choosing Butler, a black lesbian and national pro-choice activist (currently living in Maryland), demonstrated that Newsom was still pursuing a national brand.

The political energy that continued to boost Buttigieg and Newsom illustrates just how far Harris had fallen with the Democratic Party elites in Washington, DC, over her and Biden's first years in office. Why would they so easily abandon their first black woman vice president? With the growth of social media and the internet, the most important political currency is authenticity. In her first few years as vice president, Harris was revealed to the world as an ambitious, calculating, and demanding political figure. That kind of personality can thrive if one has the competence and charism to cover up the arrogance. The glowing magazine covers, softball interviews, and scripted events no longer have the same strength to prop up a politician, when short clips of authentically awkward or embarrassing moments go viral. Harris also lacked an easy villain to boost her superhero aspirations. When she was a senator, she was fighting tooth and nail against the Trump administration as politically enraged out-of-power Democrats cheered her on. When you are vice president, you are in the executive branch because you beat the other people who wanted the job and you must prove every day that you deserve the position. It was not long after the inauguration before Harris demonstrated she lacked full commitment to Team Biden. Kamala is for Kamala, but the executive branch demands more.

# YEAR THREE: REBOOTING THE REBOOT

In her third year as vice president, Harris and her staff tried to shore up their defenses and prepare for the upcoming presidential campaign, but first Biden had to make a decision about whether he would run for reelection. Donald Trump formally announced his campaign for a second presidential term on November 15, 2022, from his home at Mar-a-Lago in Palm Beach, Florida. The former president was setting up a rematch against Biden, even though Biden had not officially announced his decision to run for reelection. Biden had said for months that he intended to run, but he remained famously noncommittal about officially announcing his campaign. Democrats had no delusions about Harris's own presidential ambitions, the only question was whether she would remain on the ticket in 2024. Biden had already committed to running with Harris in early 2022. "Yes, and yes," he replied in January 2022 when asked by reporters if he was satisfied with Harris's work on voting rights and whether he would commit to keeping her as his running mate. "She's going to be my running mate, number one. And number two, I did put her in charge. I think she's doing a good job," he said. But Democrats knew that Harris's failure to launch and Trump's commitment to run again meant that they would have to rely on Biden in 2024, even as the president was not anxious to announce his official reelection campaign.

As 2023 approached, Biden told reporters he would make a final decision about running for reelection over the Thanksgiving and Christmas holiday. But he continued dragging his feet on "Biden time" and stalling the official announcement. As the weeks went by, Democrats wondered why Biden was taking so long and began looking at other candidates. Democratic governors J. B. Pritzker of Illinois, Gavin Newsom of California, Roy Cooper of North Carolina, and Phil Murphy of New Jersey all made the lists of potential presidential candidates *if* Biden turned down a bid for reelection. Few asked why Harris was not at the top of the list, or even on the list at all.

In January 2023, Harris tried to shake things up again. As she gathered with her staff after the Christmas break, the vice president asked each of them to share their word for the new year. Harris volunteered that her word for new year would be *momentum* as she spoke about her goal to break out of Washington, DC, more frequently and help promote Biden's agenda.[10] Harris had a good reason to reassess her priorities. An NBC poll in January 2023 showed her with only a 35 percent positive rating.[11]

There were still questions about whether her position on the presidential ticket was secure. Harris was confronted by her unpopularity during an interview with NBC News anchor Andrea Mitchell in February 2023. "Dozens of Democratic leaders are saying that they not only don't think that he's the strongest candidate, you know, considering the larger field that could be possible given his age and other defects, but they don't think that you're the right person to be on the ticket. Why do you think that is?" Mitchell asked. Harris dismissed the question. "I think that it is very important to focus on the needs of the American people and not political chatter out of Washington, DC," she said. Mitchell was not alone. The political chatter only grew as the visibly aged Biden faced another run for president. Senator Elizabeth Warren sparked controversy after she declined during a radio interview to endorse Harris as the president's running mate in 2024. "I really want to defer to what makes Biden comfortable on his team," she said.[12] Warren's reluctance to endorse Harris was not surprising, as she had campaigned vigorously to be Biden's running mate in 2020, but her willingness to question Harris's political future on the ticket spoke volumes. Even Hillary Clinton viewed Harris as a disappointment and certainly not the future of the party. "Two Democrats recalled private conversations in which former Secretary of State Hillary Clinton lamented that Ms. Harris could not win because she does not have the political instincts to clear a primary field," the *New York Times* reported.[13] How humiliating for Harris to have Hillary Clinton, the loser of the 2016 presidential election, cast doubt on the future of her political career.

The 2024 parlor games were cut short when finally, on April 25, President Joe Biden's staff released a video on social media officially announcing his decision to run for reelection. Campaign staff quietly recorded video footage of the eighty-year-old president at his home in Delaware in April explaining why he would again run to stop former president Donald Trump and save the "soul of America." The campaign video flashed through multiple photos and moments of Biden but also included over a dozen images with Vice President Kamala Harris. "Let's finish the job," he concluded, asking voters to donate online to his campaign. Biden's promise to be a bridge for a new generation of Democrats appeared long forgotten as Harris failed to cross it. The party's future would again have to rely on its ancient infrastructure to compete with a resurgent Trump.

It was time for another reboot. "Biden Looks to Elevate Harris' Work as Core to Re-Election Bid" was the headline of an April 27, 2023, NBC News article on Kamala Harris, discussing the "growing view among White House aides" that they needed more attention on Harris in reaction to low polling numbers.[14] Other reports noted that the White House was finally working to assist Harris, who was struggling to dig out of a political hole. A June NBC News poll showed Kamala Harris with only a 32 percent positive approval rating and 49 percent negative, including 39 percent who had a "very negative" view of the vice president. The net negative approval rating of minus 17 was the lowest in the history of the poll—even lower than Vice President Dick Cheney. Harris's ratings were worse than they were in January. Aides struggled with the grim reality that was setting in. Harris was again asked about her low approval ratings in a July 31 interview with ABC News anchor Linsey Davis, who noted she had the lowest approval ratings of any vice president. "Well, there are polls that also say I have great approval ratings!" Harris replied. That was wrong. Harris had not earned polling numbers with a net positive approval rating since October 2021. But White House chief of staff Jeff Zients suggested they keep getting Harris out in public more. "We just need to make sure that we do a good job of exposing," he explained.[15] It was not working.

There were never any reports of Team Biden having serious discussions about replacing Harris on the ticket, since Biden would never allow it. He had been deeply upset in 2011 when reports emerged of President Obama's political team quietly polling and running focus groups about the idea of replacing him with Hillary Clinton on the 2012 ticket. For Team Biden, however, replacing Harris would be a useless exercise. Biden's choice of Harris as his running mate was one of the most pandering decisions of any vice presidential pick in modern history, based almost entirely on her identity. At the time, Democrats were desperate to thrill black women and he needed their help push him across the finish line. To walk back that decision would instantly anger the black activists and voters he had tried to appease during the 2020 election. There was no way that Biden could drop out of the race and endorse Harris either. Early polls showed her getting crushed in a general election match-up with Trump. A February 2023 poll showed that 49 percent of respondents would vote for Trump in a hypothetical 2024 match-up and 39 percent would vote for Harris, a ten-point gap.[16]

Despite their dismal approval ratings, Biden and Harris would have to work together to win reelection. In an interview with MSNBC in May, Biden insisted that Harris was doing great. "She is really very, very good," he said. "With everything going on, she hasn't gotten the attention that she deserves." Perhaps she was not getting as much attention because she was still without a communications director. Her office reportedly pitched that position to veteran Democratic strategist Jennifer Palmieri, but ultimately she did not accept.[17]

Republican candidates for president continued weaponizing Biden's age and Harris's unpopularity on the campaign trail. "This uncertainty about Biden's mental competence means Americans must consider the *actual* competency of the vice president. Kamala Harris is one of the most incompetent elected officials in the country," former South Carolina governor and United Nations ambassador Nikki Haley wrote in an op-ed.[18] Haley only increased her attacks on Harris after Biden tripped over a sandbag onstage after delivering a commencement address at the US Air Force Academy in June and fell sprawling. "We are running against Kamala Harris. Make no bones about it. . . . Every liberal knows it. They know that it's Kamala Harris that's going to end up being president of the United States if Joe Biden wins this election," Haley warned in an interview with Fox News in June.[19] In August, Haley said the prospect of Harris as president "should send a chill up every American spine."[20]

Other Republicans agreed. "In a very real sense, this election, the Democrats are saying, 'Kamala Harris for president' . . . there's a very real possibility that Kamala Harris becomes the president," Senator Ted Cruz said in a May interview on Fox News. "Can you imagine Kamala sitting across from Putin? Can you imagine Kamala Harris sitting across from Xi [Jinping] . . . just cackling ineffectively and weirdly and creepily?" Other political figures, such as former representative Tulsi Gabbard, were more explicit. "The DNC's strategy to ensure the Democrat establishment remains in power is to reelect Joe Biden, no matter how old or capable he is, and then get him to resign or step aside and install Kamala Harris as president," Gabbard said. Left-wing journalist Jemele Hill, now working with the *Atlantic*, rushed to defend Harris, accusing Haley, the daughter of Indian immigrants, of being racist. "So part of the reason racism is such a terrible sickness in this country is because politicians like this know they can rally a certain base with the fear of OH MY GOD A BLACK WOMAN MIGHT BE PRESIDENT IF YOU DON'T VOTE FOR ME," Hill wrote on social media. Haley, however, defended her claim. "This has nothing to do with Kamala's gender or Kamala's race," she said. "This has everything to do with Kamala's incompetence. . . . Everything she's ever been given, she has failed at. That's not an opinion, that's a fact."

The growing attacks made the Harris team more uneasy as they faced another campaign season. Team Harris continued harboring resentment against the West Wing for not doing enough to defend her. They called on a familiar ally for help. In June 2023, EMILY's List announced they would spend "tens of millions of dollars" to promote and defend Harris, an unusual arrangement for a sitting vice president. For years the organization had been supportive of Harris, which was no accident, as the president of EMILY's List, Laphonza Butler, was a former senior advisor for Harris's doomed presidential campaign. Butler voiced a familiar complaint. The problem was not Harris, she insisted, but rather "the massive misinformation and disinformation that's been directed towards her since she's been elected."[21] In year three, Harris and her team were still using the same old excuses.

The mistakes kept happening. Harris flew to Iowa in July 2023 to criticize a statewide six-week abortion ban but stumbled while describing the economy under Biden. "Most Americans are a four-hundred-dollar unexpected expense away from bankruptcy," she said. The comment was incorrect. While surveys showed that many Americans living paycheck to paycheck could not cover an unexpected four-hundred-dollar expense without going into debt, they were not facing the drastic step of declaring bankruptcy. The comment, while wrong, also hurt the administration's attempt to sell "Bidenomics" as a radical success in the country.

Despite a more stabilized office, some staffers still headed for the exits, even as the campaign season was approaching. At the end of August 2023, Harris's chief economic advisor, Deanne Millison, and policy advisor Michael George announced their decisions to leave.

As Biden kept making more and more errors, polling revealed growing concerns about his age. The question now on everyone's mind: Was Harris ready to take over the job? Harris pointedly told voters in multiple interviews she was ready. In a September interview, CBS News anchor Margaret Brennan asked her about polls showing that two-thirds of Democrats believed Biden was too old to run for president again. "Are you prepared to be commander in chief?" Brennan asked.

"Yes, I am, if necessary," Harris replied. "But Joe Biden is going to be fine," she added.

To lighten up the mood, Harris hosted a dance party at the vice president's residence to honor the fiftieth anniversary of hip-hop. Video of the vice president dancing to "Vivrant Thing" by Q-Tip while wearing high-waisted pink pants and a nineties floral print shirt emerged on social media. Her fans cheered her willingness to get down with the beat, but her critics derided her awkward dancing as "granny moves."

## ALARM BELLS

Although Harris was confident in her ability to serve as president, prominent Democrats and journalists were having second thoughts. *Washington Post* columnist David Ignatius urged Biden not to run for reelection, or to at least choose a different running mate. He suggested Los Angeles mayor Karen Bass or commerce secretary Gina Raimondo. Liberal journalist Josh Barro wrote that it was time for Biden to replace Harris with Michigan governor Gretchen Whitmer. *New York* magazine's Eric Levitz agreed on replacing Harris with Whitmer, adding that Senator Raphael Warnock, Senator Tammy Duckworth, and Representative Lauren Underwood would also make good replacements.[22] There was something about Harris that continued to nag prominent Democrats.

The conversation continued to worm through DC social circles, prompting CNN's Anderson Cooper to question former House Speaker Nancy Pelosi on the matter in September.

"Is Vice President Kamala Harris the best running mate for this president?" Cooper asked.

Pelosi dodged.

"He thinks so and that's what matters," she replied.

Cooper repeated his question two more times.

Pelosi dodged again, speaking in circles about the Harris political instincts and the role of the vice president without answering the question. "I think she's represented our country very well at home and abroad," she finally concluded. It was jaw-dropping. The most powerful female politician in the history of American politics was unwilling to endorse Harris on Biden's reelection ticket. It was hardly the headline that Harris wanted as she prepared to hit the campaign trail in earnest.

## BACK TO COLLEGE

In September, the Biden campaign sent Harris on a "Fight for Our Freedoms" tour to several friendly college campuses across the country, where she could play her greatest hits on gun control, abortion, climate change, voting rights, equity, and environmental justice. Although Harris was on the record describing college students and young people as "stupid," she was now fawning over the youth as the paragons of leadership and inspiration. "When I meet with our young leaders, and they are all over, and I'm going to give a particular shout-out to the Gen-Z, they're brilliant!" Harris gushed during a conversation at the Congressional Hispanic Caucus Institute Leadership Conference.

During the tour, Harris repeatedly drew on a curious analogy about frogs to make her point about Republicans. During a discussion with journalist Gia Peppers and former White House official Cedric Richmond in Atlanta, Harris asked, "You know the story about the two frogs and two pots of water?" As the moderators stared blankly at her in response, she continued with a laugh: "OK, so here it goes. So. Two frogs and two pots of water. So, in one pot, the water's there and you slowly, you put the frog in the water and you slowly turn up the heat. And the frog will be hanging out like, 'Oh it's getting a little warm in here.' The next thing you know, that water is boiling, that frog perishes. The other pot of water, you first turn up the heat to boiling, then you drop the frog in it. That frog jumps out.

"Let's not be that first frog," Harris concluded.

The moderators nodded wordlessly as Peppers finally replied, "There it is."

Harris also raised the issue of "climate anxiety" with students. "Young people have told me about how they're really concerned whether they should have children, whether they should ever think about buying a home because it could be destroyed by flood or hurricane or wildfire," she said. When one somber student asked Harris where she found optimism during these dark times, Harris tried to step back. "To be clear-eyed about the challenges doesn't mean you gotta be depressed, it just means you gotta be clear-eyed, right? And know what's in front of you." It was a clumsy political exercise. Harris was trying to terrify students and inspire them at the same time.

# KAMALA'S MOMENT IN TIME: THE PATH TO MADAM PRESIDENT

*So I think it's very important, as you have heard from so many incredible leaders for us at every moment in time and certainly this one, to see the moment in time in which we exist and are present, and to be able to contextualize it, to understand where we exist in the history and in the moment as it relates not only to the past but the future.*

—KAMALA HARRIS, APRIL 25, 2023

It's a popular parlor game in Washington: How do you fix Kamala Harris? At this point, the story of the nation's first black woman vice president teeters between a tragedy and a comedy, but the conclusion of her political career is not yet written. It's no secret that Harris is "not politically agile" and is "overly cautious," as a former White House official explained to me. "She has to want to get better, she has to want to take risks. Risks that allow her to be who she is." But Harris remains protective about her privacy and very guarded in public. Vice President Kamala Harris is still in the same place despite multiple attempts at narrative resets and on-the-job training. Washington, DC, is cruel. Once you are found unworthy, there is little you can do to change people's minds. In my time spent reporting for this book, I was surprised to learn how few Democrats even like Harris, let alone respect her—unless they are personally invested in her success. Mistakes compounded on mistakes only cemented her reputation and there is little room for sympathy when you reach that level of power. There's plenty of negative chatter behind the scenes, but few dare speak publicly, for fear of being branded a racist or a sexist.

After winning the presidential nomination, Biden famously promised to select a vice president who was "ready to be president on day one" but that is not Harris. Even Harris's biggest political allies concede that she got off to a bad start. "Everybody gets a learning curve in this business," Representative Jim Clyburn admitted during an interview with CNN's Abby Phillip on September 13. "You aren't born a United States congressman. You aren't born a vice president. You've got to learn the job."[1] Clyburn is understandably ready to give Harris a pass, but on-the-job training for four years is not part of the job description for vice president.

What happened? In California, Kamala Harris was a star, the friend of celebrities, the financial beneficiary of hotshot tech moguls, and the subject of glowing media profiles. She made winning look easy. Political titans of California unleashed devastating attacks on her political rivals on her behalf, while she breezily shrugged off moments of controversy. She was politically timid but calculating, and her patience paid off as she swiftly climbed the Golden State's ladder of political power.

As a senator, Harris failed to make meaningful achievements in Congress but generated enough heat to thrill activists and media personalities to believe she could be a formidable political foil against President Donald Trump and the entire MAGA movement. Then she threw caution to the wind by running for president, and her hat into the ring, only to have it thrown right back in her face. Democratic voters in the early voting states of Iowa, New Hampshire, and South Carolina were not impressed. Harris appeared undisciplined with her campaign message, uncertain in interviews, and unable to think quickly on her feet in debates. Her campaign narrative kicked off strong, but faded as she and her political team repeatedly went back to the drawing board and rebooted the campaign. Different messages, slogans and ad campaigns failed to inspire voters, particularly from a candidate who frequently was forced to walk back and clarify her political positions and simply lacked charisma and authenticity. "The laugh" that Harris frequently deployed to smooth over rough patches and awkward moments failed to reassure the skeptics.

As vice president, Harris and her team folded under the scrutiny that comes with the job, constantly working on rehabilitating and retooling her image after her failure to launch. Part of the problem was that Harris was more concerned about her own political future than Biden's success. Her attempt to carve out her own identity separate from Biden made her a subpar vice president. When that failed, Harris and her staff tried to reset the narrative. It seems like every few weeks, her allies tried to reboot her vice presidency, but at this point there are three clear major reboots on the record.

Vice President Kamala Harris 1.0 began as a historic first woman, first black vice president, a "true partner" of President Joe Biden who would be a loyal advocate. When it was clear the Biden circle was keeping her at arm's length while dumping politically precarious issues on her lap and she blundered through political minefields, she became more cautious and uncertain. That led her to stand up for herself and protect her political future. Biden's team found her unreliable and took a hands-off approach as they waited for her to find her footing and churn through staff.

The vice president's reshuffled leadership team debuted Kamala Harris 2.0 in 2022 after her devastating first year. The new version of Kamala would break free of Washington, DC, and go to the people to promote Biden's victories. But as she went out to the people more, the people were not impressed. More media interviews led to more awkward moments. More speeches and community roundtables meant more highlight reels of word salads and confusion.

Kamala 3.0 was revealed when Biden decided to run for reelection. The new Kamala Harris was unleashed as a partisan warrior who would attack Republicans on a host of social issues like gun control, abortion, voting rights, and racial justice. But she could not be part of Biden's reelection campaign without answering the ultimate question: Was she ready for the ultimate job when it was time to replace Biden?

By the beginning of the 2024 campaign season, Harris was certainly aware of how she is perceived by the public, going back to her first failed presidential campaign. She placed blame on the media, despite obvious signs that editors pulled many punches when describing her political narrative. Not all of the reasons for this are under her control. As Biden ages, and as his aging becomes a more consistent media narrative, Harris receives more scrutiny than a typical vice president. "He's so old that people see her as a natural successor," one former White House official explained, which raises alarm from Democrats who are convinced she is not ready. But Harris is reluctant to acknowledge failure and even more reluctant to apologize. She has no intention of changing either. If you have a problem, or you don't understand her, that's your problem. Harris seems to think she has told Americans who she is, and she expects that your opinion of her will change when you change, not the other way around. She revealed her thinking in an interview with *Politico*. "You could have followed me around in Iowa. You would have seen the same thing four years ago. It's always who I've been," she said. "So, I can't get into people's heads about why they characterize things as being one way or another. It's not as though I've just found myself. I've always been here and never went away."[2]

In October, Harris pushed back against criticism from her own party, speaking to a reporter for *New York Times Magazine* about Biden's choice to make her vice president. "He chose a Black woman. That woman is me. So I don't know that anything lingers about what he should choose. He has chosen," she said.[3] Speaking to the *Atlantic* for an October magazine profile, Harris unwittingly channeled the cartoon character Popeye to reassert her identity. "You know, I am who I am. I am who I am. And I think I'm a pretty open book, but I am who I am." Harris clearly believes in her staying power in the executive branch, despite widespread doubt. But at this point, she appears more comfortable waiting in the wings than trying to push forward.

It's easy to see why Harris thinks she can wait out the critics. After all, Vice President Joe Biden was once a laughingstock among the political class in Washington after losing two previous campaigns for president. Few Democratic leaders wanted him to run for president in 2020, but he did anyway and won. Part of Harris's calculus has to be: If Biden can do it, why not me?

If Harris ever decides to run for president again, Biden has given her a boost by successfully pushing the Democratic National Committee to re-structure their primary calendar so that South Carolina is the first state in the presidential primaries. The argument from Biden and his team is that black voters in the state deserve a bigger influence in selecting the ultimate presidential nominee. (He also owes them a debt after the state saved his presidential campaign.) The new calendar could conceivably jump-start Harris's presidential aspirations with an early primary win in the future. No longer will she have to spend her Thanksgivings in Iowa or winter months in New Hampshire. Instead she'll be just a short flight away from Washington, DC, anytime she feels like it. South Carolina Democrats are also more moderate, so she could steer away from the radical socialism favored by Democratic voters in early states like New Hampshire and Nevada and focus on her own post-Biden brand.

It will take more than an adjusted primary calendar, however, to get Kamala Harris to the finish line. Something has to change if she ever wants to get elected president, but Harris is either unwilling or unable to change. That comforts her political rivals, who believe she could never run and win a presidential campaign in the future. But maybe she does not need to. It could happen any day now.

# ACKNOWLEDGMENTS

The decision to write a book is immense, and I never believed I was ready to do it. A big thanks to my family for doing the believing for me. I am forever grateful to my wife, Becca, for the encouragement during the lows, the calming support during the nerve-racking lulls, and the joys of celebrating the highs. I'll never forget our long walk-and-talks and evening bourbon conversations before setting forth on this journey. Thank you to my parents, Kelly and Sylvia, for raising me and teaching me the values of work, family, and faith while preserving a Wyoming sanctuary from the political insanity. Thanks to my siblings, Jamie, Karen, Anthony, Peter, Roseanne, Sr. Molly, Katy, Marion, and Lucy for all their prayers, support, and long phone conversations. Thank you, Michael, for watching over us all. Thank you to my children—Caroline, Maximilian, Nora, Robert, Arthur, and Julia—for doing so much to care for each other. Your unconditional love and the joyful, chaotic interruptions in my day always remind me of my favorite job as your father. It was a good year for the Kings Dominion season passes. Thank you also to my friends and extended family, including Derek and Bethany Rogers, Marc and Veronica Perrington, the Old Dominion league, and particularly Christopher and Kathleen Smith for their encouragement and support.

I'm especially grateful for my mentors, who offered much-needed intellectual support. Thank you to my first and most influential political writing mentor, David Freddoso, who helped me envision this book and get started. An enormous thank-you to my "fairy godmother," Mollie Hemingway, who stepped in to offer me advice and encouragement at a difficult point in my career. This would not have happened without your kindness.

# ACKNOWLEDGMENTS

The idea for this book was not originally mine, but it was a lot of fun to write it. Thank you to Keith Urbahn of Javelin and Simon & Shuster's Natasha Simons for the inspiration. Thank you to Javelin's Matt Latimer and Dylan Colligan for helping make the proposal sing. Our first meeting with Natasha was one of the most rewarding of my writing career, and this first-time author is forever grateful for the assistance. I'm also grateful to Natasha and assistant editor Mia Robertson for helping me sort through the jumbled first drafts and giving me critical feedback. It was a real joy to work with you. Who knew how much fun writing a book could be? I also want to acknowledge copyeditor Tom Pitoniak for patiently correcting my multiple styling and syntax errors, and catching my propensity for mixed metaphors.

Working on this book made me immensely grateful and indebted to the talented group of journalists in San Francisco, Sacramento, and Los Angeles who chronicled the early political career of Kamala Harris. The magazine profiles, the investigative reporting, the dutiful day-to-day dispatches, even the gossip nuggets make all the difference when researching the history of a political figure. I also want to thank the campaign correspondents and citizen journalists on social media who put into the record the moments that politicians would rather delete from the Internet. It all matters.

Finally, all thanks to God, who showed me a new path and gave me the courage to walk down it. *Apud Deum omnia possibilia sunt.*

# NOTES

## CHAPTER ONE: THAT GIRL WAS ME

1. Chidanand Rajghatta, *Kamala Harris: Phenomenal Woman* (New York: HarperCollins, 2021), 61.

2. David Axelrod, "The Axe Files: 'Interview with Kamala Harris,'" CNN, March 9, 2017.

3. Ashley C. Ford, "Kamala Harris Is Officially Vice President of the United States," *Elle*, April 30, 2021, https://www.elle.com/culture/a34225242/kamala-harris-interview/.

4. Alex Haley, "Alex Haley Interviews Martin Luther King, Jr.," July 22, 2020, https://alex haley.com/2020/07/26/alex-haley-interviews-martin-luther-king-jr/.

5. Matt Sedensky, "For Harris, Memories of a Warrior Mother Guide Her Campaign," Associated Press, April 20, 2021, https://apnews.com/article/0b55116cc42c4a80b3a3 4b5080e98e40.

6. Ellen Barry, "How Kamala Harris's Immigrant Parents Found a Home, and Each Other, in a Black Study Group," *New York Times*, October 6, 2020, https://www.nytimes .com/2020/09/13/us/kamala-harris-parents.html.

7. "Bad Teaching," *Stanford Daily*, November 3, 1976, https://archives.stanforddaily.com /1976/11/03?page=4§ion=MODSMD_ARTICLE11.

8. Donald J. Harris, "Universal Healthcare: Mandates or Not?" *Stanford Daily*, February 6, 2008, https://web.stanford.edu/~dharris/papers/Universal%20Health%20Care,%20 Mandates%20or%20Not%20-%20%20Stanford%20Daily%20020608.pdf.

9. Donald J. Harris, *Capital Accumulation and Income Distribution* (London: Routledge & Kegan Paul, 1978).

# NOTES

10. Joan Walsh, "Kamala Harris Has Been Here Before," *The Nation*, July 30, 2019, https://www.thenation.com/article/archive/kamala-harris-terence-hallinan-willie-brown/.

11. CNN, "Kamala Harris Rips up the Script," April 2017, https://www.cnn.com/interactive/2017/politics/state/kamala-harris-rips-up-the-script/.

12. "Bonus Episode: Our Next VP (with Kamala Harris)," *You and Me Both with Hillary Clinton*, podcast, iHeart, October 1, 2020, https://www.iheart.com/podcast/1119-you-and-me-both-with-hill-71671764/episode/bonus-episode-our-next-vp-with-72111389/.

13. Scott Duke Harris, "From the Archives: In Search of Elusive Justice," *Los Angeles Times*, October 24, 2004, https://www.latimes.com/politics/la-pol-ca-tm-kamala-20190121-story.html.

14. George Joseph, "It's Time for New Leadership: Harris," India Abroad, December 19, 2003.

15. Lisa Tsering, "TiE Forum Empowers Women," India-West, April 9, 2004.

16. "VP Kamala Harris on the Second Mother Who Inspired Her," Popsugar, March 3, 2023, https://www.popsugar.com/celebrity/vice-president-kamala-harris-black-history-month-49089374.

17. Elana Schor, "Harris Brings Baptist, Interfaith Roots to Democratic Ticket," AP News, August 12, 2020, https://apnews.com/article/joe-biden-religion-baptist-f2a91e545f44712a7ea7bd962412bcfe.

18. Jane Mulkerrins, "Meena Harris: Growing up with My Aunt, Kamala, America's New V-P," *Times* (London), January 22, 2021, https://www.thetimes.co.uk/article/meena-harris-growing-up-with-my-aunt-kamala-americas-new-v-p-rvv800kxq.

19. Peter Byrne, "Kamala's Karma," *SF Weekly*, September 24, 2003, https://web.archive.org/web/20170805043948/https://www.sfweekly.com/news/kamalas-karma/.

20. Dana Goodyear, "Kamala Harris Makes Her Case," *New Yorker*, July 15, 2019, https://www.newyorker.com/magazine/2019/07/22/kamala-harris-makes-her-case.

21. "Kamala Harris' Jamaican Heritage, Updated 14.01.2019," Jamaica Global, August 18, 2020, https://www.jamaicaglobalonline.com/kamala-harris-jamaican-heritage/.

22. "Donald Harris Slams His Daughter Senator Kamala Harris for Fraudulently Stereotyping Jamaicans and Accusing Her of Playing Identity Politics," Jamaica Global,

February 15, 2019, https://web.archive.org/web/20190218061545/https://www.jamaica globalonline.com/donald-harris-slams-his-daughter-senator-kamala-harris-for-fraud ulently-stereotyping-jamaicans-and-accusing-her-of-playing-identity--politics/.

23. Robert Samuels, "The Jamaican Connection," *Washington Post*, January 17, 2021, https://www.washingtonpost.com/nation/2021/01/13/donald-kamala-harris-father/.

24. Dan Bilefsky, "In Canada, Kamala Harris, a Disco-Dancing Teenager, Yearned for Home," *New York Times*, November 10, 2020, https://www.nytimes.com/2020/10/05 /world/canada/kamala-harris-montreal.html.

25. Robin Givhan, "Kamala Harris Grew up in a Mostly White World. Then She Went to a Black University in a Black City," *Washington Post*, September 16, 2019, https://www .washingtonpost.com/politics/2019/09/16/kamala-harris-grew-up-mostly-white -world-then-she-went-black-university-black-city/.

26. *"The Truths We Hold,"* C-SPAN, January 9, 2019, https://www.c-span.org/video /?456728-1/the-truths-hold.

27. Evan Halper, "A Political Awakening: How Howard University Shaped Kamala Harris' Identity," *Los Angeles Times*, February 3, 2021, https://www.latimes.com/politics/la-na -pol-kamala-harris-howard-university-20190319-story.html.

# CHAPTER TWO: THE REAL SLICK WILLIE

1. *Willie Brown: The Political Life*, Apple Podcasts, November 2, 2020, https://podcasts .apple.com/us/podcast/willie-brown-the-political-life/id1025864075?i=10004968 98071.

2. Robert Scheer, "The Flash: Willie Brown's Story," *Los Angeles Times*, June 23, 1991, https://www.latimes.com/archives/la-xpm-1991-06-23-tm-1753-story.html.

3. James Richardson, *Willie Brown: A Biography* (Berkeley: University of California Press, 1996).

4. Neil Henry, "California's Ex-Speaker Still Making Waves," *Washington Post*, June 18, 1995, https://www.washingtonpost.com/archive/politics/1995/06/18/californias-ex-speaker -still-making-waves/08e4ed46-9533-4c89-8ad9-3bf9c5bac986/.

5. Ruthe Stein, "Bedfellows Make Strange Politics?" *San Francisco Chronicle*, November 20, 1995.

6. Willie L. Brown Jr., *Basic Brown: My Life and Our Times* (New York: Simon & Schuster, 2008).

7. Benjamin Schneider, "Looking Back on Kamala Harris' Record in California," *SF Weekly*, August 11, 2020, https://www.sfweekly.com/archives/looking-back-on-kamala-har ris-record-in-california/article_10316c0c-29e1-5ba4-a9c3-aea9effe926c.html.

8. Michael Kruse, "How San Francisco's Wealthiest Families Launched Kamala Harris," *Politico Magazine*, August 9, 2019, https://www.politico.com/magazine/story/2019 /08/09/kamala-harris-2020-president-profile-san-francisco-elite-227611/.

9. Richardson, *Willie Brown*.

10. Herb Caen, "Cut Along Dotted Lines," SFGATE, December 14, 1995, https://www .sfgate.com/news/article/Cut-Along-Dotted-Lines-3017971.php.

11. Brown, *Basic Brown*.

12. Herb Caen, "'Twas the Day After," SFGATE, December 26, 1996, https://www.sfgate .com/news/article/HERB-CAEN-Twas-the-Day-After-3017150.php.

13. Michael Finnegan, "Fighter Right Out of Golden Gate," *Los Angeles Times*, January 15, 1996.

14. Phillip Matier and Andrew Ross, "Brown's Creative Financing Underwrites Far-Flung Trade Jaunts," SFGATE, February 2, 1998, https://www.sfgate.com/bayarea/matier -ross/article/MATIER-ROSS-Brown-s-Creative-Financing-3317408.php.

15. Matier and Ross, "Brown's Creative Financing Underwrites Far-Flung Trade Jaunts."

16. Michael Warren, "Pugnacious San Francisco Prosecutor in Tough Re-Election Race," Associated Press, October 30, 1999.

17. Jaxon Van Derbeken, "Top S.F. Prosecutor Quits D.A.'s Office," SFGATE, August 8, 2000, https://www.sfgate.com/news/article/Top-S-F-Prosecutor-Quits-D-A-s-Office -2710499.php.

18. Phillip Matier and Andrew Ross, "S.F. Mayor Makes 'Major' Play to Get New Sports Arena," SFGATE, August 9, 2000, https://www.sfgate.com/bayarea/matier-ross/article /S-F-Mayor-Makes-Major-Play-to-Get-New-Sports-3315663.php.

19. Phillip Matier and Andrew Ross, "Brown Excoriates Hallinan, Other 'Big-Mouth' Critics," SFGATE, September 10, 2001, https://www.sfgate.com/bayarea/matier-ross /article/Brown-excoriates-Hallinan-other-big-mouth-3314761.php.

# NOTES

20. Lee Fang, "In Her First Race, Kamala Harris Campaigned as Tough on Crime—and Unseated the Country's Most Progressive Prosecutor," The Intercept, February 7, 2019, https://theintercept.com/2019/02/07/kamala-harris-san-francisco-district-attorney-crime/.

21. Demian Bulwa, "Harris Raps Hallinan on Domestic Violence; Challenger Says D.A. Is Failing to Prosecute Crimes," SFGATE, December 4, 2003, https://www.sfgate.com/politics/article/Harris-raps-Hallinan-on-domestic-violence-2525957.php.

22. Demian Bulwa, "Harris Slams Hallinan on City's Gun Violence," SFGATE, November 12, 2003, https://www.sfgate.com/politics/article/Harris-slams-Hallinan-on-city-s-gun-violence-2512358.php.

23. Patrick Hoge, "No Cap on Election Outlay; Hallinan Loses Case against Harris," SFGATE, October 18, 2003, https://www.sfgate.com/politics/article/No-cap-on-election-outlay-Hallinan-loses-case-2581971.php.

24. Demian Bulwa, "Harris Denies Being Indebted to Donors; Political Machine Made Challenger, D.A. Hallinan Says," SFGATE, November 25, 2003, https://www.sfgate.com/politics/article/Harris-denies-being-indebted-to-donors-2511055.php.

25. Peter Byrne, "Kamala's Karma," SF Weekly, September 24, 2003, https://web.archive.org/web/20170117163033/https://archives.sfweekly.com/sanfrancisco/kamalas-karma/Content?oid=2149429.

26. Nick Veronin, "Alternative Facts: SF Weekly Turns 40, Takes a Break," SF Weekly, September 30, 2021, https://www.sfweekly.com/archives/alternative-facts-sf-weekly-turns-40-takes-a-break/article_c6bdc080-5902-566d-b231-fd7e26118f10.html.

27. "The Chronicle Recommends Kamala Harris for D.A.," editorial, San Francisco Chronicle, October 19, 2003, https://www.sfchronicle.com/opinion/editorials/article/THE-CHRONICLE-RECOMMENDS-Kamala-Harris-for-D-A-2552871.php.

28. Demian Bulwa, "Harris Defeats Hallinan after Bitter Campaign," SFGATE, December 10, 2003, https://www.sfgate.com/politics/article/Harris-defeats-Hallinan-after-bitter-campaign-2546323.php.

29. Willie Brown, "Sure, I Dated Kamala Harris. So What?" San Francisco Chronicle, January 25, 2019, https://www.sfchronicle.com/opinion/article/Sure-I-dated-Kamala-Harris-So-what-13562972.php.

# CHAPTER THREE: KAMALA THE COP

1. Jaxon Van Derbeken, "New D.A. Promises to Be 'Smart on Crime'; Harris Speaks Well of Hallinan, Will Continue Some of His Policies," SFGATE, January 9, 2004, https://www.sfgate.com/politics/article/New-D-A-promises-to-be-smart-on-crime-Harris-2831205.php.

2. Matthew B. Stannard, "D.A. Won't Pursue Death in Cop Slaying; Harris Fulfills Campaign Pledge with Decision," SFGATE, April 14, 2004, https://www.sfgate.com/crime/article/SAN-FRANCISCO-D-A-won-t-pursue-death-in-cop-2767716.php.

3. Phil Willon, "Kamala Harris Is a Different Kind of Prosecutor," Los Angeles Times, October 20, 2010, https://www.latimes.com/archives/la-xpm-2010-oct-20-la-me-harris-20101015-story.html.

4. Phillip Matier and Andrew Ross, "Feinstein's Surprise Call for Death Penalty Puts D.A. on Spot," SFGATE, April 21, 2004, https://www.sfgate.com/bayarea/matier-ross/article/Feinstein-s-surprise-call-for-death-penalty-puts-3313728.php.

5. "Anti-War Protesters Avoid Prosecution," SFGATE, April 3, 2004, https://www.sfgate.com/bayarea/article/Anti-war-protesters-avoid-prosecution-2798630.php.

6. Jaxon Van Derbeken, "Trials and Tribulations of Kamala Harris, D.A.; 2 Years into Term, Prosecutor, Police Have Their Differences," SFGATE, March 20, 2006, https://www.sfgate.com/politics/article/Trials-and-tribulations-of-Kamala-Harris-D-A-2521498.php.

7. Elizabeth Weil, "Kamala Harris 2020: Can She Beat Trump?" Atlantic, October 1, 2020, https://www.theatlantic.com/magazine/archive/2019/05/kamala-harris-2020-campaign/586033/.

8. "Rewind to 2005: Kamala Harris Makes Her Oprah Debut," The Oprah Winfrey Show, October 9, 2020, https://www.youtube.com/watch?v=n0zjsyjDvYA.

9. David Steinberg, "Lap Victory," SF Weekly, September 8, 2004, https://web.archive.org/web/20201029143822/https://www.sfweekly.com/news/lap-victory/.

10. Jesse McKinley, "San Francisco's Prostitutes Support a Proposition," New York Times, November 2, 2008, https://www.nytimes.com/2008/11/01/us/01prostitute.html?_r=0.

11. Heather Knight, "City Trying to Get Worst Truants to School; Help for Students, Criminal Prosecution Part of Crackdown," SFGATE, September 14, 2006, https://

www.sfgate.com/education/article/SAN-FRANCISCO-City-trying-to-get-worst-truants-246 9689.php.

12. German Lopez, "Why Kamala Harris Is Under Attack for a Decade-Old Anti-Truancy Program," Vox, February 7, 2019, https://www.vox.com/future-perfect /2019/2/7/18202084/kamala-harris-truancy-prosecutor-president-2020.

13. "Kamala Harris Speech—January 14, 2010, Commonwealth Club of California," You-Tube, https://www.youtube.com/watch?v=QKaCFmNefHA.

14. Kamala Harris, "Truancy Costs Us All," SFGATE, October 14, 2009, https://www .sfgate.com/education/article/Truancy-costs-us-all-3213456.php.

15. Aziz Haniffa, "Kamala Devi Harris," India Abroad, August 14, 2009.

16. Jaxon Van Derbeken, "Kamala Harris Accused of Withholding Vital Info," *San Francisco Chronicle*, June 3, 2010, https://www.sfchronicle.com/crime/article/Kamala-Harris -accused-of-withholding-vital-info-3186525.php.

17. Michael Finnegan, "San Francisco D.A.'s Program Trained Illegal Immigrants for Jobs They Couldn't Legally Hold," *Los Angeles Times*, June 22, 2009, https://www.latimes .com/archives/la-xpm-2009-jun-22-me-harris22-story.html.

18. Brock Keeling, "D.A. Kamala Harris Comes Under Fire," SFist, December 30, 2018, https://sfist.com/2009/06/22/kamala_harris_comes_under_fire/.

19. Peter Jamison, "D.A. Kamala Harris Wins Fewer Felony Trials Than Any Big-City Prosecutor in California," *SF Weekly*, May 5, 2010, https://web.archive.org /web/20100507165245/https:/blogs.sfweekly.com/thesnitch/2010/05/kamala_harris _felony_trials.php.

20. Phillip Matier and Andrew Ross, "Chris Kelly's Ads Will Attack Kamala Harris," SFGATE, May 9, 2010, https://www.sfgate.com/bayarea/matier-ross/article/Chris -Kelly-s-ads-will-attack-Kamala-Harris-3189358.php.

21. "When Kamala Harris Lost on Election Night, but Won Three Weeks Later," *Roll Call*, July 16, 2019, https://rollcall.com/2019/07/16/when-kamala-harris-lost-on-election-night-but-won-three-weeks-later/.

22. Carla Marinucci and Joe Garofoli, "GOP Carly Fiorina Attacks Dem Barbara Boxer," SF-GATE, August 22, 2010, https://www.sfgate.com/politics/article/GOP-Carly-Fiorina -attacks-Dem-Barbara-Boxer-3255387.php.

23. "First Woman District Attorney Kamala Harris," *Talks at Google*, YouTube, September 14, 2010, https://www.youtube.com/watch?v=aJllQ9d3pYM.

24. Aziz Haniffa, "NBC Chief Zucker Stumps for Harris," India Abroad, August 14, 2009.

25. "Kamala Harris: Drastic Repair," YouTube, May 5, 2010, https://www.youtube.com/watch?v=6viSLXP1S7c.

26. Marisa Lagos, "Corruption-Fighting Candidate Took Many Gifts," SFGATE, August 9, 2010, https://www.sfgate.com/news/article/Corruption-fighting-candidate-took-many-gifts-3256569.php.

27. Phillip Matier and Andrew Ross, "Obama Fundraiser for Democrats Shifts to Peninsula," SFGATE, October 20, 2010, https://www.sfgate.com/bayarea/matier-ross/article/Obama-fundraiser-for-Democrats-shifts-to-Peninsula-3170021.php.

28. "California: Election Results 2010," *New York Times*, n.d., https://archive.nytimes.com/www.nytimes.com/elections/2010/results/california.html.

# CHAPTER FOUR: TOP COP

1. Ben Smith, "America's Most Powerful Liberal?" *Politico*, September 24, 2011, https://www.politico.com/story/2011/09/americas-most-powerful-liberal-064299.

2. Alejandro Lazo, "Kamala Harris Pressured to Reject Bank Foreclosure Settlement," *Los Angeles Times*, September 30, 2011, https://www.latimes.com/business/la-xpm-2011-sep-30-la-fi-foreclosure-settlement-20110930-story.html.

3. "Foreclosure Victims Occupy Senate Stump Speech of Kamala Harris," Los Angeles Indymedia, May 26, 2015, https://la.indymedia.org/news/2015/05/268280.php.

4. David Dayen, "Kamala Harris Fails to Explain Why She Didn't Prosecute Steven Mnuchin's Bank," The Intercept, January 5, 2017, https://theintercept.com/2017/01/05/kamala-harris-fails-to-explain-why-she-didnt-prosecute-steven-mnuchins-bank/.

5. Darwin Bond Graham, "The Strike Force That Never Struck," *East Bay Express*, May 29, 2014, https://eastbayexpress.com/the-strike-force-that-never-struck-1/.

6. Andrew Cohen, "California's Prison Crisis Is Now a Constitutional Crisis," *Atlantic*, April 14, 2013, https://www.theatlantic.com/national/archive/2013/04/californias-prison-crisis-is-now-a-constitutional-crisis/274852/.

7. *Colman v. Brown*, https://casetext.com/case/coleman-v-brown-73.

8. Adam Serwer, "California AG 'Shocked' to Learn Her Office Wanted to Keep Eligible Parolees in Jail to Work," BuzzFeed News, November 18, 2014, https://www.buzzfeednews.com/article/adamserwer/some-lawyers-just-want-to-see-the-world-burn#.vd4dYOL6d.

9. Ford Foundation, "California State Attorney General Kamala D. Harris on the Importance of Prison Education," May 20, 2014, https://www.youtube.com/watch?v=-uWEWCrDCg4.

10. Danny Hakim, Stephanie Saul, and Richard A. Oppel Jr., "'Top Cop' Kamala Harris's Record of Policing the Police," *New York Times*, August 9, 2020, https://www.nytimes.com/2020/08/09/us/politics/kamala-harris-policing.html.

11. Bob Egelko, "Kamala Harris Sees Safeguards in D.A.s Prosecuting Police Killings," SFGATE, December 22, 2014, https://www.sfgate.com/news/article/Kamala-Harris-sees-safeguards-in-D-A-s-5972586.php.

12. Phil Willon, "Kamala Harris Should Take Bolder Action on Police Shootings, Civil Rights Advocates Say," *Los Angeles Times*, January 18, 2016, https://www.latimes.com/local/politics/la-me-pol-ca-harris-police-shootings-20160118-story.html.

13. Juliet Linderman, "Harris Eyes Reform as Candidate, Was Cautious as Prosecutor," AP News, April 1, 2019, https://apnews.com/article/kamala-harris-california-ap-top-news-ca-state-wire-politics-0e7dd2e5b2564a25b6266f0632da651e.

14. Joe Garofoli, "Kamala Harris Wins New Badges of Respect from Police," SFGATE, January 19, 2014, https://www.sfgate.com/politics/joegarofoli/article/Kamala-Harris-wins-new-badges-of-respect-from-5158187.php.

15. Jennifer Medina, "Live Analysis of the Supreme Court Decisions on Gay Marriage," *New York Times*, June 26, 2013, https://www.nytimes.com/interactive/projects/live-dashboard/2013-06-26-supreme-court-gay-marriage.

16. Howard Mintz, "California Transgender Inmates Fight for Medical Care," *Mercury News*, May 17, 2015, https://www.mercurynews.com/2015/05/17/california-transgender-inmates-fight-for-medical-care/.

17. "California Must Pay for Inmate's Sex Change, Judge Rules," CBS News, April 3, 2015, https://www.cbsnews.com/news/california-must-pay-for-inmates-sex-change-judge-rules/.

18. Jesse Brukman, "2013 Hot 100 List," *Maxim*, September 29, 2013, https://www.maxim .com/women/2013-hot-100-post/.

19. "California Attorney General Kamala Harris," *Sacramento Bee*, YouTube, August 8, 2014, https://www.youtube.com/watch?v=Yo88jvTp_1A.

20. "Commitment 2014: The Race for California's AG," KCRA 3, YouTube, August 5, 2014, https://www.youtube.com/watch?v=6kATTmxYN2c.

21. Adam Serwer, "California's Attorney General Thinks Legal Weed Is Inevitable," BuzzFeed News, November 17, 2014, https://www.buzzfeednews.com/article/adam serwer/californias-attorney-general-thinks-legal-weed-is-inevitable.

22. Michael Finnegan, "Atty. Gen. Kamala Harris Calls for More Training to Prevent Police Bias," *Los Angeles Times*, April 18, 2015, https://www.latimes.com/local/lanow/la -me-ln-kamala-harris-report-police-race-20150417-story.html.

23. Melanie Mason, "Kamala Harris Cautions against 'One-Size-Fits-All' Approach on Body Cameras," *Los Angeles Times*, May 27, 2015, https://www.latimes.com/local /political/la-me-pc-harris-body-cameras-20150527-story.html.

24. CBS Sacramento, "California Starts Tracking Police Use of Force," CBS News, September 22, 2016, https://www.cbsnews.com/sacramento/news/california-starts-track ing-police-use-of-force/.

25. Allison Terry, "California Law Boosts Confiscation of Illegal Guns: Model for Other States?" *Christian Science Monitor*, May 2, 2013, https://www.csmonitor.com/USA /USA-Update/2013/0502/California-law-boosts-confiscation-of-illegal-guns-Model -for-other-states.

26. Jasmine Wright and Veronica Stracqualursi, "Harris and Emhoff Recall First Date: 'It Felt like We Had Known Each Other Forever,'" CNN, January 15, 2021, https://www .cnn.com/2021/01/15/politics/kamala-harris-doug-emhoff-first-date-cnntv/index.html.

27. Kamala Harris, "Sen. Kamala Harris on Being 'Momala,'" *Elle*, May 11, 2019, https://www .elle.com/culture/career-politics/a27422434/kamala-harris-stepmom-mothers-day/.

# CHAPTER FIVE: SENATOR KAMALA HARRIS

1. Adam Nagourney, "Kamala Harris, California's Attorney General, Leaps to Forefront of Senate Race," *New York Times*, March 27, 2015, https://www.nytimes.com/2015/03/28

/us/politics/kamala-harris-californias-attorney-general-leaps-to-forefront-of-race
-for-barbara-boxers-senate-seat.html.

2. Ben Brumfield, "Democratic Congresswoman Apologizes for Ethnically Loaded
Gesture," CNN, May 18, 2015, https://www.cnn.com/2015/05/17/politics/california
-sanchez-gaffe-native-american/index.html.

3. Christopher Cadelago, "Kamala Harris Spending Big Chunk of Money Raised for
Senate Race," *Sacramento Bee*, January 28, 2016, https://www.sacbee.com/news/politics
-government/capitol-alert/article41873313.html.

4. "Posh Hotels and Pricey Airfare: Meet the Senate Candidate Driving Democrats Crazy,"
*National Journal*, n.d., https://www.nationaljournal.com/s/125536/posh-hotels-pricey
-airfare-meet-senate-candidate-driving-some-democrats-crazy.

5. Phil Willon, "Kamala Harris Shakes up Senate Campaign Staff," *Los Angeles Times*,
November 18, 2015, https://www.latimes.com/local/political/la-me-pc-kamala-harris
-shakes-up-campaign-staff-20151117-story.html.

6. Molly Ball, "How Kamala Harris' Senate Record Reveals What Kind of National Leader
She May Be," *Time*, August 20, 2020, https://time.com/5881589/kamala-harris-vice
-president-2020/.

7. Abby Aguirre and Zoë Ghertner, "Kamala Harris Is Dreaming Big," *Vogue*, March
19, 2018, https://www.vogue.com/article/kamala-harris-interview-vogue-april
-2018.

8. Itay Hod, "That Time Kamala Harris Called New Homeland Security Secretary at
Home to Protest Muslim Ban," The Wrap, February 23, 2017, http://www.thewrap
.com/kamala-harris-homeland-security-secretary-john-kelly-home-muslim-ban/.

9. "User Clip: Kamala Harris Questions Sec. Kelly," C-SPAN, June 9, 2017, https://www
.c-span.org/video/?c4673103/user-clip-kamala-harris-questions-sec-kelly.

10. "Central Intelligence Agency Director Confirmation Hearing," C-SPAN, January 12,
2017, https://www.c-span.org/video/?421225-1/central-intelligence-agency-director
-confirmation-hearing.

11. "Sen. Kamala Harris: We Must 'Reexamine ICE and Its Role,'" MSNBC, June 25,
2018, https://www.youtube.com/watch?v=Ctxq7a3-uIA.

12. "User Clip: Kamala Harris Questions Ronald Vitiello," C-SPAN, November 15, 2018,

# NOTES

https://www.c-span.org/video/?c4762285/user-clip-kamala-harris-questions-ronald-vitiello.

13. CBS Los Angeles, "LA Radio Personality Releases Photo of Senator Al Franken Groping Her on USO Tour," CBS News, November 16, 2017, https://www.cbsnews.com/losangeles/news/senator-al-franken-grope-leeann-tweeden/.

14. "Roy Moore Defiant Amid New Allegations," transcript, *Hardball with Chris Matthews*, MSNBC, November 16, 2017, https://www.msnbc.com/transcripts/hardball/2017-11-16-msna1039361.

15. Jane Mayer, "The Case of Al Franken," *New Yorker*, July 22, 2019, https://www.newyorker.com/magazine/2019/07/29/the-case-of-al-franken.

16. "Franken on Why Trump Has Been an 'Absolute Failure,'" *PBS NewsHour*, August 18, 2020, https://www.pbs.org/newshour/show/al-franken-on-trumps-pandemic-response-and-why-biden-would-be-better.

17. Sophia Bollag, "Kamala Harris Aide Who Resigned after Harassment Case Was One of Her Closest Confidantes," *Sacramento Bee*, December 7, 2018, https://web.archive.org/web/20181209014023/https://www.sacbee.com/latest-news/article222775590.html.

18. Alexei Koseff, "Misconduct Claim Involving Kamala Harris Aide Came to Agency Months before She Left Office," *Sacramento Bee*, December 14, 2018, https://www.sacbee.com/news/politics-government/capitol-alert/article223053155.html.

19. NOLA.com, "Wendy Vitter Is Questioned by U.S. Senate Judiciary Committee," YouTube, April 11, 2018, https://www.youtube.com/watch?v=xfT5OB6Wj_Y.

20. Matt Hadro, "Nominee Grilled over Knights of Columbus Membership Confirmed as Federal Judge," Catholic News Agency, July 24, 2019, https://www.catholicnewsagency.com/news/41872/nominee-grilled-over-knights-of-columbus-membership-confirmed-as-federal-judge.

21. Michael Gerson, "Anti-Catholic Bigotry Is Alive in the U.S. Senate," *Washington Post*, January 17, 2019, https://www.washingtonpost.com/opinions/anti-catholic-bigotry-is-alive-in-the-us-senate/2019/01/17/e0ad0a14-1a8f-11e9-8813-cb9dec761e73_story.html.

22. Rabbi Mitchell Rocklin, "Keep Religious Tests Out of the Senate," *Los Angeles Times*, January 16, 2019, https://www.latimes.com/opinion/op-ed/la-oe-rocklin-brian-buescher-20190116-story.html.

23. "Foreign Intelligence Surveillance Act (FISA)," C-SPAN, June 7, 2017, https://www
.c-span.org/video/?429451-1/foreign-intelligence-surveillance-act-fisa&start=8715.

24. Susan Chira, "The Universal Phenomenon of Men Interrupting Women," *New York Times*, June 14, 2017, https://www.nytimes.com/2017/06/14/business/women-sexism
-work-huffington-kamala-harris.html.

25. Carly Sitrin, "People Keep Interrupting Sen. Kamala Harris," Vox, June 13, 2017, https://www.vox.com/policy-and-politics/2017/6/13/15795648/interrupting-senator
-kamala-harris-sessions-hearing.

26. Abby Aguirre, "Kamala Harris Is Dreaming Big," *Vogue*, March 19, 2018, https://www
.vogue.com/article/kamala-harris-interview-vogue-april-2018.

27. "Will Senator Kamala Harris Run for President?" *The Ellen Show*, April 5, 2018, https://www.youtube.com/watch?v=ZLBusGrN0Co.

# CHAPTER SIX: STOP KAVANAUGH

1. Seth McLaughlin, "With Kavanaugh Hearing, Some Democrats See Opportunity to Bolster 2020 Campaigns," *Washington Times*, July 11, 2018, https://www.washington
times.com/news/2018/jul/11/with-kavanaugh-hearing-some-democrats-see-opportun/.

2. Serafin Gómez and Judson Berger, "Kamala Harris' Office Allegedly Rejected SCOTUS Courtesy Call: 'We Want Nothing to Do with You,'" Fox News, July 10, 2018, https://www
.foxnews.com/politics/kamala-harris-office-allegedly-rejected-scotus-courtesy-call
-we-want-nothing-to-do-with-you.

3. Carrie Severino and Mollie Ziegler Hemingway, *Justice on Trial: The Kavanaugh Confirmation and the Future of the Supreme Court* (Washington, DC: Regnery, 2019).

4. "Sen. Kamala Harris Says She Believes Kavanaugh Accuser: 'She Has Nothing to Gain,'" CBS News, September 18, 2018, https://www.cbsnews.com/video/sen-kamala-harris
-says-she-believes-kavanaugh-accuser-she-has-nothing-to-gain/.

5. Ruth Marcus, *Supreme Ambition: Brett Kavanaugh and the Conservative Takeover* (New York: Simon & Schuster, 2019).

6. Ryan Grim, "Dianne Feinstein Withholding Brett Kavanaugh Document from Fellow Judiciary Committee Democrats," The Intercept, September 12, 2018, https://theinter
cept.com/2018/09/12/brett-kavanaugh-confirmation-dianne-feinstein/.

7.  Blake Montgomery, "Sen. Kamala Harris Told Christine Blasey Ford She Will Be Remembered as a 'True Profile in Courage,'" BuzzFeed News, September 27, 2018, https://www.buzzfeed.com/blakemontgomery/kamala-harris-statement-to-christine-blasey.

8.  "President Trump Rally in Mississippi," C-SPAN, October 2, 2018, https://www.c-span.org/video/?452371-1/president-trump-rally-mississippi.

9.  "Senator Kamala Harris at The Atlantic Festival," C-SPAN, October 3, 2018, https://www.c-span.org/video/?452361-103/senator-kamala-harris-the-atlantic-festival.

10. Gabriella Muñoz and Stephen Dinan, "Democratic Senators Flee Committee to Protest Kavanaugh Vote," AP News, September 28, 2018, https://apnews.com/article/courts-judiciary-brett-kavanaugh-christine-blasey-ford-469c4394d1ccda4bcb4f7d2779032451.

# CHAPTER SEVEN: RADICAL LEFTIST REBRAND

1.  "Sen. Kamala Harris Friday Afternoon Keynote Netroots Nation 2018," YouTube, https://www.youtube.com/watch?v=m6sHK4JUiMc.

2.  *The Truths We Hold,* C-SPAN, January 9, 2019, https://www.c-span.org/video/?456728-1/the-truths-hold.

3.  "Kamala Harris Reads 'Superheroes Are Everywhere,'" Gotham Reads, May 27, 2020, https://www.youtube.com/watch?v=VowoKsMOryI.

4.  *The Truths We Hold,* C-SPAN.

5.  Edward-Isaac Dovere, *Battle for the Soul: Inside the Democrats' Campaigns to Defeat Trump* (New York: Penguin, 2022).

6.  Selena Hill, "Kamala Harris Addresses Criticism, Black Girl Magic, and More at Women of Power Summit," *Black Enterprise*, March 5, 2019, https://www.blackenterprise.com/kamala-harris-criticism-black-girl-magic/.

7.  Nia-Malika Henderson, "Race in the Race: What Kamala Harris' Identity Brings to 2020," CNN, January 28, 2019, https://www.cnn.com/2019/01/28/politics/kamala-harris-identity-2020-trump/index.html.

8.  "Don Lemon & April Ryan Have Tense Debate Over Sen. Kamala Harris," *Ebony*, February 12, 2019, https://www.ebony.com/don-lemon-april-ryan-have-tense-debate-over-sen-kamala-harris/.

9. "Kamala 2024: Doomed from the Start? W/ Charisse Burden-Stelly," *Bad Faith*, October 11, 2021, https://www.youtube.com/watch?v=MgG8R5F0d5c.

10. "'Empire' Star Jussie Smollett Tells Cops His Attackers Touted MAGA," TMZ, January 29, 2019, https://tmz.com/2019/01/29/empire-star-jussie-smollett-attacked-hospitali zed-homophobic-hate-crime/.

11. Jurnee Smollett, Instagram, January 15, 2018, https://www.instagram.com/p/Bd _BJmKAB3wg.

12. Samuel Chamberlain, "Kamala Harris Gives Awkward Response When Asked about Jussie Smollett Claims," Fox News, February 18, 2019, https://www.foxnews.com /politics/kamala-harris-gives-awkward-response-when-asked-about-jussie-smollett-claims.

13. "Michael Cohen Delays Congressional Testimony," transcript, *The Rachel Maddow Show*, January 24, 2019, https://www.msnbc.com/transcripts/rachel-maddow-show/2019-01-23-msna1187671.

14. Dana Goodyear, "Kamala Harris Makes Her Case," *New Yorker*, July 15, 2019, https://www.newyorker.com/magazine/2019/07/22/kamala-harris-makes-her-case.

15. Jeremy Barr, "Hollywood's Top Power Players Favor Kamala Harris in Early Campaign Donations," *The Hollywood Reporter*, July 25, 2019, https://www.hollywoodreporter .com/movies/movie-news/hollywoods-top-power-players-donate-more-kamala-harris -campaign-1226381/.

16. Dareh Gregorian, Benjy Sarlin, and Vaughn Hillyard, "Where Does Kamala Harris Stand on Healthcare?" NBC News, June 28, 2019, https://www.nbcnews.com /politics/2020-election/kamala-harris-walks-back-her-hand-moment-health-insurance -democratic-n1024756.

17. Gregorian, Sarlin, and Hillyard, "Where Does Kamala Harris Stand on Health-care?"

18. "Planned Parenthood Candidates Forum, Part 1," C-SPAN, June 22, 2019, https:// www.c-span.org/video/?461882-1/planned-parenthood-candidates-forum-part-1.

19. Li Zhou, "2020 Democrat Kamala Harris Has a Plan to Stop States from Restricting Abortion Access," Vox, May 28, 2019, https://www.vox.com/2019/5/28/18642558/ kamala-harris-abortion-voting-rights-act.

20. "Sen. Kamala Harris Speaks Out on Police Reform," *Good Morning America*, June 9, 2020,

https://www.goodmorningamerica.com/news/video/sen-kamala-harris-speaks-police-reform-71148188.

21. "NAACP Convention in Detroit," C-SPAN, July 24, 2019, https://www.c-span.org/video/?462804-1/naacp-convention-detroit.

22. David Sherfinski, "Joe Biden on Kamala Harris: 'I Thought We Were Friends,'" *Washington Times*, July 25, 2019, https://www.washingtontimes.com/news/2019/jul/25/joe-biden-kamala-harris-i-thought-we-were-friends/.

23. Steven Nelson, "Jill Biden Said Harris Should 'Go F--k' Herself for Debate Attack on Joe," *New York Post*, May 19, 2021, https://nypost.com/2021/05/19/jill-biden-said-harris-should-go-f-k-herself-for-debate-attack/.

24. Chelsea Janes, "'Beau's Flipping in His Grave': Biden Supporters Say Harris's Attacks Betray Her Relationship with His Son," *Washington Post*, July 27, 2019, https://www.washingtonpost.com/politics/beaus-flipping-in-his-grave-biden-supporters-say-harriss-attacks-betray-her-friendship-with-his-son/2019/07/25/6e2d922a-acba-11e9-a0c9-6d2d7818f3da_story.html.

25. Chelsea Janes, "Harris's Views on Busing Come under Question after Her Debate Criticism of Biden's Past Position," *Washington Post*, July 4, 2019, https://www.washingtonpost.com/politics/harriss-views-on-busing-come-under-question-after-her-debate-criticism-of-bidens-past-position/2019/07/04/b197c6cc-9e71-11e9-b27f-ed2942f73d70_story.html.

26. "The Sit Down: Kamala Harris," Blavity TV, October 9, 2019, https://www.youtube.com/watch?v=EryrMG6k9FQ.

27. Brian Schwartz, "Kamala Harris Raised $12 Million in Second Quarter, Trailing Biden and Other 2020 Rivals," CNBC, July 5, 2019, https://www.cnbc.com/2019/07/05/kamala-harris-raises-12-million-in-second-quarter-trailing-biden.html.

28. Brian Slodysko, "Dem Donors Swoon, and Sometimes Fight, over Pete Buttigieg," AP News, April 23, 2019, https://apnews.com/article/north-america-ap-top-news-in-state-wire-hillary-clinton-ca-state-wire-81deb09157d64b138a0b6493cac004af.

# CHAPTER EIGHT: RUNNING OUT OF GAS

1. Barbara Rodriguez, "Iowa Caucuses: Weather-Canceled Kamala Harris Event Scraps

# NOTES

Plan for 'Big Homemade Breakfast' at Waterloo Church," *Des Moines Register*, February 26, 2019, https://www.desmoinesregister.com/story/news/politics/2019/02/25/election -2020-kamala-harris-cancelled-event-breakfast-worship-service-winter-weather-storm -waterloo/2984568002/.

2. Alexandra Jaffe, "Iowa Democrats Warn That Kamala Harris' 'Star Is Fading,'" AP News, June 7, 2019, https://apnews.com/article/9d694eae41bf489e955c44b435aa 8fa1.

3. America Rising ICYMI, "Fmr. San Francisco Mayor Willie Brown Criticizes Sen. Kamala Harris' Campaign Strategy," YouTube, September 23, 2019, https://www.youtube.com/watch?v=G2lvDhyE5LQ.

4. Zachary Halaschak, "'Dude Gotta Go,'" Kamala Harris Fundraises Off Viral Debate Moment," *Washington Examiner*, October 16, 2019, https://www.washingtonexaminer .com/news/dude-gotta-go-kamala-harris-fundraises-off-of-viral-debate-moment.

5. Molly Hensley-Clancy, "Why Kamala Harris Uses Female Pronouns When She Talks About the Presidency," BuzzFeed News, October 2, 2019, https://www.buzzfeednews .com/article/mollyhensleyclancy/kamala-harris-electability.

6. Teo Armus, "'Really Not a Great Look': Chris Cuomo Apologizes for Pronoun Gaffe at LGBTQ Candidate Town Hall," *Washington Post*, October 11, 2019, https://www .washingtonpost.com/nation/2019/10/11/chris-cuomo-pronoun-gaffe-LGBTQ-forum/.

7. Alex Bollinger, "Shangela Teaches Kamala Harris to Thworp a Fan like a Queen," LGBTQ Nation, October 11, 2019, https://www.LGBTQnation.com/2019/10/ shangela-teaches-kamala-harris-thworp-fan-like-queen/.

8. Kamala Harris (@KamalaHarris), "You Asked, I Answered," Twitter, November 1, 2020, https://twitter.com/KamalaHarris/status/1323087784912048128?s=20.

9. "Thanksgiving on the Trail: Two Presidential Candidates Spend the Holiday in Iowa," *Des Moines Register*, November 27, 2019 2023, https://www.desmoinesregister.com/ story/news/elections/presidential/caucus/2019/11/27/election-2020-booker-harris- visit-iowa-ahead-thanksgiving/4237272002/.

10. Christopher Cadelago, "'No Discipline. No Plan. No Strategy.': Kamala Harris Campaign in Meltdown," *Politico*, November 15, 2019, https://www.politico.com/ news/2019/11/15/kamala-harris-campaign-2020-071105.

11. Jonathan Martin, Astead W. Herndon, and Alexander Burns, "How Kamala Harris's Campaign Unraveled," *New York Times*, November 29, 2019, https://www.nytimes .com/2019/11/29/us/politics/kamala-harris-2020.html.

12. Leora Yashari, "Kamala Harris on the Impeachment Trial, Her Marriage & the Next Chapter," Refinery29, February 7, 2020, https://www.refinery29.com/en -us/2020/02/9337937/kamala-harris-trump-impeachment-trial-senator-2020-inter view.

## CHAPTER NINE: THE VEEP PRIMARY

1. John Wildermuth, "Kamala Harris, Dianne Feinstein Are Heard from, but Not Seen, in Trump Trial," *San Francisco Chronicle*, January 30, 2020, https://www.sfchronicle .com/politics/article/Kamala-Harris-Dianne-Feinstein-are-heard-from-15014916.php.

2. Valerie Volcovici, "Harris, Ocasio-Cortez Float Plan to Lift Low-income Communities in Climate Plans," Reuters, July 29, 2019. https://www.reuters.com/article/us-usa -congress-climatechange/harris-ocasio-cortez-float-plan-to-lift-low-income-communities -in-climate-plans-idUSKCN1UO259.

3. Natasha S. Alford, "Sen. Kamala Harris Announces Anti-racism Bill to Fight COVID-19's Impact on Black Communities," The Grio, July 15, 2020. https://thegrio .com/2020/07/15/kamala-harri-anti-racism-bill-covid-19/.

4. Matt Stevens, "Joe Biden Commits to Selecting a Woman as Vice President." *New York Times,* March 15, 2020. https://www.nytimes.com/2020/03/15/us/politics/joe-biden -female-vice-president.html.

5. Naomi Lim, "Jill Biden Hints Odds Are against Kamala Harris as Joe Biden Veep-stakes Pick Up," *Washington Examiner,* March 6, 2020. https://www.washington examiner.com/news/jill-biden-hints-odds-are-against-kamala-harris-as-joe-biden-veep stakes-pick-up.

6. Jill Biden, *Where the Light Enters: Building a Family, Discovering Myself* (New York: Flatiron Books, 2019).

7. Transcript, *CNN Tonight,* May 31, 2020, http://edition.cnn.com/TRANSCRIPTS/2005 /31/cnnt.02.html.

8. Eliana Block, "Yes, at Least 150 Local and Federal Officers Were Injured during the First Week of Protests in DC," WUSA9, June 11, 2020, https://www.wusa9.com/article

/news/verify/150-local-federal-officers-injured-during-dc-protests-verify/65-8fda
f04e-df2e-47d0-abd6-a47017a699f8.

9. Lisa Lerer, "Kamala Harris Is Done Explaining Racism," *New York Times*, June 10, 2020, https://www.nytimes.com/2020/06/10/us/politics/kamala-harris-racism-police.html.

10. Samantha Renck, "The DCNF Was Months Ahead of Media on Kamala Harris' Involvement Bailing Out Accused Criminals," Daily Caller, February 17, 2021, https://dailycaller.com/2021/02/17/kamala-harris-lindsey-graham-minnesota-freedom-fund/.

11. "Joe Biden on Black Woman Running Mate, Democrats Taking Black Voters for Granted + Wiping Weed Crime," *Breakfast Club*, Power 105.1 FM, May 22, 2020, https://www.youtube.com/watch?v=KOIFs_SryHI.

12. "Sen. Kamala Harris: The Nationwide Protests Are a Movement. They're Not Going to Stop," *The Late Show with Stephen Colbert*, June 18, 2020, https://www.youtube.com/watch?v=NTg1ynIPGls.

13. Julie Pace, Dave Eggert, and Kathleen Ronayne, "How Biden Chose Kamala Harris as His Running Mate," *Detroit Free Press*, August 12, 2020, https://www.freep.com/story/news/politics/elections/2020/08/12/joe-biden-kamala-harris-vice-president-search-gretchen-whitmer/3353499001/.

14. Errin Haines, "Black Women Insist That Biden 'Write Us into History,'" The 19th, August 9, 2020, https://19thnews.org/2020/08/black-women-insist-that-biden-write-us-into-history/.

15. Steven Shepard, "Study: Black Turnout Slumped in 2016," *Politico*, May 10, 2017, https://www.politico.com/story/2017/05/10/black-election-turnout-down-2016-census-survey-238226.

16. Nicholas Wu, "Kamala Harris: 'Joe Biden Would Be a Great Running Mate,'" *USA Today*, May 15, 2019, https://www.usatoday.com/story/news/politics/elections/2019/05/15/kamala-harris-says-joe-biden-would-great-running-mate/3681075002/.

17. Sarah Mucha, "Biden Says Vice Presidential Committee 'Looking at More than a Dozen Women,'" CNN, May 2, 2020, https://www.cnn.com/2020/05/02/politics/biden-committee-search-for-woman-vice-president/index.html.

18. Natasha Korecki, Christopher Cadelago, and Marc Caputo, "'She Had No Remorse': Why Kamala Harris Isn't a Lock for VP," *Politico*, July 27, 2020, https://www.politico.com/news/2020/07/27/kamala-harris-biden-vp-381829.

19. Edward-Isaac Dovere, "Biden Ally Karen Bass Explains Her History with Cuba," *Atlantic*, July 31, 2020, https://www.theatlantic.com/politics/archive/2020/07/karen-bass-cuba-venceremos-brigade/614662/.

20. Alexander Burns, Jonathan Martin, and Katie Glueck, "How Joe Biden Chose Kamala Harris as VP," *New York Times*, August 13, 2020, https://www.nytimes.com/2020/08/13/us/politics/biden-harris.html.

21. Katie Glueck, "Why Joe Biden Keeps Missing His Own V.P. Deadlines," *New York Times*, August 19, 2020, https://www.nytimes.com/2020/08/07/us/politics/joe-biden-vice-presidential-search.html.

22. "President Trump Coronavirus News Conference," C-SPAN, August 11, 2020, https://www.c-span.org/video/?474711-1/president-trump-coronavirus-news-conference.

23. Astead W. Herndon, "What Kamala Harris Learned About Power at Howard," *New York Times*, October 14, 2020, https://www.nytimes.com/2020/10/14/us/politics/kamala-harris-howard.html.

24. Maeve Reston, "Kamala Harris' Secret Weapon: The Sisters of AKA," CNN, January 27, 2019, https://www.cnn.com/2019/01/24/politics/kamala-harris-sorority-sisters-south-carolina/index.html.

25. J. J. Abrams, "Spotlight: Kamala Harris," *Vanity Fair*, June 21, 2013, https://www.vanityfair.com/culture/2013/07/jj-abrams-california-kamala-harris.

26. Michael M. Grynbaum and Maggie Haberman, "After Resistance, Mike Pence Accepts Use of Plexiglass Barriers at Debate," *New York Times*, October 6, 2020, https://www.nytimes.com/2020/10/06/business/media/pence-harris-plexiglass-debate.html.

27. "Kamala Harris Reacts to Old Photos," YouTube, October 24, 2020, https://www.youtube.com/watch?v=5KP_Ibr-g5U.

28. Yaron Steinbuch, "Kamala Harris Calls Late Ruth Bader Ginsburg the 'Notorious B.I.G.,'" *New York Post*, September 29, 2020, https://nypost.com/2020/09/29/kamala-harris-calls-ruth-bader-ginsburg-the-notorious-b-i-g/.

# CHAPTER TEN: MADAM VICE PRESIDENT

1. Transcripts, Live Event/Special, CNN, December 3, 2020, https://transcripts.cnn.com/show/se/date/2020-12-03/segment/01.

2.  Jonathan Martin and Alexander Burns, *This Will Not Pass: Trump, Biden, and the Battle for America's Future* (New York: Simon & Schuster, 2022).

3.  Edward-Isaac Dovere, "The Huge Challenges Facing Kamala Harris," *Atlantic*, May 19, 2021, https://www.theatlantic.com/politics/archive/2021/05/kamala-harris-vice -president-impossible/618890/.

4.  NowThis News, "Kamala Harris on Political Career, 2020 Election, and Love for 'Star Wars,'" August 23, 2020, YouTube, https://www.youtube.com/watch?v=kKpf _mNAK4s.

5.  Dominick Mastrangelo, "Social Media Users Celebrate Kamala Harris's Relatability after Brief Stumble Heading to Inauguration," *The Hill*, January 20, 2021, https://thehill .com/homenews/administration/535015-kamala-harris-gives-thumbs-up-after-stumble -heading-to-inauguration/.

6.  Chris Whipple, *The Fight of His Life: Inside Joe Biden's White House* (New York: Scribner, 2023).

7.  Mike Allen, "Vice President Harris to 'Axios on HBO': Trump Left No COVID Plan," *Axios*, February 14, 2021, https://www.axios.com/2021/02/14/kamala-harris-coro navirus-covid-vaccine-trump.

8.  Kate Bennett, "After Two Months in Office, Kamala Harris Is Still Living Out of Suit-cases—and She's Getting Frustrated with It," CNN, March 28, 2021, https://www.cnn .com/2021/03/27/politics/kamala-harris-vice-presidents-residence/index.html.

9.  Emily Tisch Sussman, "'She Pivots' with Vice President Kamala Harris: Stepping into Her Power," *Marie Claire*, March 8, 2023, https://www.marieclaire.com/career-advice /she-pivots-podcast-kamala-harris/.

10. Katelyn Caralle and Adam Manno, "Harris Kisses Husband Doug Emhoff with Their Masks ON at Birthday Party Where She Shouted 'Surprise,'" *Daily Mail*, October 21, 2021, https://www.dailymail.co.uk/news/article-10116437/Harris-kisses-husband -Doug-Emhoff-masks-birthday-party-shouted-surprise.html.

11. Nusaiba Mizan, "Roger Williams Is Accurate That There Were More COVID-19 Deaths in 2021 than in 2020," *Politifact*, https:// www.politifact.com/factchecks/2022/ jan/18/roger-williams/williams-accurate-there-were-more-covid-19-deaths/.

12. Amanda Barren, "Vice President Kamala Harris Speaks Exclusively with WSAZ

about Challenges Facing Our Region," WSAZ, January 28, 2021, https://www.wsaz
.com/2021/01/28/vice-president-kamala-harris-speaks-exclusively-with-wsaz-about
-challenges-facing-our-region/.

13. Amanda Barren, "Sen. Joe Manchin Reacts to WSAZ Interview with Vice Pres. Kamala
Harris," WSAZ, January 30, 2021, https://www.wsaz.com/2021/01/30/sen-joe-man
chin-reacts-to-wsaz-interview-with-vice-pres-kamala-harris/.

14. "Kamala Harris on Biden Administration's Progress—Tha God's Honest Truth," *Hell
of a Week with Charlamagne Tha God*, December 18, 2021, https://www.youtube.com
/watch?v=0y43hm8ceSw.

15. Katherine Doyle, "Kamala Harris's NASA Video Featured Child Actors," *Washington
Examiner*, October 11, 2021, https://www.washingtonexaminer.com/news/nasa-kamala
-harris-child-actors-space.

16. Nick Miroff, "Border Agents Took 172,331 into Custody in March, Statistics Show,"
*Washington Post*, April 8, 2021, https://www.washingtonpost.com/national/march-bor
der-crossing-numbers/2021/04/07/2c252c52-97dd-11eb-8e42-3906c09073f9_story
.html.

17. Martin and Burns, *This Will Not Pass*.

18. Jeremy Diamond and Jasmine Wright, "'Her Instinct Is to Dig In': Kamala Harris'
Struggles to Answer Border Question Seen as Part of a Pattern," CNN, June 14, 2021,
https://www.cnn.com/2021/06/14/politics/kamala-harris-border-answer-fallout/index
.html.

19. Juliana Valencia and Thayma Sánchez, "Migrants Bused from Texas Arrive at VP's
Residence as Title 42 Ends," NBC4 Washington, May 11, 2023, https://www.nbc
washington.com/news/local/migrants-bused-from-texas-arrive-at-vps-residence-as-title
-42-ends/3346204/.

## CHAPTER ELEVEN: STAFF EXODUS

1. Christopher Cadelago, Daniel Lippman, and Eugene Daniels, "'Not a Healthy Environment': Kamala Harris' Office Rife with Dissent," *Politico*, June 30, 2021, https://
www.politico.com/news/2021/06/30/kamala-harris-office-dissent-497290.

2. Robin Bravender, "Ex-Kamala Harris Staffers Have Bad Memories of a Toxic Culture

in Her Past Offices and Are Texting Each Other about It," *Business Insider*, July 14, 2021, https://www.businessinsider.com/kamala-harris-staffers-toxic-office-culture-dysfunction-2021-7.

3. Margaret Talev and Jonathan Swan, "Biden Aide Charges 'Sabotage' of Harris," Axios, July 2, 2021, https://www.axios.com/2021/07/02/kamala-harris-office-dysfunction-2024.

4. Matt Flegenheimer and Sydney Ember, "How Amy Klobuchar Treats Her Staff," *New York Times*, February 22, 2019, https://www.nytimes.com/2019/02/22/us/politics/amy-klobuchar-staff.html.

5. Mychael Schnell, Bernie Sanders Demands King-size Hotel Beds, Cool Rooms, Book Says," *The Hill*, May 27, 2021, https://thehill.com/homenews/senate/555774-bernie-sanders-demands-king-size-hotel-beds-cool-rooms-book-says/.

6. Tyler Pager, "Harris Hires Two Senior Advisers," *Washington Post*, September 24, 2021, https://www.washingtonpost.com/politics/harris-hires-two-senior-advisers/2021/09/24/7e9b56e6-1d7f-11ec-914a-99d701398e5a_story.html.

7. Cleve R. Wootson Jr. and Tyler Pager, "A Kamala Harris Staff Exodus Reignites Questions about Her Leadership Style—and Her Future Ambitions," *Washington Post*, December 4, 2021, https://www.washingtonpost.com/politics/2021/12/04/kamala-harris-staff-departures/.

# CHAPTER TWELVE: WORD SALADS

1. Alex Thompson and Allie Bice, "The Creator of 'Veep' Has Thoughts on Harris, Biden, and His Other HBO Show," *Politico*, October 24, 2022, https://www.politico.com/newsletters/west-wing-playbook/2022/10/24/veeps-creator-has-thoughts-on-harris-00063214.

2. Manny Fidel (@mannyfidel), "Kamala Harris is goated at this point," Twitter, March 16, 2023.

3. Lynae Vanee, "A Parking Lot Special: Lynae Vanee Sits down with Vice President Kamala Harris," YouTube, May 15, 2023, https://www.youtube.com/watch?v=ld4_G_2F2bk.

# CHAPTER THIRTEEN: THE REACH FOR RELEVANCE

1. Katelyn Caralle, "Harris Hasn't Had an Event in 6 Day, Didn't Join Biden's Afghanistan

# NOTES

Remarks and Is Going to Asia," *Daily Mail*, August 18, 2021, https://www.dailymail
.co.uk/news/article-9904753/Harris-event-6-day-didnt-join-Bidens-Afghanistan-remarks
-going-Asia.html.

2. Cleve R. Wootson Jr. and John Hudson, "Harris, Blinken Navigate Munich Security
Conference as Europe Holds Its Breath," *Washington Post*, February 19, 2022, https://
www.washingtonpost.com/politics/2022/02/19/harris-blinken-munich/.

3. "Vice President Kamala Harris Says There Must Be Severe Consequences for
Russia's Actions," *The Morning Hustle*, March 1, 2022, https://www.youtube.com
/watch?v=RKjCSb9eixI.

4. "Remarks by Vice President Harris After Tour of the Korean Demilitarized Zone,"
White House, September 29, 2022, https://www.whitehouse.gov/briefing-room
/speeches-remarks/2022/09/29/remarks-by-vice-president-harris-after-tour-of-the-korean
-demilitarized-zone/.

5. "Public Supports Both Early Voting and Requiring Photo ID to Vote," Monmouth
University Polling Institute, June 21, 2021, https://www.monmouth.edu/polling-in
stitute/reports/monmouthpoll_us_062121/.

6. BETNetworks, "Vice President Kamala Harris Answers Questions About COVID-19
Vaccine & More | State Of Our Union," YouTube, July 10, 2021, https://www.youtube
.com/watch?v=bH_mjDE3sko.

7. Zolan Kanno-Youngs, Katie Rogers, and Peter Baker, "Kamala Harris Is Trying to
Define Her Vice Presidency. Even Her Allies Are Tired of Waiting," *New York Times*,
February 6, 2023, https://www.nytimes.com/2023/02/06/us/politics/kamala-harris-
vice-presidenct-legacy.html.

8. Rudy Takala, "Kamala Harris Praises Student Who Accuses Israel of Genocide,"
Mediaite, September 29, 2021, https://www.mediaite.com/news/kamala-harris
-tells-student-who-accuses-israel-of-ethnic-genocide-your-truth-cannot-be-suppressed/.

9. Tommy Christopher, "'Wow!' Daily Show Audience Stunned by DL Hughley's Dig at
VP Kamala Harris over Tyre Nichols Funeral," Mediaite, February 3, 2023, https://www
.mediaite.com/news/wow-daily-show-audience-stunned-by-dl-hughleys-dig-at-vp
-kamala-harris-over-tyre-nichols-funeral/.

# NOTES

## CHAPTER FOURTEEN: STRUGGLING RELATIONSHIPS

1. Edward-Isaac Dovere and Jasmine Wright, "Exasperation and Dysfunction: Inside Kamala Harris' Frustrating Start as Vice President," CNN, November 18, 2021.

2. Chris Whipple, *The Fight of His Life: Inside Joe Biden's White House* (New York: Scribner, 2023).

3. Jeff Mason, "Tethered Together, Biden and Harris Move toward 2024 Re-Election Run," Reuters, March 23, 2023, https://www.reuters.com/world/us/tethered-together -biden-harris-move-toward-2024-re-election-run-2023-03-23/.

4. Jonathan Martin, "Biden's and Trump's Performances on the 2022 Trail Sow Doubts About 2024," *Politico*, November 8, 2022, https://www.politico.com/news/magazine /2022/11/08/biden-trump-performances-2024-00065548.

5. Adam Carlson, "Dr. Jill Biden & Kamala Harris' Husband Doug Already 'Have a Real Bond,'" *People*, August 28, 2020, https://people.com/politics/jill-biden-doug-emhoff -have-a-real-bond/.

6. Hannah Yasharoff, "Jill Biden Was in My Harry Styles vs. Lizzo SoulCycle Class and It Was All the Inspiration I Needed," *USA Today*, May 17, 2023, https://www.usatoday .com/story/life/health-wellness/2023/05/17/jill-biden-lizzo-harry-styles-themed-soul cycle-class/70227290007.

7. Virginia Heffernan, "Pete Buttigieg Loves God, Beer, and His Electric Mustang," *Wired*, May 18, 2023, https://www.wired.com/story/pete-buttigieg-interview-god-beer -electric-mustang/.

8. Donald Judd, "Buttigieg Tamps Down Narrative That There's a Rivalry with Harris," CNN, November 21, 2021, https://www.cnn.com/2021/11/21/politics/pete-butti gieg-kamala-harris-rivalry/index.html.

9. Jonathan Martin, "Newsom Told the White House He Won't Challenge Biden," *Politico*, November 26, 2022, https://www.politico.com/news/2022/11/26/gavin-newsom- wont-challenge-joe-biden-00070829.

10. Eugene Daniels, "Why Harris World Thinks She May Be the Biggest Winner of the Midterms," *Politico*, January 17, 2023, https://www.politico.com/news/2023/01/17 /kamala-harris-midterms-optimism-00078039.

11. NBC News poll, January 2023, https://www.documentcloud.org/documents/23589424 -230032-nbc-january-2023-poll-v2-129-release.

12. Katie Lannan, "Warren Stops Short of Backing Harris for VP in 2024," WGBH, January 27, 2023, https://www.wgbh.org/news/politics/2023/01/27/warren-stops-short -of-backing-harris-for-vp-in-2024.

13. Katie Rogers and Peter Baker, "Kamala Harris Is Trying to Define Her Vice Presidency. Even Her Allies Are Tired of Waiting," *New York Times*, February 6, 2023, https://www .nytimes.com/2023/02/06/us/politics/kamala-harris-vice-presidenct-legacy.html.

14. "Biden Looks to Elevate Harris' Work as Core to Re-Election Bid," NBC News, April 27, 2023, https://www.nbcnews.com/politics/2024-election/biden-looks-elevate-harris -work-core-re-election-bid-rcna80996.

15. Erin Doherty, "NBC News Poll: Kamala Harris Hits Record Low for VP Net Favorability," Axios, June 26, 2023, https://www.axios.com/2023/06/26/kamala-harris-poll -2024-election-biden.

16. Madeleine Simon, "Trump Beats Biden, Harris in 2024 Match-ups: Poll," *The Hill*, February 18, 2023, https://thehill.com/homenews/campaign/3863637-trump-beats -biden-harris-in-2024-matchups-poll/.

17. Alex Thompson, "Scoop: Inside Biden's Strategy to Repair Harris' Image," Axios, April 26, 2023, https://www.axios.com/2023/04/26/biden-harris-2024.

18. Nikki Haley, "It's Time for a Competency Test for Politicians. Here's Why," Fox News, May 1, 2023, https://www.foxnews.com/opinion/time-competency-test-politicians -heres-why.

19. "'Every Liberal Knows' Kamala Harris Will Be President If Biden Wins in 2024: Nikki Haley," Fox News, June 5, 2023, https://www.foxnews.com/media/every-liberal -knows-kamala-harris-president-biden-wins-2024-nikki-haley.

20. "Nikki Haley: Prospect of a Kamala Harris Presidency Should 'Send a Chill Up Every American's Spine,'" Fox News, August 27, 2023, https://www.foxnews.com/video /6335678928112.

21. Eugene Daniels, "Harris Gets Her Cavalry: Top Group Plans to Spend $10 Million-plus to Boost Her," *Politico*, June 11, 2023, https://www.politico.com/news/2023/06/11/ kamala-harris-emilys-list-pac-00101400.

# CONCLUSION: KAMALA'S MOMENT IN TIME: THE PATH TO MADAM PRESIDENT

1. Brett Samuels, "Harris Chatter Leaves Biden Allies Seeking to Shut Down Talk of
Replacing Her," *The Hill*, September 16, 2023, https://thehill.com/homenews/admin
istration/4207017-harris-chatter-leaves-biden-allies-seeking-to-shut-down-talk-of-repla
cing-her/.

2. Eugene Daniels, "'I Can't Get into People's Heads': Kamala Harris Tries to Reshape
Her Public Image Ahead of 2024," *Politico*, August 21, 2023, https://www.politico.com
/news/2023/08/21/kamala-harris-second-act-00111913.

3. Astead W. Herndon, "In Search of Kamala Harris," *New York Times*, October 10, 2023,
https://www.nytimes.com/2023/10/10/magazine/kamala-harris.html.